CONTENTMENT AND SUFFERING

Culture and Experience in Toraja

Contentment and Suffering

Culture and Experience in Toraja

DOUGLAS W. HOLLAN

JANE C. WELLENKAMP

Columbia University Press
New York

Columbia University Press
New York   Chichester, West Sussex
Copyright © 1994 Columbia University Press
All rights reserved

Library of Congress Cataloging-in-Publication Data

Hollan, Douglas Wood.
   Contentment and suffering : culture and experience in Toraja /
Douglas W. Hollan, Jane C. Wellenkamp.
      p.   cm.
   Includes bibliographical references and index.
   ISBN 0-231-08422-6. — ISBN 0-231-08423-4 (pbk.)
   1. Toraja (Indonesian people)—Psychology.   2. Ethnopsychology.
I. Wellenkamp, Jane C.   II. Title.
DS632.T7H65   1993
155.8'49922—dc20   93-4619
                                                                CIP

Printed in the United States of America
c 10 9 8 7 6 5 4 3 2 1

To the people of Paku Asu
and to Robert I. Levy

and in memory of
Nene'na Tandi and Ambe'na Toding

CONTENTS

maps, following page 10
photos, following page 112

ACKNOWLEDGMENTS

This has been a long project, and there are many people to thank. First and foremost, we wish to thank the people of Paku Asu, especially our eleven respondents and their families, who so graciously accepted us into their lives. Without their kind indulgence, this project could not have been possible. We hope that we have accurately presented their views, experiences, and concerns here. They are often in our thoughts. We are also grateful to the Kepala Desa and the clinic workers in the area where we worked—who must remain unnamed so that the identities of our respondents are not disclosed—who throughout our stay offered us hospitality, assistance, and friendship. We are grateful, too, to two individuals—who also will remain unnamed—who spent a great deal of time providing us with traditional stories, accounts, and sayings. Several families generously shared their homes with us while we were searching for a fieldsite or attending rituals in various villages, for which we are very appreciative.

Others in Indonesia who assisted our research and who helped to make our stays enjoyable and profitable include: Mr. Napitupulu of the Lembaga Ilmu Penetahuan Indonesia in Jakarta; Mr. Chuck Darsono and his family who were gracious hosts in Jakarta; Mr. Darsono's office staff who provided us with much assistance, particularly during our first weeks in Indonesia; Professor Dr. Hardjoeno and Drs. Arief Said of the Universitas Hasanuddin in Ujung Pandang; Dr. Abdullah Baasir, former director of the Rumah Sakit Jiwa (Mental Hospital), and his staff in Ujung Pandang; Drs. Pieter Malisan and Mr. Luther Palimbong of Ujung Pandang; the Bupati's office and police, health, and court officials in Tana Toraja; and Dr. Cecilia Toban and the families of Bas Plaisier and Derrick Foster, also in Toraja.

Prior to our original departure for Indonesia, Elizabeth Young, Toby Volkman, Paul Alexander, Stuart Schlegel, Shelly Errington, Eric Crystal, and George Kahin provided useful advice and information on conducting fieldwork in Indonesia, and Shirley Strum and Robert Levy put us in contact with colleagues in Indonesia. Other Indonesianists who have commented on our work or have assisted us in other ways include: Greg Acciaioli, Kathleen Adams, Jane Atkinson, Elizabeth Coville, Ken George, Karl Heider, David Hicks, Janet Hoskins, Joel Kuipers, Steve Lansing, and Roxanne Waterson.

We would also like to express our appreciation to the faculty, staff, and graduate students of the Department of Anthropology at the University of California, San Diego during the years that we were there. The Department provided a supportive and inspiring atmosphere for intellectual growth. We owe a particular intellectual debt to Melford Spiro and Roy D'Andrade, our advisors, and to Theodore Schwartz and Gananath Obeyesekere. And we are especially grateful to Robert Levy, whose influence on our work is obvious.

Most of this book has been written during the time that we have been affiliated with the Department of Anthropology at the University of California, Los Angeles. We wish to acknowledge the Department's financial and intellectual support for this endeavor, as well as the encouragement and advice of Robert Edgerton, Walter Goldschmidt, Allen Johnson, John Kennedy, Lew Langness, Philip Newman, and Thomas Weisner. We also want to acknowledge the helpful feedback we have received from students during lectures and seminars.

We are grateful to the following for their financial support: the National Science Foundation; the National Institute of Mental Health; the Wenner-Gren Foundation for Anthropological Research; Sigma Xi, the Scientific Research Society; the Office of Graduate Studies and Research at the University of California, San Diego; the Office of the Chancellor at the University of California, Los Angeles; and the UCLA International Studies and Overseas Programs.

For their warm interest and support, we also thank Ernestine Mc-Hugh, Leslie Lloyd, Mike Miller, Phil Jones, Raymond Sigrist, Nerys Levy, and our families. We wish to acknowledge in particular the steadfast support and encouragement of our parents, Cynthia Wellenkamp, the late Jeremy Wellenkamp, and Edith and Roger Hollan.

Finally, at Columbia University Press, we wish to thank Gioia Stevens, who took an early interest in our manuscript and who guided it through to press with care and efficiency, and our reviewers, whose insightful comments and suggestions we greatly appreciated.

Certain passages of this book have been published previously. We wish to thank the publishers of the following articles for kindly permitting us to include portions of our previous work:

1988 Pockets Full of Mistakes: The Personal Consequences of Religious Change in a Toraja Village. *Oceania* 58:275–289. (Hollan)

1989 The Personal Use of Dream Beliefs in the Toraja Highlands. *Ethos* 17:166–186. (Hollan)

1990 Indignant Suicide in the Pacific: An Example from the Toraja Highlands of Indonesia. *Culture, Medicine, and Psychiatry* 14:368–379. (Hollan)

1992 Emotion Work and the Value of Emotional Equanimity Among the Toraja. *Ethnology* 31:45–56. (Hollan)

1992 Cross-Cultural Differences in the Self. *Journal of Anthropological Research* 48:283–300. (Hollan)

In press Suffering and the Work of Culture: A Case of Magical Poisoning in Toraja. *American Ethnologist.* (Hollan)

1988 Order and Disorder in Toraja Thought and Ritual. *Ethnology* 27:311–326. (Wellenkamp)

1988 Notions of Grief and Catharsis Among the Toraja. *American Ethnologist* 15:486–500. (Wellenkamp)

1991 Fallen Leaves: Death and Grieving in Toraja. In David R. Counts and Dorothy A. Counts, eds., *Coping with the Final Tragedy: Cultural Variation in Dying and Grieving,* pp. 113–134. Amityville, N.Y. (Wellenkamp)

1992 Variation in the Social and Cultural Organization of Emotions: The Meaning of Crying and the Importance of Compassion in Toraja, Indonesia. In David D. Franks and Viktor Gecas, *Social Perspectives on Emotion* 1:189–216. Greenwich, Conn.: JAI Press. (Wellenkamp)

Contentment and Suffering

Culture and Experience in Toraja

INTRODUCTION

This book is a person-centered ethnography of the Toraja,[1] a mountain-dwelling group of wet-rice farmers on the island of Sulawesi (Celebes) in Indonesia. In it we describe central aspects of Toraja personal experience, including those relating to emotions, cognition, motivation, identity, and self, and we explore how and in what ways shared aspects of Toraja personal experience are related to Toraja culture and society.

This book contributes to the ethnography of culture and psychology in central and eastern Indonesia, the dearth of which has been noted by Koentjaraningrat (1975). But it also provides an illustration of what we believe is a particularly fruitful way of conducting field research in psychocultural anthropology. Since at least the time of Herodotus, scholars and explorers of varied nationalities and cultural traditions have attempted to capture the "genius," "temper," or "character" of an unfamiliar people. Yet it is only within the last century that such attempts have been made the object of critical scrutiny and developed into a subfield of anthropological research.

This subfield has gone by various names, including, early on, "culture and personality research" and later, "psychological anthropology." We prefer the term, "psychocultural anthropology," which reflects the dual interests of the field: 1) in the sociocultural influences on personal experience and individual psychology; and 2) in the personal and psychological influences on society and culture. Researchers in the field variously emphasize one or the other of these major concerns. Researchers also vary in the degree to which they focus on universals in personal experience (e.g., to what extent does culture shape cognitive development); on psychological characteristics specific to a particular sociocultural group (e.g., how do the personal concerns and experiences of the Alorese differ from those of the Chewong); or on intracultural and individual variation (e.g., how do healers' personal experiences vary from those of non-healers, or how do the experiences of healer A differ from those of healer B). This book focuses primarily on shared aspects of Toraja personal experience, although it also describes elements of individual and intracultural variation as well.

Since one of our purposes is to suggest a way of examining personal experience cross-culturally, we begin by providing a brief history of the major research approaches in the field of psychocultural anthropology and by placing *Contentment and Suffering* within the context of recent methodological developments. Developing and refining new methodological approaches is, we believe, a central task of the field. We agree with LeVine (1982:ix) who notes: "In my view, there is no need for more theory in this field unless it is accompanied by a sturdier method of data collection. Methodology has been the central problem of culture and personality research, its greatest stumbling block." Because we feel that the collection and reporting of good data must precede elaborate theory-building in psychocultural studies, we conceive of this book primarily as a descriptive, person-centered ethnography. We offer some "deeper" interpretations where the evidence warrants it, but for the most part, we develop our theoretical speculations in more detail elsewhere (see, for example, Hollan 1988a, b, 1989, 1990, 1992a, b, c; and Wellenkamp 1988a, b, 1989, 1991, 1992), and will continue to do so in future publications.

Following a discussion of methodological issues, we present a brief overview of Toraja culture and society. We then conclude the chapter with an introduction to our Toraja respondents, whose reflections on life and living make up the bulk of this book.

METHODOLOGICAL DEVELOPMENTS IN
PSYCHOCULTURAL ANTHROPOLOGY

Langness (1987) has pointed out that many of anthropology's most distinguished forebears have been interested in psychological topics and Bock (1988) has persuasively argued that *all* anthropologists are psychocultural anthropologists to the extent that their analyses of social and cultural phenomena *must be* predicated, at least implicitly, upon assumptions about human cognition, motivation, and learning. Yet an explicit and focused concern with human subjectivity, and the relationship between culture and psychology, has been primarily a preoccupation of a segment of American anthropology, and one that first began to take noticeable shape as recently as seventy years ago.

From the 1920s until the present, the methods and theoretical foci of psychocultural research have shifted significantly. In what follows, we discuss the major approaches that anthropologists have taken to investigate personal experience and psychological phenomena in other cultures—including, standard cultural ethnography, psychological testing, observation of naturally occurring behavior, and more recently, ethnopsychology and person-centered ethnography. We begin by pointing out some of the major limitations of the early approaches. We then conclude with a discussion of the open interview—one of the primary approaches we have used in our own research.

Ruth Benedict's well-known book, *Patterns of Culture* (1934), was one of the first important works in the field. Benedict borrowed holistic theories about individual personality to develop a theory of cultural integration, arguing that culture was "personality writ large." While Benedict's intent was to offer a theory about culture, she strongly implied that by closely analyzing a culture's values and institutions and identifying its unique configuration, one could infer the psychological characteristics of (at least a majority) of its people.

Although Benedict sometimes used psychiatric terms in her characterizations of non-Western groups, and although all of her portrayals have a clear psychological cast to them,[2] the data upon which she based her analyses were general cultural beliefs and practices. Her characterization of Dobuans as "paranoid," for example, was based on an analysis of sorcery beliefs and social and familial institutions, not on clinical or psychiatric evaluations of specific individuals.

The idea that individual psychology could be inferred from an analysis of social and cultural data was perhaps developed most explicitly and cogently by Abram Kardiner in *The Individual and His Society*

(1939) and *The Psychological Frontiers of Society* (1945). Kardiner, a psychoanalyst, was specifically interested in characterizing culturally shared aspects of individual psychology—not, like Benedict, in just presenting a theory of culture—and yet he, too, relied heavily upon descriptions of general cultural beliefs and practices provided by anthropologists. According to Kardiner's theory, the "primary" institutions of a society, especially childrearing practices and means of subsistence, lead to the development of a "basic personality structure," an underlying set of conflicts, adjustments, and predispositions shared by all of the members of the society, but manifested in different ways by different individuals. The basic personality structure (BPS), in turn, according to Kardiner, shapes, and serves to integrate, the "secondary" or "projective" institutions of a society, including those concerning art, religion, healing, and explanations of misfortune.

primary institutions → BPS → secondary institutions

By knowing enough about the primary and secondary institutions of a society, so Kardiner reasoned, one could indirectly infer the basic personality structure of its members.[3]

There are several problems with the assumption that individual psychology can be inferred from social and cultural descriptions, however. First of all, without psychological data collected from specific individuals, it remains just that—an assumption. Neither Kardiner nor Benedict had data available to them to validate their assumptions about individual psychology. Second, such a methodological approach is based on, or often leads to, theoretical assumptions that may be unwarranted. For example, such an approach assumes a degree of psychological homogeneity ("the" Zuni are Apollonian; "the" Dobuans are paranoid) that is unlikely to be found in even small, monocultural populations. It also assumes that many cultural phenomena are a direct reflection or projection of psychological tendencies and needs, and thus underestimates the extent to which such phenomena also may be determined by historical, economic, political, ecological, and other important variables. Finally, the use of social and cultural data to infer individual psychology precludes exploring the possibility that aspects of culture and psychology may vary independently of one another.

In the 1940s and 1950s, several psychocultural anthropologists attempted to investigate psychological characteristics more directly by using cognitive and personality tests originally developed in Europe and the United States.[4] Not only did the analysis of test data collected from specific individuals circumvent the problem of assuming some direct relationship between cultural beliefs and practices and individual psychology, but it also avoided the assumption of homogeneity—by collecting test data from several individuals in a "representative" sample of a population, one could examine the *range* of certain characteristics or tendencies. Moreover, it was hoped that psychological tests would be more "objective" and more easily standardized than other types of psychological assessments, thus permitting researchers to make more direct comparisons of psychological characteristics within and between widely different cultures.

One notable example of the early use of more direct psychological measurements in anthropological fieldwork is Cora Dubois' (1961) study of the Alorese in eastern Indonesia. DuBois used a battery of psychological tests, along with the collection of eight life histories, to evaluate the usefulness of Kardiner's concept of "basic personality structure." Psychological tests also were extensively used by Hallowell (1955) and Miner and DeVos (1960, 1989) to study cultural assimilation and change, and by Wallace (1952) in his analysis of psychological variation among the Tuscarora.

Since their early use in the field, however, psychological tests have been the subject of debate. The basic question regarding their use has been, Can psychological and cognitive tests developed by European and American psychologists for use among European and American populations provide comparable and meaningful information when used among non-Western groups? Certainly, it is clear that lack of familiarity with, and cultural differences in the perception and interpretation of, testing materials and testing situations may greatly limit the value of such tests in cross-cultural settings (Price-Williams 1978; Cole 1978).[5] In addition to problems in administering such tests, there may also be problems involved in interpreting the results. Even if, for example, one could assume that responses to color on a Rorschach test card in all cultures indicates emotional responsiveness on the part of the respondent, are we to assume that "emotional responsiveness" has the same meaning everywhere? That is, does it have the same behavioral and diagnostic implications in different cultures?

A further limitation of psychological tests is that they are designed to measure predetermined characteristics or tendencies of interest to the Western observer and thus they may fail to detect "the most significant and meaningful aspects of the world of the individual as experienced by him and in terms of which he thinks, is motivated to act, and satisfies his needs" (Hallowell 1955:88). As a result, psychological test results, if used in isolation, may provide only a very limited understanding of why individuals in other cultures think and behave in the ways that they do.

A second major way of assessing psychological characteristics in other cultures was developed in the 1950s by John and Beatrice Whiting and their associates. In place of psychological tests, they advocated the use of systematic observations of naturally occurring behavior (Whiting and Whiting 1978:55–56). In the Whitings' approach, the occurrence of specific behaviors are recorded and coded (according to such categories as "offering help" or "seeking attention and approval") and the frequency and patterns of various behaviors are analyzed. Whiting and Edwards (1974), for example, used this approach in their study of gender differences. On the basis of detailed observations of childrearing practices and children's behavior in several different societies, they concluded that putatively universal differences in behavioral and psychological patterns between males and females could be explained as a result of task assignments in early childhood, rather than as a result of biological or genetic factors.

One major drawback of this approach is that without the actor's point of view and interpretation of events, it is difficult to know whether a particular behavior "means" what one thinks it means, or has the psychological consequences that one thinks it has, in a given cultural setting. For example, an adult's failure to respond quickly and solicitously to a child's cry can be viewed as an instance of child neglect in one place, but as an indication of concern that the child not be "spoiled" in another.

In more recent years, a general wariness concerning psychological testing and a sensitivity to the limitations of behavioral observations that do not take into account sufficiently the actor's point of view—along with the rise of meaning-centered, interpretative anthropology (e.g., Geertz 1973)—have led to another methodological approach in psychocultural anthropology: the description and analysis of ethnopsychologies or indigenous conceptions of individual behavior and experience, including ideas and beliefs about the person, self, emotion, cognition, motivation, and other aspects of psychological process. (See, for example, Rosaldo 1980; White and Kirkpatrick 1985; D'Andrade 1987; Lutz 1988; and Wellenkamp 1988b.) The focus of this research (ideally) is on "experience-near" concepts—those that move us closer to the personal experiences of the individual—rather than on more abstract psychological concepts such as "affect hunger" or "object cathexis" (cf. Kohut 1971; Geertz 1983; Wikan 1991; Kleinman and Kleinman 1991). The importance of this work lies in documenting the varieties of indigenous psychologies around the world,[6] in pointing out the futility of making "deep" psychological interpretations without a thorough knowledge and understanding of cultural context,[7] and in broadening and correcting our own (sometimes narrowly focused) theories of human behavior and psychology (cf. Howard 1985; Lutz 1988).

While the cross-cultural study of personal experience must begin with the elicitation of indigenous conceptions of thought and feeling, one must not too readily assume that such concepts, especially if derived through formal methods or the analysis of general cultural data,[8] are necessarily used in everyday contexts or that they necessarily affect individual psychology and personal experience in significant ways. To presume their "directive force" (D'Andrade 1984; Quinn and Holland 1987) or cognitive and emotional "saliency" (Spiro 1984), rather than to demonstrate such effects with data gathered from specific individuals, would repeat the errors of early researchers in the field. One must also guard against overemphasizing the ideal/typical or normative aspects of behavior—that is, the way things *should be* thought about, felt, and experienced—and underemphasizing the extent to which behaviors and personal experience may actually run counter to or contradict ideal cultural representations (Spiro 1984; Howard 1985; Wellenkamp 1988b; Hollan 1992c).

In our opinion, investigations of indigenous conceptions of personal experience must be complemented by the study of particular individuals' lives. A focus on particular individuals not only allows one to examine how people *use* public beliefs and symbols to make sense of their everyday experience (Hollan 1988b, 1989, in press), but it also allows one to explore aspects of personal experience that do not neatly conform to public, ideal conceptions.[9]

A STRATEGY FOR PSYCHOCULTURAL RESEARCH: THE OPEN INTERVIEW

We advocate, following Levy (1973), combining standard ethnographic methods, including observations of naturally occurring behavior in both ritual and everyday contexts, with an extended series of open interviews conducted with a select group of respondents.[10] Although the present work focuses heavily on interview materials,[11] our interpretation and presentation of this data is grounded in our knowledge of the everyday lives and social actions of the respondents.

In a review of three recent works based on in-depth interviewing

(Levy 1973; Kracke 1978; and Obeyesekere 1981),[12] Marcus and Fischer note that the mark of such approaches is "the display of discourse—self-reflective commentaries on experience, emotion, and self; on dreams, remembrances, associations, metaphors, distortions, and displacements; and on transferences and compulsive behavior repetitions—all of which reveal a behaviorally and conceptually significant level of reality reflecting, contrasting with, or obscured by public cultural forms" (1986:54). Levy and Wellenkamp (1989) also comment on the open interview format. What they have to say about its advantages in the anthropological investigation of emotional experience also applies to the study of personal experience and psychological phenomena in general.

> Such interviews provide two kinds of information about emotion. Individuals being interviewed are used in part as *informants*, providing their own presumably objective reports, views, and interpretations of phenomena related to emotion. At the same time they may serve as *respondents*, objects of systematic study in themselves, in which their discourse—and in particular the *forms* of that discourse and their behavior as they talk— indicates something about the organization of emotion in that particular individual. . . . In open interviews the investigator attempts to let the interview follow the respondent's lead to a large degree, in order to see how the respondent presents his or her statements on the assumption that the organization of these presentations may reveal patterning of both cultural and personal significance. In the course of the interviews, personal emotional reactions are probed for by questions such as "How did you feel about that?"; "What did you feel like doing then?"; "What *did* you do?"; "Why?" and the like. Such interviews produce rich material bearing on feelings and understandings about feelings and their transformations throughout various stages of life, on learning, on fantasy, on stress and anxiety, on moral ideas and emotions, on self-concept, and on other such personally centered dimensions of experience. While a question during an interview such as (in Tahiti) "What are the responsibilities of a chief here?" produces, for the most part, cultural information, the probe "What is it like for *you* to be a chief?" will elicit information about personal experience and organization. Many aspects of form can be put to analytic use here—facial expression and body language (capable of being recorded by video tape) as well as paralinguistic features, and a rich field of thematic clumpings, distortions, evasions, hesitations, slips of the tongue, and confusions, all amply illustrated and easily discernible in a close listening to tape recordings of interviews.
>
> (Levy and Wellenkamp 1989:223–24; emphasis in original)

Although we deliberately sought to encourage spontaneity and personal reflection[13]—in order to illuminate shared and individual patterns of personal experience as well as to generate "experience-near" concepts of thought, emotion, and behavior—we loosely structured the interviews around a checklist of topics borrowed from Levy (1973:509–11). The checklist, which covers a broad range of personal and social experiences, was amended to include experiences peculiar to the Toraja, such as participation in kickfights and possession trance (see appendix). (Because of space limitations, we report much of the data regarding aspects of the life cycle elsewhere. See Hollan and Wellenkamp n.d.) Our purpose in using the checklist was to insure that the interview materials from different individuals could be compared to one another and to similar data collected elsewhere.

The checklist provided a minimal number of topics to be discussed with each respondent. If a particular topic did not spontaneously arise in the course of a series of interviews, we took the liberty of guiding conversation into the neglected area of interest. Once the topic had been introduced, however, we allowed the respondent to direct the flow of discussion.

The quality of the interviews was enhanced, we believe, because they were conducted in relative privacy with Wellenkamp interviewing the women respondents and Hollan interviewing the men. This allowed us to ask questions about sexual behavior and other personal matters that could not have been discussed easily with others present or with an interviewer of the opposite gender. It has also allowed us to present a relatively balanced, in-depth view of both female and male personal experience, which is unusual in the anthropological literature.

We tape-recorded all of the interviews, with the respondents' permission, and later transcribed them after returning to the United States. Most of the quotations we present are taken directly from the transcript materials. Some quotations, however, are taken from tape-recorded interviews Wellenkamp conducted with other villagers regarding aspects of loss and bereavement. As part of the interview process, we also administered the Rorschach test and TAT (Thematic Apperception Test) to each respondent, and we quote a few of these responses as well. We use the test results as supplemental, rather than primary, data, however. As we noted in our discussion of the use of psychological tests above, considerable rapport with respondents is needed to administer psychological tests (which limits one's sample size), and in-depth ethnographic work is essential to adequately interpret test results.

The interview methodology we are advocating here is certainly not without its own challenges and limitations,[14] several of which we discuss in a later section, yet we believe that it provides one important means by which anthropologists can gather psychocultural data that is both sensitive to local conceptions of thought, emotion, and motivation, and yet standardized enough to allow for both intracultural and intercultural comparisons.[15] We also believe that whatever this format sacrifices in terms of sample size and difficulty of execution, it more than gains back in terms of quality and breadth of data. This sort of material allows one to begin to make limited generalizations rather than build grand theory. As LeVine (1982:293) notes, such a step may be a modest one "compared to cross-cultural hypothesis-testing, but it represents the conviction that greater ambitions cannot be fulfilled without data of better quality."

Finally, by generating extensive verbatim transcript material of both the interviewer's questions and the respondent's answers, this format enables one to give direct, contextualized voice to the subjects of study—a voice that is beginning to be heard more in contemporary ethnographies.

AN OVERVIEW OF TORAJA CULTURE AND SOCIETY

Before introducing our Toraja respondents and describing in somewhat greater detail the interviewing conditions, we present a brief overview of Toraja society and culture. We selected Toraja as a place to conduct research because there were many aspects of Toraja life that seemed interesting from a psychocultural point of view (such as elaborate and unusual mortuary practices [see Wellenkamp 1984, 1991] and rituals involving possession trance), and while psychocultural research had been done with other Indonesian groups (e.g., the Balinese, Javanese, and Alorese), it had not been done with the Toraja. We should make clear at the outset that we could not have focused our research so exclusively on aspects of personal experience had we not already known a good deal about Toraja society and culture before entering the field, and we are grateful that the Toraja have received the attention of a number of outstanding ethnographers.[16]

Our emphasis in this section is on Toraja history, ritual, and social organization. Later, in Part I, we discuss religion, world view, and other topics at greater length.

The Sa'dan Toraja,[17] hereafter referred to as "the Toraja," speak an Austronesian language and live in the highlands of what is now the Province of South Sulawesi (*Sulawesi Selatan*) on the island of Sulawesi

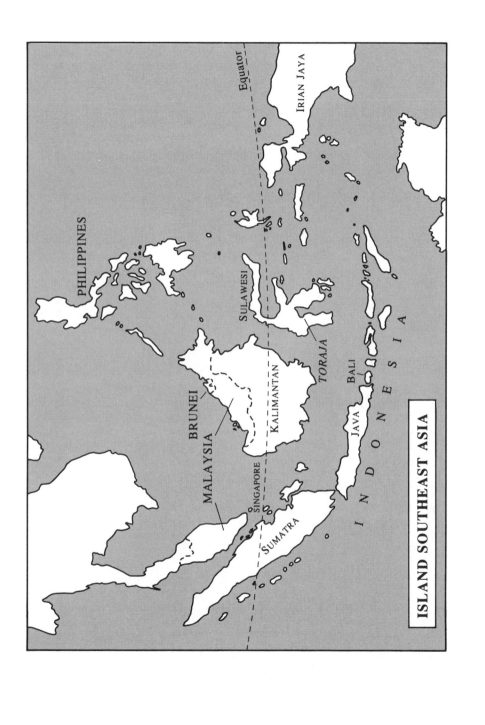

ISLAND SOUTHEAST ASIA

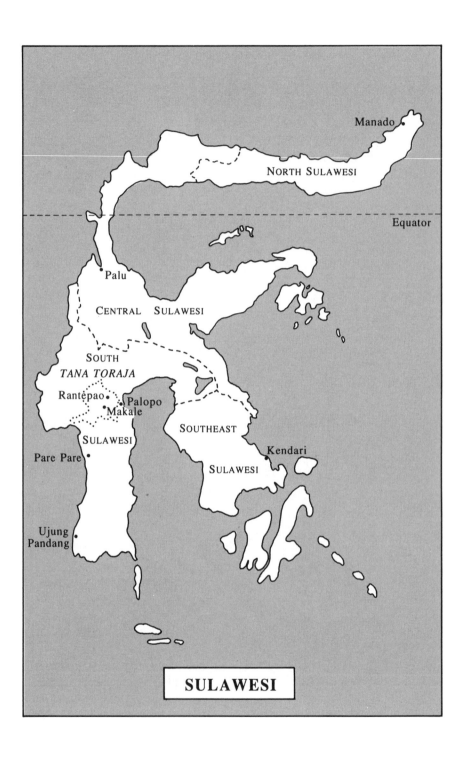

Manado •

NORTH SULAWESI

Equator

• Palu

CENTRAL   SULAWESI

SOUTH
TANA TORAJA
Rantepao •
        • Palopo
    • Makale

SULAWESI

SOUTHEAST

SULAWESI

Kendari •

Pare Pare •

Ujung
Pandang •

SULAWESI

(formerly Celebes) in Indonesia. The Toraja highlands are located within the current boundaries of an administrative district (*kabupaten*) called *Tana Toraja*.[18] The Sa'dan River valley, which forms the heart of the Toraja homeland, lies at an elevation of approximately 800 meters, but is surrounded by mountains that average 1,300 to 1,600 meters, with peaks of over 2,000 meters. The majority of the Toraja—who number approximately 350,000—make their living through wet-rice agriculture and the cultivation of small gardens of sweet potatoes, cassava, and assorted vegetables. Coffee and cloves are important cash crops. Although the market towns of Makale and Rantepao are rapidly growing, most Toraja still live in small, isolated hamlets and villages.

Historically, the Toraja were a diverse group. Regional variations—many of which persist today—existed in language, religion, social structure, and agricultural practices. In contrast to the lowland Islamic kingdoms of the Bugis and Makassar, the Toraja area remained politically decentralized prior to the arrival of the Dutch, with nobles competing for control of various local areas. Intervillage warfare occurred intermittently, and headhunting was practiced both to avenge a death and to obtain the heads that were needed for the funerals of high status persons. With the exception of a brief period of unification in the seventeenth century, political allegiance rarely extended beyond the hamlet or village. Indeed, a true sense of collective identity only began to emerge after the Dutch took control of the area in the early twentieth century (see Bigalke 1981), and even today, local ties remain an important part of the social and political landscape.

Before the last quarter of the nineteenth century, Toraja contact with the outside world was limited to sporadic encounters with the lowland Bugis and Makassar. Some of these contacts were peaceful, involving trade and intermarriage among elites and the payment of tribute from highlanders to lowlanders, but others were decidedly hostile, as the Toraja defended themselves against attack and invasion. One such attack, led by Arung Palaka of Bone, resulted in the temporary unification of the Toraja mentioned above (Nooy-Palm 1979:8).

Contacts with outsiders became more extensive in the closing decades of the nineteenth century as lowlanders, spurred by changes in international markets, became more interested in obtaining Toraja coffee and slaves. Trade alliances were established in which lowlanders provided Toraja nobles with firearms in exchange for help in acquiring desired goods. One of the consequences of these increasing contacts with the outside world was heightened political instability, as Toraja nobles used their newly acquired weapons to raid one another for slaves and coffee and to confiscate both land and livestock (Bigalke 1981).

The political situation in the highlands remained volatile until the Dutch arrived in 1906. In addition to outlawing the slave trade, the Dutch killed or imprisoned many of the most powerful Toraja nobles and froze land holdings. They also introduced and promoted Christianity, schools, and modern medicine.

The Dutch retained control of the Toraja highlands until 1942, when the Japanese occupied the area during World War II. Although the Dutch returned to power in Indonesia for a brief period of time after 1945, they eventually relinquished control to Indonesian nationalists in 1949. Tana Toraja and the province of South Sulawesi eventually became integrated into the new Indonesian national state based in Jakarta, but not before a number of lowland groups had arisen to fight for local control (Harvey 1974, 1977). These groups remained active in and around the Toraja highlands, disrupting commerce and travel, until the central government finally gained control in 1965. Since then, the Toraja highlands have remained peaceful and efforts have been made to build roads, schools, and health clinics and to develop international tourism (see Volkman 1985; Adams 1988).

The traditional religion of the Toraja, variously referred to as *Aluk To Dolo* ("the way of the people of before"), *Aluk Nene'* ("the way of the ancestors"), or simply *Alukta* ("our way"), is based on the veneration and propitiation of various gods and spirits (*deata*) and deceased ancestors (*nene'*). The central components of traditional religious practice are the *sukaran aluk,* specific rites and rituals, and the *pemali,* prohibitions, which combined, supposedly total 7,777 in all. Many of the traditional prohibitions serve to separate the "east" or "smoke-ascending" ritual sphere from the "west" or "smoke-descending" sphere.[19] The "smoke-ascending" sphere is oriented toward the *deata* and includes rituals held to promote health, fertility, and prosperity, to give thanks, and to atone for transgressions. Included within this sphere are house-building rituals (*ma'papa*), rituals involving possession trance (*ma'maro, ma'bugi'*), and *ma'bua'* rituals, which are connected to fertility and prosperity.[20] In contrast, the "smoke-descending" sphere is oriented toward the ancestors (*nene'*) and the souls of the recent dead (*bombo*) and centers around death rituals.

The Toraja are best known for their elaborate death practices. One of the more striking sights one encounters when entering Tana Toraja is the massive limestone cliffs, dotted with burial vaults and in some locales wooden balconies on which nearly life-sized statues (*tatau*) of the dead stand. Unlike other life-cycle transitions (see Hollan and Wellenkamp n.d.), the traditional cultural response to death is elaborate in Toraja, and includes two main rituals: funerals and a form of "secondary burial" (Hertz 1960; Huntington and Metcalf 1980) called *ma'nene'*.[21]

In many areas of Indonesia, death is treated as a gradual process rather than an abrupt event (Hertz 1960; cf. Ramsden 1991). Among the Toraja, there is often a lengthy interval between a person's physical demise and the performance of his or her funeral, especially in the case of wealthy, high status individuals (see below for a discussion of status). The delay is caused by several factors including the need to make preparations for the funeral (which is the responsibility primarily of the deceased's children) and the desire to await an auspicious date. During this period—which may last several weeks or even months, or in rare instances, years—the body of the deceased is kept in the house, either wrapped in several layers of cloth or injected with formalin and placed under reed mats or in a wooden coffin. For Alukta residents, the village is considered polluted by the presence of the deceased and the staging of any smoke-ascending ritual is, in principle, prohibited.

The funeral itself may take several days or weeks to conclude as the body of the deceased is gradually moved from inside the house to the houseyard, to the funeral ground (*rante*), and finally to the burial site. During this time, funeral singing (e.g., *ma'badong, ma'dondi'*), flute music, and wailing may be performed, and various effigies and memorials may be constructed, depending upon the age, status, and wealth of the deceased.[22]

The *ma'nene'* ritual involves bringing offerings to the burial tombs, cleaning and repairing the gravesites, and attending to the remains of the dead—for example, repairing damaged coffins or rewrapping the remains.[23]

All Alukta ritual is structured around animal sacrifices and offerings of rice and other substances.[24] Each sacrifice is made in conjunction with a specific, named rite. Rituals are conducted by steadily progressing through a series of sacrifices and offerings and their attendant rites. The larger rituals require a greater number of sacrifices and offerings and take place over a longer period of time.[25]

In 1982, roughly 40 percent of the population remained Alukta, while over 50 percent were Christian. While Christianity is rapidly spreading in Toraja, Christian funerals retain many traditional elements (including funeral songs and wailing, and the slaughter of pigs and water buffalo) and many Alukta beliefs have been incorporated into village Christianity, as we discuss later in chapter 1.

Traditionally, there were three main social strata in Toraja: nobles (*to makaka*, which derives from *kaka*, "older sibling"), commoners (*to buda*, "the many" or *to biasa*, "commoners"), and dependents or slaves (*kaunan*).[26] Status was primarily ascribed by birth, but some mobility was possible as a result of financial gain (which was then channeled into the competitive slaughter of livestock at community feasts) or through financial loss. While wealth generally corresponded with status since the majority of the riceland was concentrated in the hands of the nobles, it was possible for a noble to become poor through gambling or through the slaughter of livestock. Impoverished nobles were still considered "noble" by virtue of their blood, but their power and influence in the community diminished in accordance with their loss of wealth.

Today, status differences continue to be very important and status continues to be marked in a number of ways (e.g., through seating arrangements, clothing and jewelry, and the carving of houses and rice barns). In particular, the exchange and division of meat on ritual occasions continue to be important matters in which status concerns and feelings of shame and honor are prevalent. As noted earlier, livestock are slaughtered for major ceremonial events; the more numerous the livestock, the greater the prestige of the hosts. The animals are provided by the hosts of the event and by the hosts' relatives. Each animal that is contributed by a relative is considered to be a debt that must eventually be repaid; that is, the hosts are obligated to provide animals of equal value for the ceremonial events sponsored by their relatives (see Volkman 1985; Waterson 1981).

The division of meat on these occasions is often a highly elaborate, time-consuming, and dramatic event, involving special meat dividers (*to mentaa*) who distribute the pieces of meat while loudly calling out the names of recipients. The order in which one's name is called and the size and cut of meat that one receives is, in principle, determined by one's status, age, and ritual roles, and by one's previous slaughtering history (see Volkman 1985). While status is an important factor in the determination of the amount of meat one receives, it is also true that the amount one gives and receives in part determines one's relative standing in the community. Those who consistently slaughter animals for their own and their relatives' ceremonial events and who also consistently receive larger and better portions of meat are considered "big people" (*to kapua*) and are highly regarded in the community. As

Volkman (1985:82) observes: "meat is both a political medium and, at least in part, the substance of politics itself."

Currently, since even commoners and dependents have alternative sources of income, the status system is in flux, though ascribed status is still considered important (see Volkman 1985).

Descent in Toraja is traced bilaterally. A group of bilaterally related kin who trace descent from a common ancestor is called a *pa'rapuan* or *marapuan*. The house that was founded by the common ancestor is called the *tongkonan* and is important for ceremonial purposes. As Waterson (1981:34–35) observes,

> an individual can trace links to a number of *tongkonan* on both his father's and mother's side of the family, though particular houses may have particular importance for him (or her). If one side of the family is richer than the other, the link with their *tongkonan* may be cultivated, while residence near to one *tongkonan* may lead, over time, to a closer attachment there than to others more distant. As new households form over time, a string of houses will in theory link one to the *tongkonan* of the original founding ancestor-couple. Not all the houses in between will be considered important, however, or even referred to as *tongkonan*, but the original house will still be the focus for ritual activities . . .
>
> The *pa'rapuan* cannot . . . be called a descent group for it is not corporated in any real sense, nor is its membership exclusive. It is possible to belong to a number of *tongkonan* because the activities with which each is concerned are only occasional. These are chiefly rituals . . . and the rebuilding or reroofing of the *tongkonan*.

Although one's *pa'rapuan* is important for certain ritual events, it is the household (*dapo'*) around which daily living revolves and which is the most basic social and economic group. The household unit usually consists of the nuclear family but may also include an elderly parent, a married child and his or her spouse, and grandchildren.

Toraja villages were traditionally, and many continue to be, located on ridges or hilltops, surrounded by stands of bamboo and overlooking terraced ricefields and cultivated gardens. Houses are situated in rows facing north, while ricebarns face south, opposite the houses. Present-day settlements contain a mixture of traditional houses (elevated wooden houses—some of which are elaborately carved—with large, sweeping roofs made of bamboo or corrugated iron), "Bugis-style" houses (which are also elevated and made of wood), and more temporary houses made of bamboo. Nowadays, there is typically an elementary school and a simple church structure within a 20-minute walking distance of the village; junior high schools, markets, and health clinics may be located at a farther distance, perhaps an hour's walk from the village.

Currently, high schools are only located in the town areas. Paved and unpaved roads connect several parts of Tana Toraja; however, many of these are only passable during the dry season which lasts roughly from July to November.

THE INTERVIEW SITUATION

We arrived in Tana Toraja in February 1982 and immediately began looking for an appropriate field site. After some exploring, we eventually decided to settle in a village in northwest Tana Toraja, about a five-hour walk into the mountains above the central valley. In 1982, the village (*kampung*) of Paku Asu (a fictitious name) had a population of approximately 800 people spread throughout its six, widely dispersed hamlets. Over 50 percent of the residents were adherents of the traditional religion, *Alukta,* and the remainder were primarily Protestant Christian, with a handful of Pentecostals. There were three small churches in the village, two Protestant and one Pentecostal, and an elementary school with an official enrollment of 150 students. There were no all-weather roads, no electricity, no running water or other utilities, and no local markets.

Paku Asu seemed like a good site to us for several reasons. First, we were impressed by both its physical and cultural beauty. Situated on the side of a mountain and surrounded by steeply terraced rice fields and groves of bamboo, it commanded a breathtaking view of a tributary of the Sa'dan River and surrounding valley. Equally impressive was its large number of intricately carved and painted ancestral houses (*tongkonan*) and rice barns; its ritual fields (*rante*), complete with stone menhirs erected to commemorate deceased relatives; its burial grounds, carved into the limestone cliffs of nearby mountains, and its active and diverse group of traditional religious functionaries and healers.[27]

A second reason for choosing Paku Asu was that we had been treated with kindness and understanding by the head of the region (*desa*) in which Paku Asu is located. Not only did this man—a true intellectual in addition to being a highly responsible and impartial official—graciously place his office and services at our disposal, but perhaps more importantly, he also was willing to let us fend for ourselves when, for purposes of developing rapport with villagers, it became necessary for us to distance ourselves from representatives of the government. Thus we were given the cooperation of the local government in terms of satisfying various bureaucratic requirements, but we were also given free reign to conduct our research.

A third reason for choosing Paku Asu had to do with the kind of research we wanted to conduct and the working and living conditions we needed to carry out such research. Since we wanted to ask villagers about aspects of their lives that might prove uncomfortable to them if broached in a public forum, we needed to find a place where we could conduct interviews in relative privacy. As luck would have it, we found an abandoned bamboo house near Paku Asu's elementary school. Once occupied by a teacher, the house was strategically situated midway between, and yet slightly separate from, the six main hamlets of the village. This seemed like an ideal location for us since it was close enough to all of the hamlets to give us access to a wide range of households yet distant enough to afford us some privacy.

Once we decided on Paku Asu as a research site, we had the abandoned house repaired and moved there shortly thereafter. For the first seven or eight months of our stay, we concentrated on collecting standard ethnographic materials on a wide range of topics, including childrearing and family life, emotional expression and communication, conceptions of deviance and abnormality, illness and healing, death practices and beliefs, and so forth. Some of this material was collected through census work and formal interviews with various religious specialists (both traditional and Christian), local health and police officials, healers, and teachers; but much of it was gleaned from informal conversations with villagers and from observation of both ritual and everyday life.

Only after this initial phase of fieldwork, when villagers had become accustomed to our presence, did we begin to select respondents for the open-ended interviews. Because the interviews were very time-consuming both in terms of the hours actually spent talking to people and in terms of the hours spent *preparing* to talk to people—scheduling and rescheduling interviews, buying gifts, preparing and serving food and drink, reviewing past interviews in preparation for future ones, etc.— we limited our sample to eleven villagers: seven men and four women. Though this is a relatively small number of respondents, we took great pains to select individuals who were not only cooperative but also broadly representative of village life and experience. Thus, six of our respondents are of noble background (though of widely varying wealth) and five are of commoner or dependent backgrounds; four are adherents of the traditional religion and seven are Christians; seven are 45 years of age or younger, while four are over 45; two are literate while nine are either semi-literate or nonliterate; and while eight reside toward the center of the village, three live on its margins.

As it turned out, we were fortunate to have chosen the abandoned house as an interview location since we later learned from several respondents that they would not have cooperated had our conversations occurred in a more public place. Even so, scheduling was difficult. All of our respondents were busy cultivating rice fields and gardens, preparing meals, raising children, or planning and attending rituals. We thus had to be flexible enough to accommodate their schedules. Some of the respondents came to our house before dawn on their way to the fields and gardens; some came in the afternoon during a break in chores; and others came in the evening on their way home from work and occasionally spent the night with us.[28] On a few occasions, we traveled to respondents' homes (when they were alone) and interviewed them there.

On average, we interviewed each respondent a total of ten to twelve hours over a series of six to seven visits. At the lower end of the range is a person who was interviewed three times for a total of three hours and, at the upper end, is someone who was interviewed twelve times for a total of over twenty hours. The first few interviews with each respondent were conducted with as little prompting as possible; thus they more closely reflect a local version of a "life-history." In later interviews, more questions were asked to encourage the respondent to reflect upon and evaluate certain events in his or her life and to introduce topics that had not spontaneously arisen in earlier interviews. The interviews were sometimes widely spaced, depending upon the wishes of individual respondents, and this part of our research lasted about five months. None of the respondents were paid or otherwise formally compensated, though we were generous with small gifts, food, coffee, tobacco, and betel, in keeping with traditional expectations of hospitality and reciprocity.

At the time we began the open interviews, we had the choice of conducting them in the Toraja language, *Basa Toraa,* with the aid of an interpreter, since our skills in the local language had not yet progressed to the point where we could ask detailed questions about personal experience, or in the Indonesian national language, *Bahasa Indonesia,* without the aid of an interpreter. After careful consideration, we eventually opted for use of *Bahasa Indonesia.* There were two main reasons for this. First, we felt that the use of an interpreter would adversely affect our rapport with the respondents; villagers had too often expressed their fears of gossip and slander for us to assume that they would be open and forthcoming in front of someone who could later discredit them in the community. Second, we discovered that the use of *Bahasa Indonesia* would not prevent us from sampling a broad range of Toraja life and experience. This was because a larger number of villagers than we had expected could in fact speak *Bahasa Indonesia* due to their exposure to it in school, in the markets, through radio broadcasts, in interaction with government officials, and/or during travel outside the highlands. We encouraged respondents to use Toraja terms and expressions for important concepts or for thoughts and feelings that were difficult to express in the national language, and many did this of their own accord.[29]

While we feel we gained more information in the interview process through the maintenance of confidentiality and rapport than we lost through use of the national language, we do not want to minimize the problem of conducting open interviews in a nonlocal language or obscure the sampling problem of chosing respondents who were speakers of *Bahasa Indonesia*. However, because of the ubiquity of certain cultural and psychological themes, and because of careful cross-checking of information, we feel confident that the interviews provide a wealth of data about specifically *Toraja* thought and feeling.

THE "RESPONDENTS"

The villagers we interviewed varied widely in terms of age, sex, wealth, social class, social role, religion, education, personal style, village of origin, reasons for agreeing to be interviewed, and level of enthusiasm for the interview process. In the following section, we introduce readers to some of these differences and present a brief profile of each respondent. All of the respondents' names have been changed, and some aspects of their social identity have been disguised. Names are listed in alphabetical order.

AMBE'NA (FATHER OF) KONDO, THE RETICENT MEAT DIVIDER
Ambe'na Kondo was first introduced to us as one of the leaders of the village. Though still in his mid-thirties at the time of the interviews, he was already an important meat divider (*to mentaa*) at community feasts. Ambe'na Kondo is very "traditional" for a man of his age: though of noble birth and moderate wealth, he left school after the sixth grade, has rarely traveled outside of the area, and is still an adherent of Alukta—though he claims he will convert to Christianity once he has fulfilled ritual obligations to his own and his wife's parents.

Ambe'na Kondo is relatively "hard" by Toraja standards. Though he occasionally smiles or laughs, he does not do so with the ease or frequency that most Toraja do, and at times he can be sullen and uncommunicative. He is an effective and forceful divider of meat, a role that calls for a certain strength of character and decisiveness, but he has relatively little patience for other aspects of the traditional leadership role, such as the mediation of disputes or the hosting and entertainment of guests and government officials.

Ambe'na Kondo had been married two times and had had one child before he met his present wife, a slightly older woman who had also been married before and came to the marriage with two children of her own. Since being married, Ambe'na Kondo and his wife have had four children and have become deeply involved in each other's family and ritual obligations.

Ambe'na Kondo only reluctantly agreed to be interviewed—in part because he was busy and in part because, despite his surface gruffness, he is a shy man and never felt completely comfortable talking about his life. His responses and comments in the interviews were almost always short, direct, and to the point. He rarely, if ever, elaborated on any experience voluntarily, and he was no doubt relieved when the last question had been asked.

AMBE'NA PATU, THE "MODERN" CLERK AND MINISTER Ambe'na Patu, though only a few years younger than Ambe'na Kondo, is his opposite in almost every respect. Born of commoner background and modest means, he has used his education and literacy to become the village clerk and secretary, a minor government-paid position. Out of step with all but a handful of males, he shuns the politics of meat at community feasts, both because he is relatively poor and because he lacks the temerity to compete for traditional status; instead, he has set his sights on becoming a trader at the local market. He has been married only once, at a relatively young age, and has six, closely spaced children. To complete the contrast with Ambe'na Kondo, Ambe'na Patu is a Christian and preaches at one of the village's Protestant churches. If Ambe'na Kondo represents one of the last remnants of the village's traditional past, Ambe'na Patu represents, in many respects, its future: literacy, Christianity, regional and national rather than local allegiances, reliance on a cash income, and less concern with traditional means of acquiring and maintaining status.

As a earnest government employee and as a relatively low status person in a hierarchical society, Ambe'na Patu thought it his duty to help us with our research, and his cooperation in the interviews was never in doubt. It was, however, difficult for him to understand why we were interested in the lives of the more "modern" people as well as the more traditional, and he needed reassurance that his comments and evaluations were interesting and important to us. Despite his uncertainty on some topics, he is proud of his personal accomplishments, and he talked about these with relish. He was almost always interviewed late at night, to accommodate a workday that included government, farming, and trading activities.

AMBE'NA TANGKE, THE ITINERANT MASON We first met Ambe'na Tangke shortly after moving to Paku Asu when he was hired to build a water basin for us. A relatively poor man from a dependent background, he became a skilled mason to supplement his meager financial resources. Unlike some other low status Toraja, he was not overly circumspect around us, but was a willing and pleasant conversationalist. He is also unusually open and candid for a Toraja male, and in the interviews he spoke at length and with feeling about his encounters with the Holy Spirit and his subsequent conversion to the Pentecostal Church.

In his early thirties, Ambe'na Tangke was born in a neighboring village where he lived until he married his second, and current, wife. He and his wife and their two children live with his mother-in-law in a modest traditional house. Although he was an enthusiastic respondent, his interviews were widely and irregularly spaced since his work often took him on journeys away from the village.

AMBE'NA TODING, THE FREETHINKING TRADER Ambe'na Toding, who lives with his first wife and seven children, is the most "deviant" of the male respondents. Of commoner background and relatively modest means, he is the only older man—around fifty years of age—to devote much of his time to trading activities outside the village. Although he desperately wants to become wealthy, none of his many business ventures have proven successful, and he often wonders why the gods and ancestors—despite his many offerings and prayers, and despite his many religious conversions (from Alukta to Protestant Chistianity, to Alukta again, and then to Pentecostalism)—have not given him better fortune (dalle').

He also has a reputation as one of the village subversives. Not

only does he openly voice his opinion that the national government and churches should do more to eliminate the vestiges of a
feudal order, but his fearlessness in traveling to the most remote
and reportedly magic-infested regions of Tana Toraja clearly suggests to others that he himself must possess extraordinary, and
perhaps harmful, powers.

Even more distinctive, however, is his candor and humor in
discussing sexual behavior. Elsewhere (Hollan and Wellenkamp
n.d.) we present our respondents' comments on sexual behavior,
and Ambe'na Toding's observations stand out among those of
the other male respodents. While most of the other men were
rather bashful and reserved in their remarks about courtship and
marriage, Ambe'na Toding was downright ribald. He took great
pleasure in giving detailed descriptions of sexual acts he had
either seen, heard about, or personally engaged in, and he jokingly told us not to believe anyone who said they did not like sex
or implied that it was an unimportant part of human life.

Ambe'na Toding's motives for participating in the interviews
were mixed. As a free-thinker and malcontent, he enjoyed having
an audience for his heterodox views, but he also never failed to
believe that we might one day invest in one of his business ventures and thus enable him to escape from his relative poverty and
despair.

INDO'NA (MOTHER OF) RANTE, THE LOQUACIOUS TRADITIONAL-
IST Indo'na Rante, in her early forties and of noble background
and moderate wealth, is an Alukta adherent and is one of the
most traditional of the women respondents. She is married to one
of the meat dividers in the village, her first husband, and while
she has lost several children, she has five surviving ones, the
youngest of whom, at the time of the interviews, was still breast-
feeding. She is a very lively, outgoing, uninhibited person, and by
the standards of the other female respondents, unusually straightforward and talkative. Her participation in the interviews was
equally straightforward and matter of fact.

INDO'NA SAPAN, THE DEVOTED CHRISTIAN Indo'na Sapan is a
bright, attractive woman of upper commoner status but moderate
wealth in her late thirties. She has a friendly, gentle demeanor,
but is unusually reticent by Toraja standards and once suffered a
long and severe "illness" that, by Western standards, would be
considered depression. Although she has two grown sons who
now live outside of Tana Toraja, she has been divorced for many

years from a man whom she was pressured to marry by her family. She was an early convert to Christianity and remains a prominent and devoted member of the Protestant Church although she is also very knowledgeable about traditional ways. Born in Paku Asu, she lives with her mother and step-father—who remain Alukta—and is a close friend of Indo'na Tiku (see below).

Though Indo'na Sapan was quite willing to talk to us on an informal basis, she was at first somewhat reluctant to be interviewed, and like Ambe'na Patu, she had to be reassured that her views and opinions were important to us. After some initial hesitation, however, she became more comfortable with the interview process and spoke at length about some of her more difficult life experiences.

INDO'NA TIKU, THE TRUSTED TEACHER Indo'na Tiku, a woman in her early forties, has been a teacher at the elementary school in Paku Asu for many years and lives in a modest teacher's house with three of her five children and a foster child. (Two adult children have moved away.) She was raised from an early age by two different foster parents, one of whom is a prominent and wealthy noble.

Although long divorced from an older man of considerable wealth and aristocratic status, Indo'na Tiku takes great pride in the fact that she maintains her ties to important families and individuals by slaughtering livestock at ritual feasts; she does this despite the fact that slaughtering is viewed as a predominantly male preoccupation and despite the fact that as an educated person, she should "know better" than to spend time and money on such supposedly wasteful traditional pursuits.

Indo'na Tiku is highly intelligent, sociable, and articulate, but also relatively unassuming and even-tempered. She is one of the few people in the village who seems to be trusted by almost everyone—wealthy or poor, Alukta or Christian—and as a consequence, she is often put in charge of community funds and the organization of public meetings.

From the outset of our stay, Indo'na Tiku was informative and helpful, offering us assistance first in establishing a household and later with various aspects of our work. She proved to be an excellent respondent—open, responsive, and thoughtful.

NENE'NA (GRANDFATHER OF) LIMBONG, THE ALUKTA ARISTOCRAT Nene'na Limbong is the epitome of the traditional Toraja noble. Born to wealth and power, he is at once refined, measured, and charming, yet self-confident and opinionated. He is the largest landowner in Paku Asu, and though barred from official government office because he once served the Dutch, his influence is courted by local officials and he remains a major force in village politics. Despite his age—almost 70—and declining health, he is also a meat divider and plays an important role in the resolution of village disputes. Like many other aging nobles, he currently watches with dismay as the spread of literacy, a cash economy, and Christianity rapidly works to undermine his traditional rights and privileges.

Nene'na Limbong took it for granted that we would want to interview him. He was, after all, the tacit, even if not the official, head of the village, and by his own reckoning and that of many others, he knew as much or more about traditional custom and taboo as did the local religious experts. From his perspective, if we were to learn anything about Toraja life and culture, we would have to begin with him. Nevertheless, he seemed ambivalent about participating in the interviews. He sometimes canceled or missed scheduled appointments but then appeared later when we were gone or busy. When he was interviewed, he enjoyed talking about his personal accomplishments and his exploits with outsiders, and he could be very informative about political, religious, and cultural matters, but he tended to shy away from a discussion of other topics. At one point it looked as if he had given up the interviews for good, but he eventually returned when he saw that other people continued to talk to us and when he realized that we were willing to drop the interviews rather than continue trying to secure his assistance.

Nene'na Limbong has been married twice, his first wife having died when he was still a young man, and he has thirteen children and numerous grandchildren.

NENE'NA TANDI (MALE), THE CHRISTIAN ORATOR We interviewed both partners of a married couple, and in keeping with Toraja naming conventions, we have used the same teknonym to refer to both individuals. To clarify matters, however, we place (m) after the name to indicate the male partner and (f) to indicate the female partner.

Nene'na Tandi(m) contrasts with Nene'na Limbong in much the same way that Ambe'na Patu contrasts with Ambe'na Kondo.

Though over sixty years of age, he has been a Christian for at least thirty years, is currently a prominent elder in the Protestant Church, and is an articulate spokesman for the modernist, egalitarian point of view in the village. Like Ambe'na Patu, he eschews the politics of meat and claims that the competitive slaughter of livestock at ritual feasts is both pointless and wasteful. Despite such views and criticisms, however, his knowledge of traditional customs and religion is extensive, owing in part to the fact that his father was a religious specialist (*to minaa*) and his mother a midwife (*to ma'pakianak*).

Nene'na Tandi(m), who grew up in a neighboring village, inherited little land from his commoner parents, but he is nevertheless relatively wealthy due to his marriage to Nene'na Tandi(f) and to the fact that despite three marriages, he is the father of a single step-child, and so he and his wife have not had to divide their land among several offspring. He and his wife have been close companions for over thirty years, and he is the step-grandfather of four.

Nene'na Tandi(m) has a boyish quality to him and enjoys being the center of attention. He often brags about his oratory skills—which are in fact exceptional—claiming he has the ability to sooth and hearten people when they are sad or upset, move them to action when they are tired or indecisive, and make them laugh when they are anxious, angry, or simply bored. While some people dislike his cockiness, his verbal and communicational skills do give him greater influence in the village than he otherwise deserves and they also make him an extraordinary and entertaining respondent. Always prepared to talk on virtually any subject, he can turn an account of the most mundane events into a notable or moving story.

Nene'na Tandi(m) is far more extroverted than any of our other respondents and he had probably decided he would play a central part in our research plans long before we had thought of asking him to become a respondent. Indeed, he took us under his wing early in our stay and his paternal attitude and feelings toward us were alternately touching and frustrating. His participation in the interviews was wholehearted and sincere.

NENE'NA TANDI (FEMALE), THE OUTSPOKEN NURTURER Nene'na Tandi(f), who grew up in Paku Asu as a middle child in a noble, wealthy family, is the wife of Nene'na Tandi(m). Though she is our oldest female respondent, in her mid-fifties, she is a determined, energetic person who continues to possess a great deal of physical stamina. Although she was married twice briefly before, and has one child from her second marriage, she has lived with Nene'na Tandi(m) for most of her adult life. By Toraja standards, the couple spend an unusual amount of time together, both working and relaxing, and their devotion to one another is evident. Like her husband, Nene'na Tandi(f) was one of the village's earliest converts to Christianity and she is an outspoken critic of "backward" beliefs and practices, even though her own life and that of her husband are clearly rooted in traditional patterns and rhythms.

By Toraja standards, Nene'na Tandi(f), though very warm and nurturant, is an unusually "masculine" woman. At public celebrations, instead of working with other women to prepare and serve food, she prefers to sit with the high status men of the community and discuss politics. She also occasionally smokes cigarettes and drinks palm wine, behaviors that are much more characteristic of men than women. The fact that she has only one child is an important part of her identity. Because of this, she says her extra-familial relationships are all the more important to her, and she makes a point of befriending others.

If her husband played the role of our foster father, Nene'na Tandi(f) played the role of our foster mother. Although she seemed somewhat embarrassed by the attention focused on her during the interviews, she was a cooperative participant and her interpretations and evaluations of married life provide an interesting contrast to those of her husband.

To Minaa Sattu, the Ritual Specialist To Minaa Sattu, approximately forty-five years of age at the time of the interviews, is one of the four remaining specialists of the traditional religion in Paku Asu, thus his title of *to minaa*. Although he "inherited" this title and position from his father,[30] who was himself a well-known and respected religious expert, he is not particularly adept at his calling. Indeed, his fellow villagers sometimes say that his knowledge of traditional custom and metaphor-filled ritual language is relatively limited and concrete, and they do not pay him a great deal of respect. The uncle of Ambe'na Kondo, To Minaa Sattu is of noble descent but he is relatively poor, having inherited only a small portion of his parent's modest rice fields, and he and his wife struggle to support their seven children.

To Minaa Sattu may not have been as clever or knowledgeable (*manarang*) as other religious experts, but he is sincere and earnest in his devotion to Alukta and he hoped that we might preserve as much of it as possible for future Toraja generations. Thus he had a professional interest in participating in the interviews and in helping us with our research. But To Minaa Sattu appeared to enjoy the deference and hospitality we showed him, which he was not used to receiving, and like Ambe'na Toding, he apparently hoped that he could directly or indirectly benefit from our relative wealth and status. He became one of our most dependable collaborators and made sure that we kept abreast of village events and gossip. If anything, he sometimes overidentified with us, becoming jealous if we spent too much time with other people and hurt if we failed to seek his aid and advice.

ORGANIZATION AND MAJOR THEMES

Our book is divided into two parts. In part 1, "Basic Psychocultural Orientations," we examine major themes in Toraja culture and experience. Chapter 1 discusses religious, moral, and philosophical orientations. Although this chapter presents more general cultural description than other parts of the book, it provides essential context for the interpretation of more person-centered data in the later chapters. Chapter 2 presents a review and examination of focal interpersonal relationships. While touching on aspects of sibling, spouse, and parent-in-law ties, it underscores the importance of the child-parent bond in Toraja society and culture. The emotional saliency and centrality of the child-parent relationship is, however, evidenced throughout the book.

In chapters 3 and 4, we present aspects of Toraja ethnopsychology. Chapter 3 examines elements of Toraja identity and self, including the commonly shared sense of being vulnerable to, or acted upon, by other humans or outside forces. Chapter 4 concerns mental states and processes, and examines notions of spirit or soul, dreaming, sense perception, cognition, aspects of morality and conscience, and aspects of emotional expression and control. Here we note especially the value that the Toraja place on emotional equanimity and the avoidance of overt hostility and aggression in everyday life, and we examine contexts in which more expansive emotional expression is encouraged or at least tolerated.

In part 2, "Suffering," we examine elements of Toraja discontent and suffering—topics of great emotional saliency for our respondents, and ones that came up repeatedly in the interviews. These chapters reflect as well our own efforts to touch upon an area of study that, historically, has been underreported in the anthropological literature (Edgerton 1992).[31] Like other recent studies in the anthropology of suffering and misfortune (e.g., Worsley 1982; Farmer 1988; Kleinman and Kleinman 1991), we examine indigenous conceptualizations of social and mental disorder and in other ways situate such phenomena both socially and culturally. Chapter 5 focuses on prevalent interpersonal concerns and anxieties—such as being robbed, and being tricked and deceived—while chapter 6 examines more intrapersonal dysphoria and disorder, including feelings of anxiety, somatic complaints, disturbing dreams, suicide, and mental disturbances. These chapters underscore that for many villagers, happiness and contentment can best by defined as the occasional and fleeting *absence* of suffering and hardship.

In chapter 7, we examine the ways in which Toraja villagers attempt to make sense of and cope with disorder and dysphoria. Here we examine aspects of traditional healing and other social mechanisms of repair and reconciliation, but focus especially on "emotion work" (Hochschild 1979, 1983)—that is, the ways in which villagers consciously attempt to shape and manage their own emotional experiences as well as those of others.

Our final chapter, chapter 8, is a summing up of significant themes in Toraja culture and psychology and a discussion of how Toraja personal experience is both shaped by, and shapes, aspects of culture and society. (Some readers may wish to consult our summary of major themes and topics found on pages 215-217 before beginning the book.) We discuss, among other things, the emphasis on social harmony and nonaggression that coexists with interpersonal cautiousness and mistrust; the importance of emotional constraint, and the role of emotion work in maintaining such constraint; and finally, the emphasis on suffering.

NOTES ON TRANSLATIONS AND STYLE

1. Unless otherwise noted, all of the quotations from respondents we present here are taken directly from transcripts of the open interviews. Translations were made in the following manner: We left Toraja or Indonesian words in a quote whenever we felt that an English translation would be imprecise or misleading; otherwise we translated them. When translating, we made a deliberate effort *not* to convention-

alize the English translation, but rather to preserve as much as possible a sense of local idioms of expression. For example, we translated the Indonesian word "dia," a third person singular pronoun that does not specify gender, as "he/she" when the gender of the person was not clear from the context. Such relatively literal translations are, of course, awkward at times, but we believe that they are valuable in conveying a sense of indigenous ways of speaking and thinking.

2. Most personal and place names have been changed.

3. We use the term "respondent" to refer to those who took part in the open interviews; we use the term "informant" to refer to all others who provided us with information.

4. Within the excerpts from the interviews, we use parentheses to set off our own questions asked during the interview, and brackets to offer an expansion or clarification of a respondent's remarks or occasionally to provide other editorial information.

PART I
Basic Psychocultural Orientations

In this section, we discuss basic psychocultural orientations, including conceptions of the person, self, emotions, and interpersonal experience. We begin with explicit moral and spiritual beliefs and move to more implicit conceptions of the self and intrapersonal processes.

1

RELIGIOUS, MORAL, AND PHILOSOPHICAL ORIENTATIONS

At that time when, so we are told,
heaven and the broad earth still lay on each other,
all was chaos, then, so it is said,
the all-enfolding still touched the regions of the earth,
all was still in disorder.
The wide flat land was still invisible,
clusters of rock were still not to be seen,
the channels in the fields, dug by the lords,
were not visible.   (van der Veen 1965:67)

According to van der Veen's published version of a ritual invocation that narrates the origin of the world,[1] the world was created when the initially undifferentiated universe was separated into the heavens, the earth, and the underworld. The earth then was divided into rice fields, mountains, rivers, and other geological features characteristic of the present-day landscape, and Puang Matua, the "Old Lord," used his bellows to create the ancestors of humans and of certain plants and animals, who later descended from the upper world to the earth.

The first humans purportedly enjoyed direct access to the upper world via a ladder or staircase, and they lived in close contact with the gods (*deata*). Later, however, after an important taboo was violated—in one account, a prohibition against brother-sister incest, in another, a prohibition against theft—the ladder to the upper world was destroyed (Nooy-Palm 1979:145). The gods then became "inaccessible," "unapproachable," and "not to be beheld" (van der Veen 1965:31–33). They became "enclosed inside a curtain" and "enfolded within a wall;" they became "sleeping ones" and "slumbering ones" who must be aroused and awakened by prayers (van der Veen 1965:33–35).

The gods later established another, more comprehensive set of ritual prescriptions (*aluk*) and prohibitions (*pemali*) that continue to guide Alukta practice today. As noted in our introduction, it is the observation of these rites and prohibitions that forms the core of traditional religious practice. In return for compliance with these regulations—many of which concern the making of sacrifices and offerings—spiritual beings are thought obligated to provide humans with bountiful crops, thriving livestock, and numerous, healthy children. However, should the prescriptions and prohibitions be ignored, then humans can expect illness, misfortune, and death to follow.

There are a number of themes contained in Toraja origin myths that resonate with the concerns and interests of contemporary villagers. These include an awareness of the tension that exists between order and disorder (see below); the nostalgic sense that times were once better, either in one's own life or in the past; and the importance of rules for the orderly conduct of life. Also noteworthy is that relations between humans and spiritual beings are conceptualized in reciprocal and pragmatic terms: one can expect spiritual blessings (*tua'*) of fortune and prosperity, but only if one gives of oneself or one's property in return. Nene'na Limbong, an expert on traditional beliefs and practices, once compared the process of obtaining spiritual blessings to getting water from a spring. The water may be available, he said, but one needs a *lampa* (a bamboo carrying vessel) to be able to make use of the water. Thus, sacrifices and offerings to spiritual beings are the tools by which blessings are secured. Similarly, omissions or transgressions of the *aluk* and *pemali* are viewed in practical terms as "debts" that must be repaid.

SPIRITUAL BEINGS

As suggested by the foregoing, Alukta adherents—and many Christians as well—believe in the existence of a number of nonhuman beings, which we refer to here as "spiritual beings." In the following few pages, we present brief portraits of those beings which have particular salience for the people of Paku Asu. *Deata, nene'*, and *bombo* all play prominent roles in the traditional religious system. *Sadang, lobang boko'*, and *po'pok*, on the other hand, are more horrific beings which have little to do with religious beliefs per se; their significance in the lives of villagers varies somewhat from person to person.[2]

Deata. According to traditional religious belief, there are several major and minor gods residing in the upper and lower worlds as well as many local ones that are associated with particular geographic locales such as streams, trees, rocks, and mountains. These beings may be invisible or they may take human or animal forms—appearing as snakes, horses, monkeys, etc. Some *deata* are male, some are female, and for some the gender is unclear or varies according to region and to informant. Many of the older gods play important roles in the wider cosmos but have minimal contact with the living.[3] Puang Matua, the "Old Lord," is the most important of the gods in terms of current religious practice.[4] As noted above, he is said to have created the ancestors of humans and of the more important plants, animals, and objects; he is also said to have established the first rituals (Nooy-Palm 1979:110). Although *Puang Matua* is a very important and powerful god, he is considered to be more distant than the lesser gods, who are more concerned with human affairs and who occasionally manifest themselves to villagers during the course of *ma'bugi'* and *ma'maro* ceremonies.

Humans may use or traverse the geographical areas where earthly *deata* reside, but only if they carefully follow certain procedures; otherwise, there may be severe repercusions. Thus Alukta adherents may not use the water of one of the streams that flows through Paku Asu to cook the meat of an animal killed at a funeral or to wash black clothes, since both of these activities are associated with funerals and death and are anathema to the *deata* that resides there. One of our *to minaa* informants attributes at least three deaths in the village to violations of these rules.

Of our eleven respondents, only Nene'na Tandi(m) reports an encounter with a *deata* spirit outside of a dream or a ritual context: he claims that a *deata* that looked like a monkey with a pig's head once jumped over him as he crossed a bridge to a nearby hamlet. Ambe'na Toding, however, says, "It's nonsense if someone says, 'I've seen a *deata'*. . . . Because *deata* [look] the same as humans [and so cannot be readily distinguished]." Although people's ideas about, and experiences with, *deata* vary, most villagers are reluctant to walk alone at night, when *deata* are thought most likely to be about.

Nene'. The word *nene'* is used to refer to living grandparents, as well as to the souls of deceased relatives and ancestors.[5] As noted before, the traditional religion is sometimes referred to as Aluk Nene', "the way of the ancestors." One cannot overemphasize the importance of deceased ancestor figures for the Toraja. Such beings, together with the *deata,* are thought to watch over the living. If the living have conscientiously fulfilled their ritual obligations to the dead, the *nene'* may be relied upon to bestow blessings. For example, as we note later, *nene'* may appear in dreams, bringing with them cures for disease or information on how to locate amulets (*balo'*) that can be used to obtain prosperity and well being. Conversely, if the *aluk* and *pemali* are neglected or ignored, *nene'* may cause illness and other forms of misfortune. Generally speaking, however, they are viewed as having a more protective role in their relationships with humans than are the *deata,* of whom villagers are more fearful.

Some ancestors—those for whom the highest level of funeral is performed and for whom sacrifices are made at subsequent rituals (the *ma'nene'* and *ma'maro* in the Paku Asu area)—are said to eventually become *deata* (*membali puang, mendeata*). In general, long-dead ancestors are said to be more powerful than the recently dead, and yet it is the more recent dead who figure most prominently in villagers' lives. Many of our respondents, both Christian and Alukta, believe that they have been assisted by the souls of dead relatives at some time in their lives.

Bombo. *Bombo* are the souls of the recently dead or those near death. Although some villagers openly doubt that *bombo* manifest themselves to humans, Indo'na Tiku claims that it was her fear of such beings that led her to quickly entomb her foster mother after her death, and To Minaa Sattu is one of a handful of villagers who claim to have actually seen a *bombo.* Here is how he describes his first encounter:

> (Have you ever seen a *bombo?*) When I was [still] herding buffalo, I saw one. [The *bombo*] of a person who had not yet died.] (Not yet died?) Yes. Not yet died. There was a funeral going on— this was before I was married—and I had gone there to *ma'badong* [sing a funeral chant]. [After it was over], all the people went home. [But] I stayed at the rice barn and sat for awhile. [Then] I decided to go home, and I started down the trail. Just as I started, I met someone in the middle of the trail. I asked, "Who is it? Who is it?" but she didn't answer. I looked [and thought], "Oh, this is a *bombo.*" She had a string of coins around her waist, and a piece of cloth on her head. And she had a plate on her head [picking up a plate to demonstrate]. [The appearance of the apparition is identical to that of a female *tatau*—an effigy of the dead that is constructed during traditional funeral

rites]. I looked [and thought], "This is a woman from X who has come to Paku Asu. She heard the *badong,* and her *bombo* has come." I met her in the middle of the trail and asked, "Who is it?" But she didn't answer! I looked [and thought], "This is a *bombo.*"

[Then] I ran straight [back] to the dead person's house. I entered the house, and there she [the *bombo*] was! She was sitting behind the dead person. She ate the betel and sweet potato that the dead person had been given [as an offering]. And she drank the palm wine [that the dead person had been given]. And after she had eaten meat and sweet potato and corn, she took some betel and chewed betel. Her name was Ne' Bua. (Did you know her?) Yes, I knew her because she was a relative of mine. When I went home, I told people that I had seen Ne' Bua and that she would soon die [in accordance with the belief that a person's *bombo* is only visible if he or she is near death]. And sure enough, about one week later, she [Ne' Bua] died.[6]

[The second time To Minaa Sattu encountered a *bombo*]: I was still small [holding out a hand to indicate his height]. There was a funeral, and I went. I sat by a boulder [menhir] where they were slaughtering a buffalo. I sat, and then a man slaughtered a buffalo. The meat was thrown here and there. [He refers here to the division of meat which occurs at many rituals.] I saw someone get up and start eating some [raw] meat! [Normally, meat is taken home and cooked before being eaten.] But I didn't know [he was a *bombo*], because I was still young. I said, "That person is eating [raw] meat!" And then I was thrown about [he is whispering here]. (By the . . .) Yes, by the *bombo.* I was thrown about by the *bombo.*

(What did it look like?) A man! He had buffalo horns on his head [similar in appearance to a male *tatau*]. After I had been taken home and recovered—because my consciousness had disappeared—my parents asked me, "What did you see?" I told my father, "I saw a *bombo* eating meat. That's what hit me." But I knew the man! (Who was he?) A relative of ours. . . . (Why did he hit you?) Because I said his name [out loud]. (Were you frightened?) Yes, I was frightened. Of course I was frightened.[7]

Sadang. Sadang, seen only at night, appear as shining torches that move through the rice fields or across the face of a mountain. Believed to be the disembodied heads of people who were particularly courageous (*barani*) in life, they are said to leave the graves at night in search of food. *Sadang* are generally avoided, since they may attack and devour humans. Yet it is said that if one has the courage to capture and subdue them, they can be transformed into stone amulets with healing and protective powers.

Lobang boko'. Lobang boko' ("hollow back") are the potentially dangerous spirits of women who have died in childbirth.[8] From the front, the spirits are said to have the appearance of a woman, but their backs are invisible. Nene'na Tandi(m) claims to have once been chased by one, and Indo'na Rante was fearful of being hurt by one following the death of a relative in childbirth (see chapter 6). Both respondents also provide descriptions of how people can defend themselves from *lobang boko'*. Indo'na Rante says, "If a woman dies in childbirth [and so has the potential of becoming a *lobang boko'*] . . . eggs must be placed in her hands. Because her spirit is *angry* at people. But when she wants to hit someone, she must guard the eggs in her hands [lest they be broken] . . . and thus she can't [hit anyone]." Nene'na Tandi(m) says that if a *lobang boko'* is encountered, it is helpful to know that "when they laugh, their mouths open so wide that they can no longer see. It is then that you must run, since they can't see you. But don't just run straight down the trail, cut off into the bush. Because as soon as they stop laughing they'll follow the trail to catch you."

Po'pok. Po'pok are sickly persons whose spirits leave the body at night to devour the blood and organs of healthy people. In their nighttime form, *po'pok* are said to be very thin, with dry skin, and long, beaklike mouths. Although *po'pok* do not realize their souls are feasting on others, their identities are often widely known or suspected, since they are thought to often be the same people who become possessed at *ma'maro* and *ma'bugi'* ceremonies. Though a *po'pok* may cause illness through its bite, it also has the power to heal its victims by blowing. If such a cure is attempted and succeeds, then this is considered evidence confirming the *po'pok*'s identity.

VILLAGE CHRISTIANITY

Christianity, as it is practiced by village adherents, particularly those living in areas, like Paku Asu, that are some distance from the market towns of Makale and Rantepao, is infused with elements of the traditional religious system. Many of the fundamental beliefs of Alukta have been retained by directly substituting Christian terms for concepts found in the traditional religion. This has occurred both because early missionaries made a self-conscious attempt to graft Christian doctrine and beliefs onto preexisting indigenous concepts—in keeping with their view that primitive religions had devolved from belief in an authentic Christian-like God to a corrupted state of spirit worship and polytheism (Bigalke 1981)—and because villagers themselves readily make these substitutions.

Indo'na Rante, for example, who had once become a Pentecostal while living in the city of Ujung Pandang but later reverted to Alukta when she returned to the village, states, "I equate the ancestors and gods with God. They are the same. If we believe in the ancestors and the gods, it is just the same as being sheltered by God."

And Nene'na Tandi(m), a prominent member of the Protestant Church, says, "Christians say that the bridge to God is Jesus Christ. The *Aluk* people also have a bridge to their creator, [namely] the *deata*. There is no difference. They [Jesus Christ and the *deata*] are both the same." He also directly equates the *pemali* of Alukta to the Ten Commandments. Village Christians and Alukta adherents also hold very similar beliefs about death and the afterlife and Christian funerals retain many traditional elements and symbols (see Wellenkamp 1991, 1984).[9]

Although some Christians, such as Indo'na Tiku, no longer abide by the traditional prohibitions, others, such as Nene'na Tandi(m), attempt to discover, by trial and error, which of the traditonal rules can safely be abandoned and which cannot. Nene'na Tandi(m) says:

> [We] cannot eat meat [from a death ritual] and then work in the fields. . . . Also, if we go to work the fields, we can't eat corn. We can't eat cassava, those are orders from the ancestors. It can't be said that [Christians] are divided from villagers [Alukta adherents]. [The orders of the ancestors] are still held onto. . . . [One] can't follow/agree with people who say, "I don't believe there are *pemali*." There are indeed *pemali*. . . . For example, if there is a dead person recently buried . . . [and meat from the funeral is distributed and eaten] and then we go work in the fields, the rice will be like grass. Sweet potatoes will be eaten by insects. Everything is spoiled. And when someone is born, the birth is not perfect [there are birth defects].
>
> [Elsewhere in the interview he says]: Or if we eat meat [from a death ritual] and then pull weeds from [our] coffee plants, the

coffee will die. . . . And if we Christians . . . do that it dies, too! It must die. Because [once] I felt/thought . . . "Better if I try this out one time [test the *pemali*]." So I planted some peppers. Then [one day] I ate some [buffalo] meat and I went and got some of the peppers. Three days later I went back to look at the pepper [plants] and all of them were dead! Dead! As dead as a dead person. So I thought, "Wah! It's not true when people say [there are no *pemali* for Christians] . . . there must be *pemali* for Christians, too, if it's like that!"

There are a few major differences between Alukta and Christian beliefs that cannot be easily reconciled, however. Whereas Alukta adherents worship the gods and ancestors by avoiding the transgression of numerous prohibitions and by performing rites and rituals—an important part of which are costly offerings and sacrifices—Christians worship God by praying, by contributing to the church, and by upholding Christian tenets of conduct. The Christian belief that God will provide prosperity and well-being in return for such seemingly simple acts of worship strikes village Christians as both welcome and at times, puzzling and disconcerting. Generally speaking, most villagers, Christian and Alukta alike, see Christian means of worship as a liberation from the more exacting demands of the traditional religion. From their perspective, Christianity offers a relatively short list of prescriptions and prohibitions, the Ten Commandments, in place of the extensive rules of the *aluk* and *pemali*.

But Christian villagers' reaction to their religious liberation is mixed. On the one hand, many feel relieved that they no longer have to abide by a moral code that often feels burdensome. Christian regulations are felt to be less "heavy," both psychologically and financially, than those of the traditional religion. On the other hand, there is a recognition that in certain important respects the "permissiveness" of Christianity violates basic cultural understandings about the nature of relationships. Many Christians say that they and the community as a whole pay a price for the freedoms they enjoy under the new religion. They claim that falling rice production, decreasing human longevity, and infestations of rats, insects, and other pests are part of the general decline in the quality of life that has occurred during recent years as Christian and modern influences have penetrated the region.

Another major difference between village Christianity and Alukta is that Christians are officially barred from holding most "smoke ascending" rituals and from participating in the *ma'nene'* ritual.[10] These restrictions stem from the 1920s, when the Dutch mission in Tana Toraja began to hold conferences and established a commission to devise guidelines for distinguishing between religious practice, *aluk,* participation in which would be barred for Christians, and customary practices, *ada',* which Christians could continue to follow (Bigalke 1981:221). Although there continues to be a great deal of discussion and uncertainty regarding the lines of separation between religion and custom, these early guidelines are still officially endorsed today (see Wellenkamp 1988; Hollan 1988).[11]

We will have more to say later about how Christians and *Alukta* adherents perceive one another. In the next two sections, we discuss conceptions which both groups share.

NOTIONS OF FATE AND FORTUNE

One of the implications of believing that prosperity is linked to compliance with the *aluk* and *pemali* (Alukta) or Ten Commandments (Christians) is that wealth becomes symbolic of moral and spiritual standing. If one prospers, it is generally assumed it is because one has fulfilled one's obligations to spiritual beings; if one fails to prosper, it is suspected that one has failed in one's obligations. Lack of prosperity, then, ultimately reflects negatively on one's own or one's family's moral and social worth.[12] In our interviews, this was a frequent topic of discussion, one that obviously preoccupies many of our respondents during less fortunate periods of their lives. Several respondents commented on illnesses or deaths which, they thought, had resulted from wrongdoing. Indo'na Rante, for instance, says that she did not eat rice during her mother's funeral (as required by mourning taboos), but that after awhile:

> I couldn't tolerate not eating rice [and so she resumed eating it prematurely]. Often my father would say, "It won't be long before you lose your teeth" and indeed that was true. . . . [About the time] I had Rante, my teeth started to *hurt* and then [they] came out. My father would say, "That . . . is a sign [that she had broken a *pemali*]!"

We will have more to say about how one may absolve oneself of wrongdoing, and so enhance one's prospects for prosperity, in chapter 7.

Few villagers would assert, however, that compliance with religious rules and practices guarantees wealth and prosperity. This is because many also hold the view that good fortune is at least partially dependent on one's practical efforts and labor. It is more accurate to say, then, that villagers believe that spiritual beings offer the opportunity for wealth and prosperity—through compliance with specified rules of conduct—but that the realization of such prosperity requires an expenditure of personal energy. Thus, for instance, while spiritual beings might assure that the rice seed will germinate and that the fields will eventually fill with water, it is left to villagers to plant and care for the rice seedlings and so bring them to fruition. This notion that one must actively seize the good fortune offered by spiritual beings is a recurrent motif in both folktales and in our respondents' accounts of their life experiences. In one very common scenario, a person begins with a single chicken. Through careful husbandry and the beneficence of spiritual beings, the chicken reproduces and is eventually sold to buy a piglet. The piglet is then raised and sold to buy a buffalo, which in turn is sold to buy rice land. Here, for example, is how Ambe'na Patu describes how his father began to accumulate wealth:

> Indeed, my father was a hard worker. [First] he sold coffee. That was all he had. [Then] before getting married, he started growing sweet potatoes and other things. After several years, he sold [his garden produce] and started raising pigs and chickens. [After selling the pigs and chickens], he started buying rice land. [Then] he could start eating rice [rather than sweet potatoes or other less valued foods].

> [Later in the interview, he describes his own work habits as a youth]: I began growing plants in the fourth grade [for profit]. I raised white onions. . . . I sold a bag of onions and bought a pig. [Then] I raised the pig. After I graduated [from grade school], I sold the pig and bought a buffalo. Like that. When I entered high school, I sold the buffalo to pay for my expenses.

The accumulation of wealth and prosperity thus is not seen as instantaneous or effortless, but rather requires patience and perseverance. One may enhance the results of one's efforts through the accumulation of both practical and magical "knowledge" (e.g., of astronomy and meteorology, of propitious names and days of the year, of magical or spiritual powers, including dream portents, and of the spiritual beings who bestow such powers, etc.), but the labor itself cannot be avoided.[13]

Even though Toraja believe that lack of prosperity reflects negatively on one's moral or spiritual standing, there is also the belief that there are limits to human agency and responsibility. Thus villagers say that ultimately, one's fate lies in the hands of spiritual beings. One can long for good fortune and work hard to attain it, yet all prosperity, in actuality, is a "gift."

Ambe'na Toding says, for example,

> Prosperity is never a certainty, because it comes from . . . [spiritual beings]. All we can do is work. We don't know if prosperity will come to us. No. All we can do is work [and hope that prosperity will come].
>
> [Elsewhere, when discussing what happens when one makes a mistake, he says]: We don't know whether [there will be a repercussion] in the coming [days] or not. We are merely like blind people. All we [can do is try] to make a living.
>
> [In yet another interview, Ambe'na Toding remarks]: If we're going to be poor [that is, if it is our fate], even if we have ten buffalo, they will all die.

Ambe'na Patu, the Christian minister, holds remarkably similar views: "My thoughts/desires are always blooming, but nothing is ever certain. We humans have many plans, but it is God who determines such things. So we have many plans and ambitions, but it is God who controls things."

NOTIONS OF ORDER AND DISORDER

The traditional Toraja world is highly structured and carefully ordered. Spatial and temporal orientations are important components of this ordering. Like many other Southeast Asian groups (Milner 1978; Fox 1980), the Toraja are highly cognizant of directions—marking in their speech the direction in which they move (north, south, east, west, up, down, across, etc.)—and they are highly attuned to the timing of particular events in their lives. Numerous traditional rules regulate the proper orientation of objects, plants, people, activities, and so forth, in space and time.[14]

Belo (1970) and Bateson and Mead (1942) have conveyed similar concerns of the Balinese regarding the proper placement of things and people, as Errington (1983a, 1983b, 1989) has done for the Bugis of Luwu (South Sulawesi). Mead (Bateson and Mead 1942:7; cf. Swellengrebel 1960) reports, for example, that among the Balinese, "the head is the highest part of the body and . . . a flower which has fallen to the ground may not be picked up and placed in the hair again." Errington (1983a:567) reports that among the Bugis, "shoes are placed on the floor at the foot of the bed, never at the head; and, when a pile of clothing is made, sarongs must be placed under blouses, never the reverse." Much of the Balinese and Bugis preoccupation with such matters stems from a desire to maintain proper relationships between things and people of different status and value or power (Anderson 1972; Errington 1983a).

Some of the Toraja concern with temporal and spatial arrangements similarly is related to notions of hierarchy and to a desire to distinguish between different levels, including levels of social status and of ritual. High status villagers, for example, are buried in the vaults at the top of limestone cliffs while lower status people are buried near the bottom. "Smaller" or "lower" rituals are held earlier in the agricultural year than "larger" or "higher" rituals (Wellenkamp 1984:31; cf. Weinstock 1987:93–95). But in addition, the Toraja concern with proper placement stems from the division between "smoke-ascending" and "smoke-descending" ritual spheres, each of which has its own set of directions, time of day, plants, food, vocabulary, and so forth.[15]

Objects and activities associated with one sphere should be kept strictly separate from the other sphere (with some exceptions; see Crystal 1986). Most of the traditional prohibitions (*pemali*) in some way serve to keep these spheres separate. It is taboo, for instance, to wear black clothing to a "smoke-ascending" ritual, to harvest rice or remove rice from one's ricebarn after having eaten meat from a funeral, and to cook any meat received at one type of ritual with meat received from the other. As we have noted, if such prohibitions are violated, misfortune in some form such as illness, famine, infertility, or death is believed to inevitably follow.

For example, when Indo'na Rante's older sister developed blurry vision in one eye, specialists determined her symptoms to be caused in part by a member of her family violating the taboo against cooking eggs with meat received at a funeral. To Minaa Sattu explains that he once had a bad infection that he believes resulted from his having attended *rambu tuka'* and *rambu solo'* activities in quick succession: "There were some people tying up a pig, and I went to watch. Someone threw a piece of bamboo cord, which I picked up. But it cut my hand! . . . A lot of blood came out! It became very sore. . . . [For] five months my hand festered [in infection]! . . . People said it was . . . because [I] was going here and there [mixing ceremonies]."

The normally strict segregation of the two spheres is such that we were even instructed to keep separate notebooks for recording information on "smoke-ascending" and "smoke-descending" events.

Despite the strict segregation, the relationship between the ritual spheres is perceived as a complementary one. As one ritual specialist explained, the relationship between the two spheres is similar to those between husband and wife, and between the verbs, "leave" and "return;" that is, each entails the other.[16]

Although the traditional prohibitions and regulations are extensive, there are mechanisms that allow for some flexibility in an otherwise minutely regulated environment. According to one person, for instance, the prohibition against holding smoke-ascending and smoke-descending rituals on the same day can be circumvented by taking a nap in between the two rituals. In some cases, violations of prohibitions can be safely ignored provided that the violation is not openly acknowledged or labeled as such (see Wellenkamp 1984:35).

Along with the emphasis on temporal and spatial orientations in Toraja life is a general concern with detail and orderliness. Nooy-Palm (1975:71) comments that, "the Toraja like order: ricefields are laid out in a neat pattern, houses are decorated with motives in a geometric design. Everything has its place in the system." Similarly, Volkman (1985:14) notes that "one of the striking patterns that emerged in many fieldwork contexts . . . is the Toraja penchant for order and completeness. To discuss a ritual sequence, for example, one must proceed from the beginning to the end and leave out nothing in between." For the Toraja, it is a matter of aesthetic (and, at times, religious) importance that activities (ranging from ritual to language instruction) be conducted with an attention to detail, and with an emphasis on progressing step-by-step from one end to the other—from low to high, small to large, outside to inside, etc.[17]

The Toraja concern with order is expressed in ritual verses as well (Hollan 1988b). Here, images of order, such as combing through tangled hair, are used to suggest atonement and the correction of errors, while images of disorder, such as walking through dense undergrowth, are used to represent mental confusion and illness. Quiet, undisturbed water, in contrast to the turbulence and opaqueness of rapids or cataracts, is also used to suggest a state of health and vitality after a period of illness (van der Veen 1965:144). The meticulous and orderly weaving together of disparate threads into cloth is used to suggest the order and peace of a united community (van der Veen 1965:100) and the strict form and proper order of a successfully executed ritual (van der Veen 1965:27). The correct and proper way of executing a task, including ritual, is also suggested by the straightness and clean, unambiguous lines of a bamboo stalk (van der Veen 1965:27).

Related to the concern with order in Toraja life is an emphasis in everyday behavior on personal constraint, "coolness," and stability, and on maintaining smooth interpersonal relations. However, there are times when "heat" and lack of constraint are expected and encouraged. One occasion is *ma'maro*, a ritual held for various reasons (Hollan 1984:244) but in general concerned with healing, purification, and transformation. Another occasion are kickfights (*sisemba'*). At both of these events—in contrast to the normal state of affairs—disorder, lack of constraint, and "heat" are associated with personal and community well-being. We examine both the *ma'maro* and kickfights in greater detail in chapter 4.[18]

THE VALUE OF SOCIAL UNITY AND INTERDEPENDENCY

A fundamental assumption of Toraja villagers is that life centers around interdependent relationships. The living, of all ranks, are dependent on spiritual beings for wealth and prosperity and for protection from disease and misfortune; the landless and the poor are dependent on wealthy patrons for work opportunities and other support; young children are dependent on their parents for nurturance and protection; and so on. While in some contexts, a person provides aid and comfort to others, in other contexts, he or she expects to receive aid and comfort. The high value attached to the system of mutual aid is suggested by Indo'na Rante: "Here [in Tana Toraja], it is really good. If there is something we need, whatever, if we don't have it, we can go to someone else's house and ask for it." Indo'na Rante gives as an example a pig that she needs for a funeral. If she hears that someone in the next hamlet has a pig, she goes and asks to borrow the pig, agreeing on the pig's value and setting a date for repayment. "And also if, for example, the agreed time elapses, and the pig isn't repaid, the person *isn't angry*. This is the way of the Toraja people. If he/she comes to request [the return of the pig], and we don't have it, he/she just waits patiently!"

Although people often are not so patient in such matters as we discuss later, Indo'na Rante is voicing the ideal response, at least as concerns outward, public behavior. Villagers are fond of saying that if you need a sacrificial animal and do not have one, you can borrow it; anyone who requests a piece of meat at a ceremony will be given one;

and if you are very hungry, you may help yourself to another person's sweet potatoes.[19] While stealing is considered a very serious crime, people often say that there is no reason to steal because one only has to request (*palaku*) whatever it is one needs.

This is not to imply that the Toraja value altruistic giving. Those who would give without consideration for eventually receiving something in return, are considered irrational. Thus, when a "crazy" woman in the village climbed up to her ricebarn and began passing out bundles of rice to passersby, her behavior was perceived as further evidence of her insanity. What is valued, then, is reciprocal exchange.

Such exchanges are so highly valued in part because they come to symbolize and validate the very existence of a relationship (see Coville 1988).[20] Under these circumstances, requests for assistance are not dismissed lightly—since a refusal could imply a denial of relationship—and when requests do go unfulfilled, the person whose assistance was sought often feels constrained to explain his or her behavior. Conversely, those who receive assistance are said to have a moral duty to reciprocate.

In many contexts, exchanges are expected to be relatively balanced. Adult children are expected to feed and care for their aged parents as their parents once fed and cared for them in childhood (see Hollan and Wellenkamp n.d.). And a person who provides a pig or buffalo for a relative's funeral assumes that he or she will eventually be repaid with an animal of equal value. In other contexts, however, where the status, wealth, or power of the parties are unequal, the exchange is unbalanced (cf. Valeri 1985:65–67). This is particulary true of exchanges with spiritual beings, from whom villagers expect to receive a bounty of wealth and prosperity in return for comparatively small amounts of offerings. Villagers' expectations regarding the bounty they expect to receive from spiritual beings are reflected in the *merok* feast, when the *to minaa* ask the gods to bring villagers limitless amounts of wealth: "All the goods of all kinds, all the possessions together ... riches in quantity, like foliage; precious things, like the branches of the tree" (van der Veen 1965:65). Similarly, the slaughter of water buffalo at funerals is viewed as only a temporary financial outlay which will eventually be repaid in manifold by the ancestors. We will have more to say about some of the advantages of the subordinate position in an exchange relationship when we discuss aspects of hierarchical relationships in the next chapter.

Related to the orientation toward social interdependency in Toraja is an emphasis on social unity and an avoidance of interpersonal conflict. Beginning with the kindred and extending to the wider community, fellow members are enjoined to have *sanginaa* or *misa penaa:* one mind, one breath, one course. As in Java and other parts of western and central Indonesia, interpersonal relations should be conducted with a minimum of outward conflict, and important decisions should be made jointly or collectively. Actions that contribute to the maintenance of social unity, such as the making of compromises and the smoothing over of potential conflicts, are highly approved. Actions that promote social discord and disunity meet with strong disapproval.

The emphasis on social interdependency and on maintaining social unity reflects a real need for cooperation between fellow family members and villagers in important areas of life such as wet-rice agriculture and house construction. Arrogant behavior, even on the part of community leaders, is widely condemned and one reason for this is that arrogance is an affront to the notion of social interdependency. That is, those who act arrogantly are in effect stating that they do not need other people. Favoritism is also condemned because of its erosive effect on social interdependency and unity. Thus it is felt that one should not discriminate between one's friends and neighbors, and particularly between one's close family members. That this emphasis on sharing and egalitarianism may sometimes contradict an equally strong value placed upon status, privilege, and prestige will become clear in chapter 2.

THE MORAL PERSON

Not surprisingly, many of the personal characteristics and habits the Toraja most admire are those consistent with the social and moral values discussed above.[21] One particularly esteemed complex of traits—having to do with generosity, honesty, and trustworthiness—is closely linked to the importance of reciprocal exchange in establishing and maintaining ties among people. Many times in the interviews, people talk about the importance of maintaining trust so that help is given when and if it is needed.

In talking about his father's funeral, Nene'na Limbong says:

> There were buffalo, there were pigs—in other words, many people helped [with the funeral arrangements]. . . . So many people were willing to help me. . . . Some gave buffalo, some gave money . . . But I repaid everything! When they [those who helped him]

had to arrange a funeral, I paid back everything that was lent to me. So I in turn helped others."

Nene'na Tandi(m) reports:

That's the most important attitude for me, truthfulness. . . . If I say to you, "Give me some money, I need to borrow some money," and then I don't pay it back, some would call that trickery or deceit. But I call that a lie [which is even worse than trickery and deceit].

Ambe'na Toding says:

I am . . . well thought of and respected. We must have that [people's respect]. If even one time we can't be trusted, how many times are we going to be helped? . . . If we can be trusted, we will be helped—with a good heart like that. We must think about these things.

To Minaa Sattu remarks that a dishonest, untrustworthy person is shunned:

If a bad person like that goes to someone's house, he/she isn't given anything. Because he/she is a bad person! People say, "That person is a bad person. Don't give him/her rice. Don't give him/her drink. Don't give him/her betel." . . . If a good person walks by [one who can be trusted], he/she is invited in. But if a bad person like that is seen walking by, the door is shut.

He continues this discussion by claiming that he himself has proven to be a trustworthy, generous person by responding to our requests for research assistance:

I have come to instruct you because I have a good heart. Even though you are from far away, I must give you my knowledge. Because you want to ask questions of me, I must answer. So if you ever wonder, "Is the to minaa a good person or not?", think first. If I had even the slightest bit of untrustworthiness in me, certainly I wouldn't have come [to help you]. . . . Whatever you have asked, I have given you.

A second complex of highly valued traits, which includes patience, tolerance, and interpersonal sensitivity, has to do with the importance of social and familial unity. The high value attached to these traits is perhaps most clearly reflected in the criticism directed toward those who engage in verbal disputes with others.

Thus Nene'na Tandi(m) comments, for example:

> We feel that if there are arguments/disruptions in the village, inside one village, everything is ruined! Heart/soul is ruined. Thought is ruined. Development is ruined. Farming is ruined. Prosperity is ruined. So everything is ruined. The first thing ruined is the unity/oneness of the community.

Divisive arguments, he explains, are like "poison:"

> For example, you and I buy a buffalo. Half-interest for you and half for me. After awhile you say to me, "You have only a quarter share in this buffalo." Then I respond, "No!" Then you say, "That buffalo will be dead before you get it!" Truly, that [the curse] is like poison." [He then gives a second example]: Imagine you and I have adjoining rice fields. You say to me, "You've taken part of my field!" Then I say, "It's you who've taken my land!" And then you say, "You'll be dead before you take any crops off that land!" That, too, is like poison.

Ambe'na Toding is equally critical of those who engage in verbal disputes or harangues. He tells the following story: It is cassava-planting time and X needs seedlings for his garden. Without asking permission, he goes to Y's garden and removes some seedlings. Y discovers the missing plants and begins to publicly curse X for his thievery. According to Ambe'na Toding,

> If we curse like that, we can only expect to be cursed by others. Y was really angry! The point is, everyone could hear. He shouldn't do that, curse like that: "Fuck your mother!" Everyone could hear. He's not the only one in the village. We're all family. . . . We must have shame, we can't say things like that. [It is considered highly inappropriate to use sexually explicit curse words in front of opposite gender family members.] He shouldn't get angry and curse like that because we're all related.

Ambe'na Toding claims that rather than curse, Y should have just given X the plants he needed: "I would have said, 'Here, take my seedlings! Help yourself.'" Ambe'na Toding is voicing here the widely held view that a public and socially disruptive reaction to a breach of conduct may be considered even more reprehensible than the original breach.[22]

Angry outbursts are condemned, in part, because they may stimulate angry, aggressive responses in others, thus leading to greater social turmoil. According to Indo'na Sapan:

> Someone who is always angry, we don't like someone like that. Because a person like that is always saying bad things until we [those listening to the bad things] get upset and angry too. [She goes on to explain the difference between a patient, tolerant person and an angry one]: An angry person is called a *to sengkean* [from the root *sengke*, meaning angry]. A good person is called *to sa'bara'* [a patient, tolerant person]. An angry person, he/she throws it out [expresses their anger], but a patient/tolerant person, he/she stores it [does not express anger]. . . . If you respond to someone else's anger [by yourself getting angry], that is bad. . . . If it [the anger] is always thrown out, there are always difficulties. It is better if we remain patient/tolerant.

The preservation of social unity is achieved not only by the suppression of anger and hostility, however, but also by the active promotion of courtesy and respect toward others. This leads to consideration of a third highly esteemed complex of traits, including friendliness, helpfulness, and a proper sensitivity to feelings of embarrassment and shame, which have to do with the cultivation and maintenance of social etiquette. By cultivating social etiquette, the Toraja, like many other Asian and Indonesian peoples, attempt to maximize the predictability of social behavior and so minimize the inadvertant frustrations and insults that may lead to socially disruptive behavior.

A proper sensitivity to feelings of embarrassment/shame (*malongko'*, *masiri'*) is perhaps the most essential element in this complex of attitudes and behaviors,[23] for it is the fear of being shamed and humiliated that explains, in part, why Toraja villagers abide by conventional rules of etiquette. Those who violate these standards and act in a manner seen as offensive are said to "not have *siri'*" and are compared to animals, young children, and insane persons. *Siri'* also orients one to the social hierarchy: If persons are accorded the deference and respect due their place in society, they feel honored/respected (*dikasiri*). But if their position is challenged in some way, they are likely to feel embarrassment/shame/humiliation.

For socially mature persons, an element of shame enters into many interactions occurring outside the intimate family or with members of the opposite sex within the family. Ambe'na Kondo gives some examples:

If I'm about to meet someone I've never met before, I must be slightly embarrassed/ashamed.

For example, if people have just begun to eat and then I arrive [unexpectedly], I must be embarrassed/ashamed. There must be embarrassment/shame in a situation like that.

If it is a female child I must instruct [toilet train], I must be embarrassed/ashamed.

It is a person's own sensitivity to embarrassment and shame that leads him or her to act in a way that reduces the chances that others will feel shame. In day-to-day behavior, this is done by extending to people the courtesy and respect due their social position. Passersby, for example, deserve the courtesy of being offered drink and shelter. Though it is understood that this is a formality and that one should not always accept such invitations, to not offer aid and comfort to a visitor could shame or humiliate them. Most people also deserve not to be criticized or disparaged too openly and publicly; thus critical remarks are generally avoided or expressed only indirectly. The command of allusive speech (*gora-gora tongkon, ponto bannang*) is highly valued among the Toraja, and proverbs which express the inappropriateness of open, blunt, or crude speech are common (Kobong et al. 1983:19).[24] It would be considered rude, for example, to directly refuse an offer of drink or shelter. Rather, one responds, "I'll return later," or "I'll drop by one of these days." To speak in a polite, softened manner is to *ma'kada melo,* literally "to speak well/pleasingly." People who express themselves in this way are called *to masipa* ("polite/well-behaved people").

Besides using pleasing words, polite people avoid the empty gossip that can cause someone to feel shame or humiliation. Such rumor-spreading is likened to bird calls: it has no purpose or aim, and is therefore pointless.[25] *To masipa* also avoid boastful, bragging talk, since by inflating oneself, one inevitably deflates and embarrasses others.

The cultivation of courtesy and respect does not mean that people are overly circumspect or shy, however. To the contrary, the Toraja highly regard those who speak easily and well and have the ability to make others laugh. Such highly verbal, socially skilled people have greater success in establishing ties with others and in gathering aid and support when in need. As we have noted, villagers recognize that feeling too much shame and embarrassment can be a liability.

Throughout the interviews, respondents speak of the importance of social etiquette and proper behavior. The following excerpts are taken from interviews with Nene'na Tandi(m), who is himself a master of social skills. He comments on his own interpersonal style and on the advice he gives others regarding appropriate attitudes and behavior:

That is what we need . . . goodness and honesty. We shouldn't brag, "I am brave." "I am rich." We can't do that. We are not respected [if we brag] . . . The most important thing is to have a good heart. And sweet words. And honesty. Those are the three things we need.

Our parents [give us advice] for when we travel or when we go anywhere. One piece of advice is, "When you travel, no matter what village or area you enter, don't brag about your wealth. Don't brag about how smart you are. What you must take is a good heart. You must not steal. Don't take anything, not even food, unless it is given." This is their advice . . . This advice—indeed we may say the *commands* of our parents—their advice . . . is like wealth [it is very valuable].[26]

I have a good heart. It is not wealth that is wanted . . . but sweet words and a good heart . . . I am not intelligent/successful, but I have a good heart and sweet words.

The extent to which a command of social etiquette is considered necessary for creating and maintaining good will among people is suggested by Indo'na Rante when she criticizes a couple who lack such skills:

Indo'na La'lang, she doesn't know how to get people's sympathy/ care. It's not good if we don't know how to behave. Even if we are rich [as are Ambe'na and Indo'na La'lang]. Who knows when we'll be stranded on the road? Who will feed us then? If someone doesn't receive help, it's because they don't know how to behave. But if I were to be stranded . . . people would give to me [because she knows how to behave]. They'd say, "There's a good person." That's important. . . . But Indo'na La'lang and Ambe'na La'lang aren't like that. They just think, "We're wealthy." But that's not enough.

The Toraja vision of the ideal, moral person is summarized in the concept of *penaa melo*, a phrase literally translated as "good breath." People with *penaa melo* are courteous, fair, and sensitive to others' feelings of shame. They give willingly, refrain from gossip, and avoid inciting anger and hostility in others. When, despite their best efforts, they become embroiled in disputes, they remain tolerant and patient and make every effort to avoid a breakdown of social unity and harmony; they are essentially nonaggressive. Above all else, the ideal person acknowledges that the peace, security, and unity of the family and village take precedence over individual interests. Identity and self-esteem are affirmed within the community, not apart from it.

2

Aspects of Interpersonal Relationships

THE NATURE AND BASIS OF ATTACHMENTS

There are two important bonds upon which interpersonal relationships among the Toraja are presumed to be based. The first bond is that of shared ancestry, which distinguishes one's "family" from all "others." Volkman (1985:45) notes: "The Toraja social world consists, most broadly stated, of family and other people. In this respect the Toraja resemble the Bugis, for whom, as Errington (1979) has shown, these two categories define the trusted and comfortable as opposed to the unknown and the potentially threatening." *Rara buku,* literally, "blood bones," is a central element in the Toraja conceptualization of family bonds. As Volkman (1980:81) describes it, "the idea is that these substances [blood and bones] are shared by members of the family, and the term is in fact a shortened version of *sang rara sang buku,* or 'one blood, one bones.' " *Sikande rara,* another way of referring to family, "is literally 'reciprocally eat blood,' with the sense of being so closely joined that there is no gap, like broken bones that grow together (*sikande*) as they heal" (Volkman 1980:81–82).[1]

Botanical terms and metaphors also suggest the "natural" and biological nature of ties between fellow kin:

> Several nuclear families that share a common ancestor are called *sang sape*, a single branch of the rice plant. A cluster of *sape* is called *sang to'*, the clustered strands of a rice plant. When many people (many 'clustered strands' or *to'*) acknowledge a common ancestor, the term *sang rapu* or *pa'rapuan* is applied. *Rapu* is a clump, as in a dense bamboo stand or a group of coconut trees, growing together as if from a common root, but with each tree branching separately.   (Volkman 1985:46)

Both botanical metaphors and notions of shared blood and bones are commonly used in everyday conversations and in interviews when discussing relationships to fellow family members. Nene'na Tandi(m) describes how he compared himself to a leaf on a tree to remind his Alukta parents of the permanent nature of family bonds so that they would not disinherit him when he converted to Christianity:

> He told his parents, "There is not a person in the world who can be separated from his/her parents. Just like . . . there is not a leaf that can be separated from the tree [it grew from]. All of them [the leaves], even if they fall, fall beneath the tree [they grew from]. They do not fall away from the tree. I am the same to you. . . . Blood bones, that is something that can't be broken/separated . . . If you want to throw [reject] me with your right hand, I will still be in the left [hand]. If you want to throw [reject] me with your left hand, I will still be in the right."

Many people assume that shared ancestry in and of itself ensures a greater commonality of interests. We discuss this further in the section on "Parental Surrogates."

The second important bond recognized between individuals, as we noted, is one based on reciprocal exchanges.[2] Social life in Toraja revolves around reciprocal exchange, especially the exchange of food or foodlike substances, such as *pangngan* (areca nut, betel, and lime). Daily socializing centers around sharing *pangngan* and tobacco, cigarettes, cups of tea or coffee, and occasional snacks such as roasted corn or boiled sweet potato.[3] The most dramatic and costly exchanges of food, of course, take place on ritual occasions when large numbers of livestock may be given to hosts before they are in turn slaughtered and their meat distributed to those in attendance.[4] As we have noted, relationships between humans and spiritual beings also are based on reciprocal exchanges.

If on the one hand, the offering and sharing of food and other items (such as cloth and pieces of clothing, labor, medicinal, magical, and ritual knowledge, and even children) is seen as establishing and strengthening interpersonal relationships, the withholding or misappropriation of food and other items of exchange may, on the other hand, express disruptions in those relationships. For example, parents who are particularly upset with their children's behavior may not allow them to eat a meal. Calling a man's name out of order or offering him a small or less desirable piece of meat in the division of meat at a ritual may indicate a deliberate attempt to belittle the man or to challenge his status and prestige in the community. Slights in hospitality at feasts or in casual visits may be read as hostile comments on the status of a relationship. Spiritual beings, too, are thought to communicate their displeasure with humans by, among other means, depriving them of food sources through drought or pestilence.

Regarding the emotional component of interpersonal attachments, parties to a close relationship are said to "love" (*ma'pakaboro'*, *mamali' lako*) one another. To "love" someone means to be concerned about their welfare and to feel sorry for them and have compassion (*mamase*) for them in times of need. It also means to be accustomed to their presence and to think about them and yearn for them (*ma'inaanaa*) when they are away.[5]

FOCAL RELATIONSHIPS

Among family members, generally speaking, child-parent, sibling, and grandchild-grandparent relationships are the most central in Toraja, both culturally and personally.

Child-Parent Relationship

By far the most salient relationship of those listed above is the child-parent relationship. Children are highly valued in Toraja for many reasons. Volkman (1985:50–51) writes:

> Aside from their economic value (as laborers in fields and houses), their social value (they join houses in alliance), their ritual value (they sacrifice animals for their parents), and their emotional value (they are generally adored), they are valued as affirmations of self (childlessness is considered a severe and pitiable lack) and as a sign and promise of good fortune (*dalle'*). . . . "If our fortune is good, we will bear a child on each hip and another on each shoulder; they are our treasure."

Many villagers consider the birth of children to be one of the happiest moments in life. Indo'na Tiku, for example, when asked when she has felt the most joyful (*parannu*), laughs and replies, "Oh . . . when I took my [teacher's] exam and was told [I had] passed. . . . And also when I had children!"

The birth of one's first child establishes a person as a truly "adult" member of the community. This change in status is reflected in naming practices. In place of one's personal name, a teknonym is used once a child is born. Thus a parent is called "Mother of" or "Father of" and with the birth of a grandchild, "Grandparent of".[6]

It is clear from the interview material that conventional naming practices have a phenomenological basis. That is, children are perceived by respondents as extensions of the self; they are also perceived as "replacements" for deceased relatives, and for the self as one ages (see chapter 3).

According to cultural doctrine, one important basis for the child-parent bond is the biological tie uniting child and parent. This tie is presumed to be an immutable one (although, as indicated by Nene'na Tandi's(m) concern over his parents possibly disinheriting him, in actuality even close biological ties may not prevent estrangement between individuals). The presumed immutability of the child-parent bond is reflected in the practice of planting the child's umbilical cord next to the house, an act that symbolizes the child's permanent tie to his or her natal house and village. Also, a child is considered to be forever indebted to his or her mother for bearing the burden of pregnancy and childbirth.

From a Toraja perspective, the second basis underlying the child-parent bond is the sustenance and care that the parents provide the child. That parents take their nurturing responsibilities seriously is suggested by respondents' claims that decisions about divorce (see below) and remarriage are strongly determined by considerations regarding the welfare of one's children. Ambe'na Toding, for example, says:

> Many times I have felt like finding another wife [because of domestic quarrels]. But I have remained [because] I love/pity my children. So that's how I feel. When she argues with me . . . I feel like leaving her. But when I am 'conscious' again, I [remain]. . . . Some people leave for a year and then return. Some leave for two years and return. Some leave for only a week or two but then return, feeling the suffering of their children.

For such parental care and concern, the child is thought to be heavily indebted to the parents. Eventually, the child repays his or her debt when as an adult, he or she sends gifts such as money and clothes to the parents. But most important, the debt is not considered repaid until the child provides for the parents' funerals (see chapter 3) and if the parents are Alukta, performs other related duties. These obligations are taken very seriously: Children often travel long distances and spend large amounts of resources for their parents' funerals; and some children of Alukta villagers postpone becoming Christians while others may revert to Alukta in order to fulfill ritual obligations for their deceased parents.

To fail to acknowledge one's relationship to one's parents or children is considered a grave "sin" or "mistake," as Ambe'na Toding relates in the following story:

> There was a man who was working [outside the highlands]. After a while, his father followed after him [but] he didn't know which city [his son was living in]. He [the father] met someone who said, "I have seen your child." So he followed the person to his child. Once he got there, the child said, "You are not my father." At that, the father started to cry! The father had brought rice and other things, but the son did not want to acknowledge [him] because he had become rich!. . . . So he was ashamed by his father. After the father had cried, he picked up his rice and other things and returned to the house [where he was staying], because the child had said, "Take all of your things with you. I am not your son." When he got home, he cried again and then he got angry [and said], "We must acknowledge our father and mother even if [they are] only [a piece] of wood, a dog, or a pig. [If not], we sin." Then . . . [the son, feeling regretful] hurried to find his father. . . . When he found him . . . he climbed out of the vehicle and then another car came [and hit] him and he died!

Respondents' comments suggest that children, of whatever age, generally perceive their parents as important providers and protectors whose love and nurturance is highly valued and sorely missed when it is lost. In speaking of his mother's death, To Minaa Sattu says, for example:

> When my mother died, I thought, "Where will I live?" That's why I was sad. Sad . . . [he pauses]. When my mother died, my body felt broken/out of order, [and I thought], "Where will I live now?" Because I was still young [around 10 years old] and already an orphan [biung pu'pu'] [his tone of voice is soft and subdued]. So [I thought], "Who will feed me?" I was still too

young to feed myself. When I went to school, I would see my friends and tears would come to my eyes. I would look at my friends [and think], "Most of these children still have their mothers. I am the only one whose mother has died." That's why my heart was sad.

His comments about his father's death are similar:

(What did you feel when your father died?) I felt sad when my father died. I cried morning, noon, night because I [had become] an orphan. . . . That's why I cried. Because I was still young. [I thought], "Where will I get another father?" I was just a child and my father had died [his tone of voice is again soft and subdued]. That's how I felt when my father died! . . . To this very day, I still remember my father. . . . Whenever I see large groups of people, tears come to my eyes. I look at them [and think], "If my father were still alive, he'd be here." That's how I feel. I see large groups of people and I must cry.

In another interview To Minaa Sattu comments on why he was not frightened when he got sick as a child:

When I got sick, my father and mother were still alive. And every day, I was sung to by my mother. That's why I wasn't afraid. If my father and mother had been dead, of course I would have been frightened.

When he is asked when life was most difficult for him, he replies:

When my mother and father were still alive, I was happy a little. When they died, things became difficult. Ever since then—I am an adult now—it has been difficult to make a living.

Nene'na Tandi(m) also bemoans the loss of his parents, especially their advice and counseling. At several different times in the interviews, he mentions the positive effect his parents' advice has had on his life, and he talks of the necessity of providing similar advice to one's children. After discussing some of the particular items of advice given by elders and parents (e.g., don't be arrogant, don't steal), Nene'na Tandi(m) says:

So I think elders are like judges. . . . they give us advice. There is "evidence" with all those people I have seen who have not stored well, or didn't hold on tightly to those requests of our parents. . . . All of those people . . . are [now] poor. Why? Because [they] threw away all of them [items of advice]! . . . Although they are called "lessons," I myself think they are [valuable] possessions.

In a later interview, he returns to this topic:

[He is talking about some Christian villagers who have been quarreling and fighting] They don't pay attention to [the fact] that us Toraja, what we remember first are the requests of our parents. It's like I already told you, the requests that our parents give us are like gold. . . . you shouldn't ignore those requests, but these people who are doing all these things, indeed they haven't been given advice by their parents. . . . [they] can't be taught, [they] are like wild animals. When people understand/follow . . . those requests, indeed [it is as if] they have been given gold by their parents.

Nene'na Tandi(m) says that since his parents' deaths,

I haven't been that happy, what I mean is, I've felt lonely. . . . [When they were alive] I could lean on them, tell them . . . about the difficulties that I faced, and they could tell me secrets/strategies [to use]. But now [that] my parents are gone . . . I have only my thoughts to answer me.

The central importance of parents as opposed to other relatives in Nene'na Tandi(m)'s life is suggested by his wife, who comments on why he no longer visits his natal village:

It has been years since he has visited his [natal] village. Sometimes I get angry and say, "Go and visit your older sibling!" But he replies, "I have no desire to go." [And I say], "Why don't you want to go?" And he says, "It's true that Randan is my [natal] village, but my mother and father are no longer there. So when I go there, I begin to think of my mother and father. I become sad. That's why I don't visit there anymore." [pause] [Then] I say, "But you have an elder sibling there who is like a mother [to you]." And he says, "An older sibling is not the same as our parents." [pause] So that's why, sadly, he doesn't visit there anymore.

Although feelings of sadness and loss in connection with temporary separations between family members are sometimes downplayed especially in public settings (see Wellenkamp 1988b:490–91), some respondents report greatly missing their parents and children during absences.

Both Indo'na Rante and Indo'na Sapan, for example, returned to Paku Asu from travels outside the highlands in part because they missed their parents. Indo'na Rante relates:

My mother told me to go to Ujung Pandang [to earn money for school clothes]. Sadly, I went. . . . I went to Ujung Pandang and got clothes, [but] I also remembered my parents. I often cried. I cried, remembering my mother. I thought, "It would be better if I went home to my mother." . . . Nothing can hurt us if our parents are still alive.

Indo'na Sapan says:

We're only happy when we're together [with our parents]. [pause] If we're separated, we're not happy. Like when I went to Manado [to live with her husband]. I was not happy for even one night— what a pity—because I was thinking of my parents. When I returned [to Paku Asu], I was happy again, and sad when I had to go back.

Indo'na Sapan says she often dreamed of her mother when she was away:

Every night I dreamed I was with my mother. I would get up [and realize], "Oh, I'm here [in Manado and not in Paku Asu]." I was very cheerful when I dreamed I was with her. According to the elders, if you dream you're with someone, it means they [the person you dream about] remember you. [It means] they don't forget you, so they say. [It means] they always remember you.

Other common dream experiences also suggest the importance respondents attach to their parents' care and nurturance. As we note in other chapters, many of our respondents whose parents have died have had dreams in which the souls of their parents come to them offering gifts and advice. These dreams are thought of as "real" experiences that validate the existence of ancestor spirits (*nene'*) and demonstrate that parents continue to be interested in one's fate even after death. In the following, for example, Nene'na Tandi(m) tells of a dream in which his deceased parents offered him advice:

(What did your parents say [in the dream]?) They said, "If you follow our advice you will lack for nothing. Raise/nurture your grandchildren well. And don't get angry at your wife, or hit her. Don't. All that you possessed before [his bad ways], throw it all

away. . . . don't ignore [our advice]. [Don't let it] disappear."
They spoke to me just as they always did!

He then goes on to say that he and his wife, Nene'na Tandi(f), continue
to receive help from her deceased parents as well:

> Nene'na Tandi has also met with her mother [in a dream]. . . . I
> asked her, "What did your parent bring you?" And she replied,
> "Two *sarongs*—one for you and one for me [which prophesied
> good fortune]." . . . [And] right away, we bought two rice fields!

Indo'na Rante, after relating that she has had several dreams of her
deceased mother bringing her something, says:

> Often when I sit like this, I just remember/think of my mother.
> Usually if I really remember my mother, a few nights later, I
> *dream* [of her], I see her again. (What do you feel when you
> dream of your mother?) I feel very sad. When I get up, oh deh
> deh. My heart, [I feel like], "I'm here, I'm alive with my mother."
> [pause] Then I remember, "Oh, [she's] dead. It was a dream."

In a later interview, the discussion returns to dreams of deceased
relatives, and this time Indo'na Rante suggests that her dreams are a
pleasant experience:

> (You have dreamed of your mother.) Yes. Usually when I wake
> up from the dream, I feel happy. [pause] [I think], "Oh last night
> I saw my mother." I imagine her body. (Oh.) Yes! It's like she's
> there! And sometimes we talk to one another.

Pleasant reactions to seeing one's deceased relatives in dreams appear
to be more typical of our respondents and other villagers than distress-
ful ones.

Respondents generally emphasize the positive aspects of the child-
parent bond, yet many child-parent relationships are not unambivalent.
While dreams in which deceased parents bring gifts or advice appear
frequent, respondents also report dreams of deceased parents that have
more ominous meanings or are characterized by anxiety (see chapter
6). Also, fear of possible spiritual punishment may motivate children
to fulfill ritual obligations to their deceased parents. Finally, at least
some respondents are made anxious, rather than comforted, by a reliance on parental figures. In explaining why he chose to establish his
own household as quickly as possible after marriage,[7] Ambe'na Patu
comments:

This is the problem. If we get used to living with our parents, we're happy to let them make a living [for us]. We don't have to work ourselves. We rely on our parents. But when they die, things will be difficult. . . . If we live with our parents, we don't lack for anything. If we have a need, they provide it. If we have no salt, they provide it. If we have no rice, they provide it. But if we live in our own house, if there is a need, we must provide it [ourselves]. . . . That's how we learn that we must work before eating.

The cultural emphasis placed on the child-parent bond in Toraja is also reflected in conceptions of relationships obtaining between children and various parental surrogates.

Parental Surrogates

There are many circumstances under which a child comes to be raised by persons other than its parents by birth. The first is when individuals or couples who do not have children of their own, or who would like to have more children, ask to have a relative's child come live with them. For example, a couple with no children may ask to raise a sibling's child; a grandparent whose children are all living elsewhere may ask to raise a grandchild; an unmarried woman with no children of her own or a divorced woman who already has children but who would like another child, may request one from a sibling or a cousin; or, an older sibling moving to town may take a younger sibling along to help with household labor and to provide company. The couple, Nene'na Tandi(f) and Nene'na Tandi(m), for instance, have fostered 10 children over the years, and Indo'na Tiku has fostered two (one of whom came to live with her before she was married, and the other, after she was divorced).[8]

According to cultural doctrine, a request to raise a close relative's child cannot be refused. In practice, however, parents often seem reluctant to give up a child unless the arrangement offers some advantage (e.g., the child would receive a better education).

A second circumstance under which children come to be raised by those other than their parents by birth is when the parents die or divorce, and relatives then take over the care of the children. Indo'na Rante and her husband and To Minaa Sattu and his wife have both cared for children under such circumstances. Also, relatives living in town may be asked to care for a child temporarily while she or he attends school or looks for work.

The age of a child at the time that residence is taken up with parental

surrogates varies considerably, although generally children are not separated from their parents until after the child is weaned (after 9 to 15
months or so). Requests to raise a relative's child are made only after a
birth has occurred.[9] According to our census of one of the hamlets in
Paku Asu, over one-half of the households (15 out of 26) have either
given children to relatives to raise, or are raising or have raised relatives' children.

In her discussion of children in the traditional legal system, Nooy-
Palm (1979:37–39) distinguishes between various statuses, including
children who are "adopted" as opposed to those who are "fostered."
She uses the term "adoption" to refer to the Toraja practice of formally
including an individual into the nuclear family by way of a small
ceremony. The second, more informal arrangement whereby children
are cared for by relatives either on a temporary or permanent basis but
without the performance of a formal ceremony, she refers to as "fosterage."[10] Waterson (1981:294–97) also distinguishes between adoption
and fosterage. Adoption, according to Waterson, entails not only the
performance of a formal ceremony,[11] but also the assumption of certain inheritance rights and certain obligations toward the adopted
parents (or parent),[12] including caring for the parents in old age and
providing for their funerals. Usually, the adopted child is given *tekken*
(land that is given to the child for his or her use until the parent's
death, at which time the child becomes the legal owner).[13] Adoption
has no effect on the rights and obligations obtaining between the child
and the parents by birth, which remain intact.

While Paku Asu villagers are aware of the possibility of formal
"adoption," it seems to be uncommon and most people do not distinguish between foster and adopted children.[14] Mostly, villagers talk of
those who are raised (*to dipakasalle*) as opposed to those who were
given birth to (*to didadian*); also, children who are taken at a young
age are called *passarak*,[15] while those taken when they are older are
called *to diala anak*. For lack of a better term, we use "fostering" to
refer to children raised by those other than their parents by birth.

Fostering usually takes place between close kin; often foster children
are close kin of the foster mother. This is especially true for *passarak*,
who are usually grandchildren or siblings' children. Toraja parents
would feel uneasy giving their child to a nonrelative to raise;[16] similarly, a prospective parent would prefer to raise a relative's child. The
preexisting kinship bond between the parents is assumed to assure that
the child will be well-treated and that possible future conflicts of interest will be avoided.

Ideally, the bond between foster children and their foster parents is as close and strong as that obtaining between children and their parents by birth. In cases where sibling's children are fostered, kinship terminology remains the same both before and after the child is fostered. That is, while specific terms of reference exist for one's parents' siblings,[17] in practice parents' siblings are simply referred to as one's "mother" (*indo'*) and one's "father" (*ambe'*). Similarly, siblings' children are technically *pa'anakan* but are usually referred to simply as one's "children" (*anak*). In their treatment of children, parents are expected to not discriminate against their foster children in favor of their other children, if they have any. And parents claim that they do not, in fact, discriminate between their children, that to them, foster and children by birth are "just the same."[18]

Nevertheless, careful distinctions regarding the foster status of children are maintained. When Indo'na Tiku was asked what was the name of her youngest child, she replied, "Tangke," referring to her youngest child by birth, even though she has a still younger foster child, Sampe, who she requested and has raised since he was weaned and who has since had little contact with his natural parents. Similarly, the couple Nene'na Tandi(f) and Nene'na Tandi(m) frequently remarked how it was a pity that they only have one child, neglecting to mention that they have several foster children. Others in the community are also quick to distinguish between a couple's children by birth and their foster children, and children learn at a young age who in the family is a "raised" child and who is not.

In addition to the careful distinction that is maintained between raised children and children by birth, there is a notion expressed by some that parents by birth are more likely than foster parents to spoil and indulge a child. Correspondingly, foster children are perceived as being inherently drawn to their parents by birth and to be likely to leave at any time to return to their home. While in many cases, foster children do return to live with their parents, this latter sentiment is expressed even when the possibility seems unlikely such as in the case of Indo'na Tiku's foster son, Sampe. When asked if she thought Sampe would feel anything when he is told he is not her son by birth, she replies:

> Yes, indeed, that child is going feel, "Later when I'm already grown, it would be better if I leave for my mother by birth." Indeed, raised children are like that. If they know that they have a mother by birth, usually they run to their mother by birth. [pause] Like Sampe later. Maybe he will already have left by the

time he is 10 years old. (Really?) Yes. [pause] Thus, it's difficult for the raised child to stay continuously with the mother who raised him. Always he will follow his parents. (Why would he follow his parents if he has always lived with the mother who raised him?) Oh. [pause] Because the raised child has more love for his mother by birth than for the mother who raised him. Indeed, that's the way it is." [19]

It is not uncommon for villagers to feel sorry for those who have been raised exclusively by foster parents. Many people commented, for instance, that Indo'na Tiku's mother had left her with relatives when she was a young child and has never returned. One woman said that Indo'na Tiku was probably upset over the fact that she never knew her real parents. Not surprisingly perhaps, the only ones who do not always make careful distinctions between raised children and children by birth are those who have been fostered. For example, when one of us asked a young man who was being raised by the couple, Nene'na Tandi(m) and Nene'na Tandi(f), about his parents whom he visits periodically, he seemed reluctant to talk about them. Instead, he emphasized that he considers Nene'na Tandi(m) and Nene'na Tandi(f) to be his real parents.

There are, we think, many factors that contribute to the maintenance of the distinction between foster children and children by birth. One factor is that children are never unconditionally transferred over to the foster parents. But in addition, it seems that the distinction serves to highlight and reinforce the cultural notion that the child-parent bond is the strongest and most enduring bond in Toraja society. That is, one of the cultural messages that is conveyed by the maintenance of this distinction is that even though foster children and parents share a close biological tie and hence their relationship is assumed to be characterized by a sense of security and trust, nevertheless, the relationship is not as close as that between a parent and child. As Indo'na Sapan says, even if one has a second mother, "it does not matter how rich she is [or] how pretty she is, she's not the one who gave birth [to you]."

There is a considerable difference in the way in which foster relatives are perceived as opposed to stepparents with whom stepchildren may share little direct biological connection. Whereas the treatment of children by foster parents is asserted to be the same as, or at least closely approximating, that by parents, stepparents are commonly depicted as callous to the needs of their stepchildren. The situation whereby a child would come to live with what we have termed a "stepparent" is one where one of the child's parents dies or leaves because of divorce, and the remaining parent remarries. Both stepfathers (*ambe' poro'*) and stepmothers (*indo' poro'*) are portrayed as typically insensitive and unloving toward their stepchildren (*anak poro'*). Indo'na Tiku says, for example, that one reason she has not remarried since her divorce is her apprehension that any man she might marry would be likely to behave maliciously toward her children.

Although some relationships between stepparents and stepchildren appear close and harmonious (such as those between Nene'na Tandi (m) and his stepdaughter, and between Indo'na Sapan and her step-father), others are more conflictual. Ambe'na Toding, for instance, recalls that when his father remarried after his mother's death, the marriage was short-lived due to his father's disapproval of his second wife's treatment of Ambe'na Toding and his siblings. While people assume that stepparents in general are to be mistrusted, stepmothers, since they spend more time with their stepchildren and are responsible for their daily care,[20] are presumed to present a greater risk to stepchildren than stepfathers. Indo'na Tiku says: "For a stepchild with a stepmother it is a hardship; because when the father goes out to work, only the mother remains at the house. [pause] It is fortunate if [the stepchildren] are given kind words at the house, if they are pleasantly given food, if the father is not present. *But,* if—! Yes, maybe the reverse would be given if the father is no longer there! Not until later when the father returns is [she] sweet to her stepchildren."

The following, taken from Indo'na Rante's response to TAT card number 13MF (which depicts a woman lying down with her breasts exposed and a man standing nearby with one arm covering his face), further illustrates the negative way in which stepmothers are typically characterized.[21]

> This woman is dead. What a pity, this person is crying. The husband here is crying. [long pause] He is crying, he is thinking "What am I going to do?" If, for example, he has children, children who are still young. He has children, he thinks, "Oh, what a pity, who is going to cook for them? Even if I go out and look for food, who is going to cook at the house?" Nothing can compare to having a mother and a father. When the man looks for food, the woman stays behind and cooks. And tends to the children. Even if [the father] remarries, a stepmother is not the same. It's not possible that she would provide good care [for the children]. At the most, she would feed them once [a day]. They

wouldn't be given baths, they wouldn't be looked after. What compares to having a true mother! . . . This is what is giving this man cause to think, what a pity, assuming he has young children.

The remarks quoted above illustrate not only the undesirable qualities of stepmothers but also the special relationship that is presumed to exist between a child and his or her parents. Close consanguineal relatives in general, but particularly parents are symbols of stability and security. Villagers often express the notion that no one else cares for you as your parents do. Those whose parents are dead—whether the parents died when the person was still young or have died during the person's adulthood—feel decidedly at a disadvantage in relation to others whose parents are still living. For some, such as Indo'na Tiku, having children may be a way of replacing a sense of security that one's parents previously provided. Referring to her desire to have children, Indo'na Tiku says, "My parents are no longer. There is only me to increase myself. We are now six in all [she and her five children]. Indeed, if there are only a few people [in a family], they will want to expand by having lots of children."

Siblings

Like the parent-child relationship, the sibling relationship is an emotionally significant one. Ideally, according to Indo'na Rante, younger siblings should feel the same degree of love and respect for their older siblings that they feel for their parents. Older siblings, in turn, are expected to demonstrate parental concern for the welfare of their younger siblings, which may include helping to pay for their education. Older siblings also are given significant child care responsibilities, and their early interactions with younger siblings are intimate. When opposite-gender siblings begin to approach a sexually mature age, however, their behavior around one another becomes much more modest and self-conscious due to a strong brother-sister incest taboo.[22]

Some siblings, such as Nene'na Tandi(f) and her younger brother, remain close throughout life; others, however, can be distant and aloof or argumentative with one another. One of the things adult siblings tend to fight about, according to Indo'na Rante, is the inheritance of their parents' rice fields:

[A younger sibling might say to an older sibling], "Why did you get more of our parents' rice fields [than me]?! They should be divided up evenly." [And the older sibling] will answer, "Because

I'm the oldest child." [And the younger sibling will respond], "No! . . . Each child must get an equal share."

Outside mediators are occasionally called in to help resolve disputes between siblings, as occurred once following a dispute between Indo'na Rante and her older sister.[23]

Tensions and conflicts between siblings also are expressed in dreams and folktales. While explaining that some people hold onto anger and resentment for many years, To Minaa Sattu says:

> Many people store [their anger]. Many. Many people [hold onto their anger] into old age! For example, there once were two brothers who were angry with one another. [The older] brother said to his children, "If I should die [before my brother], don't allow him to be buried in the same gravesite." And then the [older] brother died and was buried. Later, the [younger] brother died. . . . [But the younger brother's] children forgot that he was not supposed to be buried [in the same gravesite] with his brother.. . . They took him [to the family gravesite where his brother was buried] and put him in. Later that night, the gravesite collapsed! It is there in X [a nearby village]! It fell down! Because the [two brothers] had started to fight [again]! The *bombo* [spirits] of the two [brothers] were angry and started to fight! And then the gravesite collapsed. It is near the ritual field in X. . . . The ruins are still there.

Husband-Wife Relationship

While the conjugal pair is very important in social structural terms in Toraja, the emotional, and to some extent, sexual aspects of this relationship are culturally relatively muted. For example, proper public behavior between husband (*muane*) and wife (*baine*) serves to de-emphasize conjugal intimacy. Seating at public gatherings is usually segregated by gender, and rarely are there any overt public displays of affection between adults of the opposite gender, although physical contact and displays of affection are common between children, between adults of the same gender, and between adults and children. We soon found that it was not clear on the basis of public behavior alone who was married to whom.

Furthermore, it is said to be the desire for children that motivates marriage; thus, it is often said that widowed or divorced parents with several children have no reason to remarry because they "already have children." Indeed, it is the couple's children that are seen as providing the link between husband and wife. The use of teknonyms primarily highlights the tie between child and parent or grandparent and only secondarily reflects the tie between husband and wife as co-parents or co-grandparents of a child. Polite forms of address also reflect this emphasis: the polite way to refer to the husband or wife of a person being addressed is to say "the father of your children" (*ambe' anak-komi*) or "the mother of your children" (*indo' anakkomi*).

The lack of emphasis on marital attachments also is illustrated by Indo'na Rante's TAT response quoted above. Her emphasis is not on the husband-wife bond and the pain the husband might be expected to feel upon his wife's death. Instead, she focuses on the father's concern for his children in the face of their mother's death. This is not to say that the husband-wife relationship is considered to be devoid of emotional intimacy. In some instances, feelings of love between young partners are sentimentalized and marriages may be based on mutual attraction rather than parental choice (see Hollan and Wellenkamp n.d.); but the existence of feelings of love and intimacy is considered more as a desirable possibility and less as an assumption regarding all marital relationships. (However, see chapter 5, where we discuss reactions to a spouse's infidelity.)

In addition to the relatively low public profile accorded the emotional attachment between husband and wife, there is an implicit assumption that the marital relationship is not inherently stable. The existence of a divorce payment (*kapa'*)—which is paid by the partner who seeks to dissolve the relationship—is both an indication of the desirableness of marital stability and a recognition of the possibility of marital instability.

Marital discord is considered detrimental to the well-being of the household. This is because it interferes with the family's attempt to make a living in both practical and spiritual ways. Household harmony is considered a prerequisite for attaining good fortune and prosperity. Furthermore, prolonged interpersonal discord, and negative emotional experiences in general, are believed to possibly cause illness and even death, as we discuss in more detail later. Given this, there is a strong incentive to resolve marital disputes before they become chronic or severe.

Disputes between spouses are handled through a negotiation process that involves the help and advice of esteemed, older villagers. These elders, according to several of our respondents, assess the ways in which the partners are at fault, and use their moral authority to strongly encourage reconciliations. Ambe'na Patu claims that even minor disputes may require outside intervention to be resolved:

> (Do you ever fight with your wife?) Well, actually, we often argue about one thing or another. There are times that we argue, but we haven't divorced yet! (What do you argue about?) Usually about little things. We fight about whether there is drinking water or not, whether the pigs have been fed, about how the children are raised. (And how do you settle these things?) Smart people don't try to do it alone. When people fight, they should call someone who can make peace—elders or a preacher.

Of course not all marital disputes are resolved, even with the help of mediators, and the Toraja, like many groups in Southeast Asia (Reid 1988:152–53), have a relatively high divorce rate—despite the existence of the divorce fine.[24] Six of our eleven respondents have been divorced at least once, and of these six, three have been divorced twice.[25] Such separations appear to involve little stigma, however, especially when they occur during the early years of a marriage.[26] There is a notion that spouses either mutually "agree" (*siporai*) with one another or they do not. If they do not "agree," there is little virtue seen in prolonging a conflictual and unproductive relationship. Indeed, as we have noted, Toraja believe that such conflict and discord can be harmful, leading to ill health and misfortune.

Parents-In-Law

Ideally, parents-in-law should be considered the same as one's own parents. Formal kin terms exist for father-in-law and mother-in-law (*matusa muane, matusa baine*) and son-in-law and daughter-in-law (*mamintu muane, mamintu baine*), but they are rarely used in practice. Instead, parents-in-law are usually referred to as "mother" (*indo'*) and "father" (*ambe'*) while the spouse of one's child is simply referred to as "child" (*anak*). Tensions within these relationships are, however, openly acknowledged to exist. For instance, while Indo'na Tiku reports that she considered her parents-in-law, when they were alive, to be just like her own parents, she goes on to say that she has known cases where parents-in-law are despised, especially by their daughters-in-law. For Indo'na Tiku, it makes no sense that someone would like his or her spouse and yet despise the spouse's parents. And while she finds behavior that is motivated by such feelings despicable, she says that it is not uncommon. Similarly, there is an assumption that spouses will be reluctant to provide large sacrifices for the funerals of their parents-in-law. Because of this assumption, spouses may actually be more insistent on staging a costly funeral for their in-laws than the children of the deceased. According to one person, Ambe'na Rempa, it is a common practice for sellers at the Rantepao livestock market to attract prospective buyers by calling out "Your *matusa* is dead; buy a nice buffalo!"

VERTICAL VERSUS HORIZONTAL RELATIONSHIPS

Like many other groups in central and western Indonesia, the Toraja value sharing, mutual aid, and equal treatment as well as status, privilege, and prestige. In reference to the second orientation, Geertz and Geertz (1975:163) have said of the Balinese that "What matters to a man—or to a woman—is public repute: the social deference it brings, the sumptuary rights it confers, the self-esteem it engenders, the cultural assertion it makes possible." The contradiction between the second orientation and the first is why they also add that "*Homo hierarchicus* and *homo aequalis* are engaged in Bali in war without end" (1965:167).

Some contradictions between a hierarchical social structure and cultural values emphasizing sharing and interdependence are evident in Toraja as well, and are reflected in contrasting styles of interpersonal interaction. When interacting with more powerful people or spiritual beings, villagers employ an interpersonal style that makes use of persuasion, coaxing, and "appeal" (see Wellenkamp 1992). Appeal is a term we borrow from Schieffelin (1976, 1985a, b), who contrasts it with "assertion" when describing prevalent behavioral styles among the Kaluli of Papua New Guinea. Assertion, according to Schieffelin, involves the demonstration of personal initiative and dynamism, whereas appeal involves an attitude of need and dependency: "If assertion exerts its influence by provoking, intimidating, exciting, and inspiring, . . . appeal exerts its force through the evocation of a sentimental intimacy, pathos, and compassion" (1985a:112).

The use of appeal, which conveys respect and humility, is an appropriate mode of interacting with superiors and is commonly used in other situations as well (cf. Atkinson 1989:50, 54–55). Such an interpersonal strategy presupposes that others will come to one's aid in time of need. The following examples illustrate the importance of appeal in Toraja, and the salience of the cultural expectation that people should feel sorry for, and help, those who are distressed or in need:

1. In folktales, frequent mention is made of those who are needy being helped by others. One in particular in which this theme appears repeatedly is "Polopadang and Deatanna." Polopadang is married to a

goddess named Deatanna. When Deatanna takes their child and returns to the upperworld, Polopadang sets out to find them. Along the
way he encounters numerous, seemingly insurmountable obstacles. Each
time he runs into trouble, he sits down and cries miserably, until a
creature of some kind—an eel, a water buffalo, a cat—asks him why
he is crying and then out of a sense of compassion, offers to assist him.
With the help of the various creatures, Polopadang eventually is reu-
nited with his wife and child and brings them back to this world
(Nooy-Palm 1979:154–56).

2. Both Nene'na Limbong and Nene'na Tandi(m) relate trying situations that left them feeling very dejected and discouraged; both stories
end with someone unexpectedly offering them aid and comfort.[27] Nene'na Limbong related the following incident. He had been staying in
the coastal city of Ujung Pandang during a period of political unrest
when he received news that his wife, who had stayed behind in the
village, was seriously ill (in fact, she had died). An army driver offered
to take him up to the mountains the following day in an army convoy.
Nene'na Limbong agreed and paid him in advance for the gasoline.
The next day, Nene'na Limbong, accompanied by two of his children,
boarded the army vehicle, but at the last minute they were ordered out,
while the driver who had arranged the trip was nowhere to be found.
Nene'na Limbong recalls, "That was a hardship. I cried!" The remainder of the story describes how he was befriended by the head of the
army convoy, who not only took him and his children to Toraja, but
also paid for hotel accomodations along the way and insisted that they
spend the night at his house in Rantepao before they began their hike
up to the village.

Nene'na Tandi's(m) story concerns his unsuccessful visit to Irian
Jaya where he went to seek his fortune as a trader. While he was there
he says he found little to eat but dog meat. He recalls, "I wanted to eat
sweet potatoes, but there weren't any. I wanted to eat rice, but there
especially wasn't any rice. . . . Thus, I cried." Eventually a ship arrived
that was headed for Sulawesi. Once aboard the ship, the captain looked
after him and gave him rice to eat and beer to drink.

In both accounts, the men say that they "cried." By this they mean
that they felt very unhappy and discouraged; it is doubtful that they
literally cried. (See chapter 4 for a discussion of cultural restrictions
regarding the expression of sadness and crying.) But it is noteworthy
that both men can speak of "crying" without any sense of embarrassment or shame.

3. Many of the stories respondents give in response to the TAT

concern people who are troubled or ill, and in some cases crying. Often they are offered assistance and comfort by others. For example, one TAT card portrays the back of a person sitting slumped over, with his/her head and one arm resting on a piece of furniture. Indo'na Rante's response to this card was: "[This person] is either sick or upset. If they are upset, someone will come and give them some advice and they will be content again. If they are sick, someone will come and give them some medicine and they will recover."

Nene'na Tandi(f), responding to the same card, said: "This person collapsed, crying. They are upset. Because their head hurts, or they heard bad news, or they were fighting [with someone]. . . . They are thinking long/hard. Someone may come and tell them, 'Don't think like that, think happy. And pray to God. So God will bless you. Lots of other people [have experienced trying times]. You should only be a little upset. You must divide your heart so that [your distress] won't lead to illness.' This person doesn't continue to 'faint.' Someone sees them and gives them a warning/advice."

If a crying person makes a direct request to be given something (e.g., assistance, goods), such a request is said to be particularly difficult to deny. Parents say, for example, that they may ignore or deny a child's request, even a request made repeatedly, until the child begins to cry, at which point they feel compelled to fulfill the request.[28]

While appeal is a common behavioral style in Toraja, in informal settings and among close kin and friends, villagers are less mindful of status differences and more demanding of equal treatment and of an equal distribution of food, love, respect, etc. The interpersonal style in such contexts, though not exactly "assertive" in Schieffelin's sense, is less deferential and more likely to include displays of pique.

INSIDERS VERSUS OUTSIDERS

The definition of insiders and outsiders is not fixed, but rather shifts according to the context and the speaker's purpose (cf. Errington 1989). As noted earlier, in the context of relationships among close kin, stepparents and parents-in-law are more openly acknowledged as potential objects of mistrust, due in part, we think, to their position outside of the family. In the context of the community, those living outside of the general vicinity of the village and with whom one has no kin ties are portrayed as particularly threatening and dangerous. Many villagers seemed surprised by our willingness to travel to other villages and we were often warned of the dangers of being tricked, robbed, or poisoned while in unfamiliar territory. Newcomers to the village—especially teachers (who come from various parts of Tana Toraja) but also those who have married in—although they should, ideally, be accepted unilaterally into the community, in practice, may never completely lose their status as newcomers and may always be considered somewhat suspect. The threatening aspects of other unrelated Toraja, however, are surpassed by those of the neighboring Islamic groups, the Bugis and Makassar. The Toraja perception of these people is that they are hostile and particularly dangerous because of their reliance on weapons and physical violence as a means of solving disputes, in contrast to the more measured, verbally oriented ways of the Toraja.[29]

The wariness regarding "outsiders" is to some extent a realistic one rooted in a history of political instability and of intervillage headhunting, although it also reflects, more generally, prevalent interpersonal concerns and anxieties (for a discussion of these, see chapter 5).

3

ASPECTS OF IDENTITY AND SELF

The sense of who one is, or one's "identity," as we use the term here, shifts somewhat depending on the context and on who or what one is comparing oneself to. We first examine aspects of collective identity before discussing aspects of village, family, class, adult, religious, gender, and individual identity.

COLLECTIVE IDENTITY

Bigalke (1981) has pointed out that it was not until the Dutch began to impose an administrative structure on the highlands of south Sulawesi early in this century that a sense of collective identity began to emerge among the Toraja. Before that time, people did not refer to themselves as "the Toraja," but as "the people" of particular villages or hamlets, for example, *To Tikala,* the people of Tikala. With the introduction of Christianity and public education, the inclusion of the highlands as an autonomous administrative district within the Indonesian national state, and the development of an international tourist industry, a sense of collective identity has begun to develop rapidly (Volkman 1984; Adams

1988). The Toraja now see themselves as distinct, culturally and ethnically, not only within Indonesia (where Toraja cultural practices have received extensive media coverage), but also in a worldwide context, as a growing number of tourists from Europe, the United States, and Australia travel long distances to view Toraja funeral rituals, carved ancestral houses and effigies of the dead, and cliffside burial vaults.[1]

Although a sense of national and international cultural uniqueness is increasing among rural villagers, it is in contrast to their more immediate and familiar neighbors, the lowland Bugis and Makassar, that Paku Asu residents tend to define themselves most readily. One characteristic that for villagers serves to define Toraja as Toraja is the collective response to death—the way in which villagers come to the assistance of, and share in the grief of fellow Toraja who have experienced a death (see Hollan and Wellenkamp n.d.). Other key contrasts drawn by villagers are: the Islamic Bugis and Makassar do not eat pork, while the Toraja do; they are easily angered and violent, while the Toraja are friendly and pacific; thefts occur often among them while for the Toraja, theft is taboo; they are large in number and strength, while we, though few in number, are clever and quick-witted; they avoid manual labor and spend their earnings on fine clothes, while we are willing to work hard, and save our resources for rituals or schooling.

The largely negative portrait of the Bugis and Makassar is rooted in part in past experiences of the Toraja with their lowland neighbors (see our Introduction and Bigalke 1981). As we have noted, the Toraja periodically were subject to invasion, the exacting of tributes, and slave raiding by Islamic outsiders. But the use of negative images of the Bugis and Makassar to promote a positive group identity also is a reaction to a lowland stereotype of the Toraja, namely, that the Toraja are crude, former slaves who continue to practice many of the backward ways of their ancestors.

The image that Toraja have of themselves as a cultural group is not a completely positive or flattering one, however. Criticism by the national government, which has portrayed Toraja ritual practices as irrational, extravagant, and wasteful, has contributed to doubts many Toraja now voice about the wisdom of spending years of savings on a ceremony that may last only a week or less. Sometimes villagers jokingly refer to themselves as "foolish" or "stupid" people who are better at creating debts—by borrowing and slaughtering large numbers of livestock—than at making a living for themselves. Even Nene'na Limbong, a staunch Alukta adherent, once commented that there would be no need to ask for blessings from the gods and ancestors if everyone just stopped slaughtering livestock at rituals, because then everyone would be rich anyway![2]

VILLAGE, FAMILY, AND CLASS IDENTITY

Other aspects of identity come to the fore when villagers compare and contrast themselves with other Toraja. Village or hamlet affiliation continues to be an important source of identity. Not infrequently, villagers from one hamlet in Paku Asu comment upon the differences between them and the residents of another hamlet (regarding, for instance, their ability to get along with one another, or their diligence in repaying financial commitments).[3]

Another important source of identity is that of shared biological kinship. As we noted earlier, those of one family are said to share "one blood, one bones." In chapter 2, we provided some illustrations of the strong sense of shared identity that obtains between family members. In addition, there is a sense that family members literally replace one another through the generations. Nene'na Limbong comments: "Here [in Toraja] we say that one inherits blood bones. When my father died, I replaced him. I replaced his blood bones. Later, when I die, my children will replace me." Naming practices—which include the use of teknonyms and the practice of naming children after deceased forebears—also reflect as well as promote a sense of shared identity with family members.

In other ways, too, individuals' lives are seen as closely entwined with those of fellow family members. For instance, one feels *ma'siri'*, "shame/embarrassment," not only for oneself, but for one's immediate kin. Similarly, people believe that they may incur misfortune not only for their own personal mistakes but also for those committed by members of their families, whether alive or already long dead.

Another important source of identity is one's class or social status. Up until recently, social status was primarily determined by birth, which established a person as a noble, a commoner, or a dependent.[4] Nobles' claims to superior rank were largely based on the belief that they were the direct descendants of beings (*to manurun*) who long ago descended from the upperworld (*Langi'*) to earth. A noble's or commoner's relative standing in the community, however, was determined by their slaughtering history—that is, the amount of livestock they contributed to ritual celebrations.

Currently, the basis on which social status is determined is a topic of much local debate (see Volkman 1984, 1985). The introduction of Christianity has undermined the traditional religious and philosophical justifications for differences in rank, and with the development of public education, a cash economy, and employment opportunities outside the highlands, some commoners and former dependents now have additional resources to compete for status by buying and slaughtering livestock at rituals. In the Paku Asu area, however, individuals considered noble by virtue of their birth alone are still recognized at meat divisions, even if their families are no longer wealthy, while the newly rich are called *to sugi'*, "rich people," to distinguish them from true *to makaka*.

ADULT IDENTITY

Adulthood—for our purposes, the period of life that begins with marriage and parenting but precedes old age—provides the Toraja with a number of valued experiences, including the challenges of building a household, the opportunity to validate and enhance one's status through the slaughter of pigs and water buffalo at rituals (see Volkman 1985 and below), the sense of pride and economic security that comes from having children, the accumulation of "knowledge" and wealth, and the sense of satisfaction associated with repaying obligations to parents, relatives, and deities through the organization and execution of rituals. Yet when given an opportunity to talk about adulthood and how it compares to other periods of life (see Hollan and Wellenkamp n.d.), our respondents focus less on the satisfactions and pleasures of maturity, and more on its difficulties.

In contrast to childhood and early adolescence—commonly remembered as times of relative freedom and comfort—adulthood is generally conceptualized as a period of hard work and heavy responsibilities. One struggles not only to "make a living"—that is, to feed and clothe oneself and one's family—but also to pay for the education of one's children and to fulfill one's ritual obligations. It is the combination of these (often conflicting) demands that at times seems overwhelming to our respondents, and which leads many of them to compare mature adulthood unfavorably with earlier years of life. Below we illustrate the pervasiveness of these themes by quoting at some length from the interviews.

> AMBE'NA KONDO: (Were you happier before or after you got married?) [He laughs] Before I was married, I still thought like a child. After I was married, my thinking changed. (How did it

change?) When I was still young, I didn't have to think about anything in particular. But now, there are many things I must think about: How do I make a living? How do I pay my [ritual] debts? I think about what I'll feed my children tomorrow or later today. . . . (And when you were still young?) When I was still young, I just played around, looking for happiness! . . . (When you think about your life up until now, have there been more good times or bad times?) The two periods are different. There was happiness in both periods, but now there are more difficulties because now I have [ritual] debts. . . . And I have to think about work and other things. When we're children, we don't have to think or worry about anything. We just wait for our parents to give us everything. . . . But now, I think about many things. For example [I think], "Where will I find rice to eat? What will we cook later today?" Things like that. Or [I think], "If a debt comes due and I must slaughter a pig, how will I pay for it?" There is no relief.

TO MINAA SATTU: [He has just finished a discussion of childhood games and activities.] And then I looked for a wife. And then after marrying, I had children. And from that point on, all I've done is try to feed my children. It has been difficult [speaking in a low, subdued tone of voice]; looking for clothes and whatever else they need.

[In another interview, he is asked when life was most difficult for him. He replies]: When my parents were both still alive, I was happy. After they died, things got difficult. From then until now— I'm a [mature] adult now—I've had to make a living. . . . Because I already have children. They ask for rice, sweet potatoes, they ask for everything.

INDO'NA TIKU: (When have you been the happiest?) When I was still in school. Because when I was still in school, I didn't know about the things that make us think/worry. If I asked for money, there was money. [I got] whatever I needed. And it wasn't me who had to find it! So indeed, [I] . . . was happiest when I was still in school.

[In the next interview, she is asked whether she has experienced more happiness or more hardship in her life]: It can't be said that I'm never happy. Often I'm happy, too, but in my experience, there has been more suffering than happiness [pause]. Moreover, ever since [my] children have been in school, I've really experienced suffering, I haven't experienced happiness ever since. (Really?) Yes! [I'm] always lacking, lacking, lacking. . . deprivation is the number one [cause of my suffering]. . . . Because these children ask for money one moment and then the next moment, they ask for [more] money. Where [is the money], moreover, to pay [ritual] debts? I buy pigs to pay, water buffalo to pay. . . . Thus, that's why I say that in my life I've experienced more hardship than happiness. Maybe when I was still small, maybe I was just happy! I didn't experience any deprivation then. But ever since I separated from my parents, indeed, I've experienced a lot of hardship.

INDO'NA RANTE: (Which feelings are the worst here? Like when you think, "Oh, I don't like it when I feel . . ." How?) Yes. (Could you talk a little about that?) About distress/hardship? Oh, yes I can. For example, when we're upset, we think/worry . . . for example, you know . . . the person who died [recently]? [When someone dies], we think, "How are we going to get a buffalo to slaughter?" Indeed you understand Toraja customs now. So when there's a dead person, we must slaughter buffalo or pigs. So that's what we think about, Belo. Where will I get the money to buy [livestock]. That makes us distressed.[5]

[Later in the interview, she is asked when she has been the happiest.] When I was still [unmarried]. . . . Once I married . . . I felt very troubled. How couldn't we feel troubled, Belo?! We had to buy betel, we had to buy, the point is, everything. We had to build a house. We had to find food. . . . Then slowly our path was fortunate, until now I wouldn't say we're happy, [but] we have a simple life, Belo. We're neither distressed, nor happy. Do you understand?

INDO'NA SAPAN: (When were [things most] difficult [for you]?) Once I was older! . . . (About how old?) I don't know. But now all that I think about are my children. And my parents, you know. Because there's no one [but me] to support them. . . . That's what makes me troubled. Even when I sleep at night, I just think, I remember and remember my children. They want to go to school, how can we make it?

NENE'NA TANDI(M): (Have you had more happiness or more hardship in your life?) When I was young, I was happy, because I didn't lack for anything. Things became difficult once I got married. That's when I suffered most. Why do I say suffered? Because we couldn't live on the amount of rice we were growing then. So that's when I felt most sad and discouraged.

The Slaughtering of Livestock

While respondents describe their ritual obligations—which are chiefly fulfilled through the slaughtering of livestock—as a considerable financial burden, they also indicate that the slaughtering of livestock is one of the most significant and emotionally charged activities of adulthood.[6]

Although it is men who dominate the public roles involved in the slaughtering of livestock and in whose names the meat is distributed (with the exception of divorced or widowed women), women also contribute to the exchange of livestock and view this ritual activity as highly meaningful.

The conscious motivations for slaughtering livestock at rituals are complex and overdetermined. One of the main reasons that people slaughter livestock is for the funerals of their parents and other close family members. People generally feel a strong obligation to provide livestock for their parents' funerals to repay their parents for their love and support over the years. Nene'na Tandi(m) explains:

> When we were still small, we were carried everywhere by our mother for one year [during pregnancy]. Then mama gave birth to us, and from when we were one night old to one year, mama couldn't leave us. . . . After that, when we could walk, our papa cradled us at celebrations or at the market [and that] we must repay. Even if we cried, papa had to find a way to make us content, whether it was [by giving us] fish or cookies, [and] all of that cajoling from papa . . . we must repay.

In some instances, too, inheritance may be determined by the number and type of livestock that children provide for their parents' funerals (see Wellenkamp 1984; Volkman 1985; Waterson 1981).

The importance of providing water buffalo for parents' funerals is indicated by Indo'na Rante, who says that if, for example, one's mother is soon to be buried and "we do not yet have a water buffalo, we feel like we are going to die." In another interview, she imagines what it would be like for someone whose siblings could afford to contribute buffalo to the parent's funeral but he or she couldn't:

> [They] would gather together in one house. [Someone would say], "Just say if you can't [provide any livestock]. When can you bring

[something] for your mama?" . . .What can we slaughter if we don't have any [livestock]?! For example, if our sibling says, "I'm going to slaughter two [buffalo]!" [Another says], "I'm going to slaughter three!" Whereas this one [sibling], what a pity, can't [slaughter any].

Similarly, when Nene'na Limbong is asked when Toraja are likely to feel sad, he replies:

Usually Toraja feel sad or humble if when their mother or father dies, their siblings slaughter [buffalo at the funeral] but they don't have anything to slaughter. They feel sad because their siblings are able to repay the labor of the mother and father, but they can't. . . .Then, they [may] cry sadly, and feel humble. . . .Or the siblings may say words. . .that aren't good [words of scorn]. . . .Then the person feels discouraged or sad.

Another reason that slaughtering is important is because it is the primary means of validating or enhancing one's own and one's family's social status. The social and political motives for slaughtering have been discussed at length elsewhere (see Volkman 1985; Crystal 1974; Nooy-Palm 1979); a brief discussion of these follows.

When discussing their own involvement in slaughtering, respondents tend to emphasize the "social" rather than the political aspects—that is, they emphasize that providing livestock for ritual celebrations is a way of demonstrating respect and concern for family members, affines, and (for Alukta villagers) spiritual entities. As Indo'na Tiku puts it, "[The slaughtering of livestock] is a sign of respect among family members."

Respondents stress that, ideally, livestock should be given freely and willingly, and only in accordance with what one can afford to give. Indo'na Tiku says, for example:

If it is [for] a distant family member, usually we only bring pigs [to be slaughtered]. But if it is a close family member, we must bring buffalo, if there *are any* [speaking emphatically]. No one is forced [to give].

Similarly, Nene'na Tandi(m) comments:

[The slaughtering of livestock should be] in accordance with one's wealth and desire. No one can order [someone] to slaughter, and no one can forbid it.

Indo'na Sapan claims that one must want to give, or one should not give at all:

> (Would someone slaughter an animal for an unrelated person?) Yes, perhaps, if there were any [animals to give]; because it [the giving] must come from the heart. Even if someone is related, if you are enemies with him/her, the elders say it is forbidden [to contribute livestock to his/her celebration].

Nene'na Tandi(m) even says that one is eventually rewarded by spiritual beings for gracious giving, but neglected for giving in a hesitant or grudging fashion:

> If we feel happy. . .[giving], and forget [about the expense and trouble], people here say that it is not we [those who provide the animal] who must pay, but the deceased person [for whose funeral the animal is provided] who [eventually] will give us the good fortune to pay for everything. But if we feel afraid or hesitant [to give], then the deceased person will say, "You don't even acknowledge your own family [therefore] it's better that you not be given any [good fortune]."

Despite respondents' claims that no one is forced to engage in slaughtering, as Indo'na Tiku admits people often feel pressured to do so: "We have to give. . . . We feel pressured actually." By pressured, she means that she would feel ashamed (*ma'siri'*) not to give and would be constantly preoccupied until she found a way to make at least a small contribution to a relative's ritual celebration. Many villagers are willing to do without basic necessities and to incur substantial debts in order to give what is expected of them.

According to Nene'na Tandi(f), disagreements between spouses over the contribution of livestock to ritual events can lead to divorce:

> (Does it sometimes happen that maybe the man wants to bring a pig or a buffalo [to a celebration] but the woman doesn't want to?) Oh. . .if the woman didn't want to . . . [the couple may] divorce. . . .Because [the man] is ashamed, you know. It's better to divorce than to be ashamed [she pauses]. But that doesn't happen that much. . . .Because it's all our shame, you know [that is, the wife and husband share in each other's shame]. How could it not be?!

The burdensome nature of slaughtering is lessened for some by the realization that the livestock one contributes to relatives' celebrations function as "investments." Indo'na Tiku, for instance, says that she knows that if she provides a pig for her niece's baptism, "it will be returned to me [later]. So. . .[the pig] is invested [*dipandan*]. . . . If I have a need later [for livestock at a celebration], that which I brought will be returned, actually."

While respondents emphasize that the exchange of livestock is both an obligation and a sign of respect, it is clear that villagers also derive much satisfaction from the renown that slaughtering can provide. Nene'na Tandi(m) comments:

> We are happy to pay [for the livestock slaughtered] for our parents [at their funerals], because then it can be said that, indeed, our parents were rich and well known.

The following statements from Indo'na Tiku also illustrate this point:

> (Is it usual for a woman to slaughter livestock by herself?) Yes, it's nothing [not unusual or of note], as long as there are [livestock to slaughter]. As long as [one] is willing [to do it]. . . .I've slaughtered tens of pigs! Ever since I began work [as a school teacher]. For example. . .in October [of the year before]. . .I gave five pigs to be slaughtered [she says this with much pride and satisfaction]. . . .When that older person [a relative] died at Laka I slaughtered one buffalo and one pig [she pauses]. Ah, three days later, I went again to a *ma'papa* [a house-building celebration]. . . .Ah, I got a pig that cost 80,000 [rupiahs]! I bought it at the market [she pauses]. (So when—) That was three days later!

Not everyone participates in slaughtering to the same extent, however, or finds the political aspects equally engaging. For example, Ambe'na Patu, as a young, aspiring trader and government official, actively avoids such activities. Nene'na Tandi(m) also believes that slaughtering is a waste of time and resources, but his attitude is more contemptuous, and seems to stem, at least in part, from his envy of those who use slaughtering to enhance their status. He comments:

> Why should we get angry about [the politics of meat]? This meat—indeed people call it meat, but I think of it as shit! Shit. Once we eat it, it becomes shit, right? It doesn't increase our wealth. After eating it, we sleep, and the next morning we go to the edge of the village and defecate. If it's like that, why get upset about it? (But some people say it's the most important. . .) Those are people who try to be big. Rich people. For one day [the day

of slaughtering], they can be rich. But they don't stay rich. Those who stay rich, ah, they sell rice, they sell pigs, they have nice houses. Ah, those are the happy ones. [Those are the ones] who are truly rich. But those who are rich for only an hour or two. . . .I look at them [and think], they're all stupid.

Unconscious Meanings of Slaughtering

Many villagers, Christian and Alukta adherents alike, show intense interest in the slaying of water buffalo at funerals, despite the fact that they have witnessed many such killings.[7] Our photographs of such events show people staring intently or grimacing, with some women holding a hand cupped over an open mouth.

That there is some unconscious identification with the animal being killed is suggested by the fact that two of our male respondents report "sacrifice" dreams (see chapter 6) in which they envision themselves or someone else being killed and butchered in the way that livestock are killed at rituals. For at least one man, Nene'na Limbong, such imagery seems to represent a sense of being entrapped and "preyed upon" by those, both human and spiritual, who require one to make extensive personal sacrifices before one can be assured of receiving their blessings or assistance (see Hollan 1989).

Psychological identification with sacrificial animals probably is increased by the fact that domestic animals are raised with considerable care: pigs, for example, are given specially prepared, cooked meals, and prize water buffalo are named, washed, and groomed.[8]

RELIGIOUS AFFILIATION

Religious affiliation also is an important aspect of identity. While from an etic perspective, village Christianity is infused with elements of the traditional religious system, and thus the similarities between Christian and Alukta world views appear great, from a local perspective, whether one is a Christian or Alukta adherent is central to one's identity. But the differences that villagers emphasize are not so much spiritual and philosophical, as social, political, and economic. Christian villagers see Christianity as the religion of the future and associate it with modernity, social and political egalitarianism, education, Western-style medicine, employment in the cash economy, and nationalism (cf. Atkinson 1983). Christians often view Alukta adherents as elitist, backward, and conservative.

Alukta adherents, on the other hand, see themselves as the last guardians of a rapidly dying way of life. Some, like To Minaa Sattu, remain committed to Alukta as a religious and philosophical system. They fear the misfortune that will befall the highlands once the traditional ways are gone for good, and they hope that anthropologists and other scholars will record and preserve the traditional beliefs for a time in the future when Alukta will experience a revival, a development that they believe is inevitable. Other Alukta adherents, like Ambe'na Kondo, are less committed to the traditional belief system per se, but continue to participate in the traditional rituals in order to carry out their ritual obligations to deceased relatives. Ambe'na Kondo and his wife say that once their ritual obligations to their deceased parents have been fulfilled, they plan to convert to Christianity. Still other Alukta adherents, like Nene'na Limbong, spurn Christianity, in large measure because it presents a threat to their power and position as *to makaka* and as descendents of the earliest ancestors of the village.

While many Christian and Alukta villagers prefer to minimize differences between themselves at the purely philosophical and religious level—in part because of the strong value placed on consensus and social and familial solidarity—there is a tendency among both groups to blame the other for misfortune and misbehavior. For example, Alukta adherents may blame a poor rice harvest on the Christians, who no longer observe the traditional rice ritual (*aluk pare*), while both Christians and Alukta adherents claim that adultery is more common among members of the other group (see chapter 5).

GENDER

From a cross-cultural point of view, gender differences are not given much cultural elaboration among the Toraja (cf. Waterson 1981).[9] The Toraja language, for instance, does not have separate pronouns for males and females, and terms for siblings and grandparents are gender neutral. Further, adolescent initiation practices are relatively unelaborated, and they do not serve to dramatically highlight differences between males and females (see Hollan and Wellenkamp n.d.).

While there is segregation by gender in public places, and while men appear to dominate the cultural spotlight at many public events—through their participation in the slaughtering of livestock and the division of meat, and through their role as adjudicators during legal disputes—women play prominent roles on some ritual occasions, especially the smoke-ascending ritual of *ma'bua'* (see Nooy-Palm 1986; Volkman 1985). Also, some prominent male roles are closely identified with feminine functions and characteristics: for example, the traditional leader and coordinator of rice-growing activities and rituals in the village is called *Indo' Padang*, literally, "Mother of the Ground."

Reflecting in part the cognatic organization of society, women and men share similar legal and economic rights: they each inherit property, including rice land; they may manage and control their own sources of income; they may foster or adopt children on their own; and they each may engage in competitive slaughtering at rituals (see Waterson 1981).

Behaviorally, also, from an American perspective, men and women do not seem that different. Males as well as females are involved in child care, for example, and while girls and women are primarily occupied with household activities, both males and females move beyond the confines of the village when working in gardens, buying and selling in markets, or, until relatively recently, herding water buffalo. Both men and women are physically demonstrative with friends and relatives of the same gender: men, like women, may sit with elbows and legs touching during public events or walk through the village with arms around one another; and boys, like girls, may hold hands and relax in one another's laps. For neither men nor women is it considered shameful to admit fearfulness regarding spiritual punishment or encounters, strangers, adolescent initiation rites, and so forth.[10]

Where men and women do appear to differ somewhat is in terms of personality and interpersonal style. It is our impression that men are generally more cautious, withdrawn, and less gregarious than women.[11] Yet there also is much individual variation among members of the same gender. Nene'na Tandi(f), for instance, smokes cigarettes, drinks palm wine, and sits with the men during the division of meat at rituals, all activities more commonly associated with men. Similarly, Indo'na Tiku, who in demeanor seems "feminine," contributes numerous livestock to ritual events, while both Nene'na Tandi(m) and Ambe'na Patu shun the politics of meat and so opt out of a key male activity.

While the outsider's impression is that gender differences are not highly elaborated among the Toraja, villagers themselves maintain that there are some distinctions between males and females. Generally speaking, males are thought to be more clever and bolder, while females are thought to more easily experience certain feelings such as sadness and compassion. The following are some responses to the question, "Are there any differences between males and females?"

NENE'NA TANDI(F): Boys are usually smarter . . .Girls are more polite/respectful, I guess. Yes. . . .How could boys be polite/respectful?! They [boys] like to go play [outside]. [But] girls—what a pity—stay in the house. They [girls] just play in the house. [But] boys go wherever they want, they run, run, run off!

NENE'NA TANDI(M): Indeed, there is a difference. The thought of men is long and high, [while] for women, it is low and weak. So that is the difference.

TO MINAA SATTU: Some are different, some are the same. If a woman's brain is sharp, she is the same as a man. (If [it's] sharp?) Yes. (And if not?) She doesn't. . .understand as well. [In another interview, he says]: Sometimes [women] become angry if there is something. . .eh, that [they] don't agree with. . . .If the man does something that she doesn't follow/agree with, the woman will become angry. . . .So that's a small difference [between men and women].

NENE'NA LIMBONG: Boys are stubborn. . . .[With boys], when the father arrives [home], of course [he] will be searched [and asked], "Where are the sweets you brought?" And if he doesn't have any, oh, they will cry! Nonstop. If we try to frighten them [in order to socialize them], they aren't frightened! Girls, too, are ill-behaved sometimes, but if we try to frighten them, indeed, they are frightened. But boys, they oppose us!

AMBE'NA PATU: Men do not have many feelings, but women have many feelings. Another difference is that men are strong and women aren't. [In another interview, while discussing people's reactions to funeral singing, Ambe'na Patu says that when someone suddenly feels upset] we cry at the house. Women are always crying. (Do women cry more or men?) Women! They have many feelings. (Why is that?) Women just have more feelings. (Feelings like . . . ?)They easily suffer/hurt. They are easily emotional. (Regarding all of their feelings, or [just some]?) Oh, all of them! . . .I don't know what it's like in other places. . .but in Tator [Tana Toraja], [women] may cry for an hour or two. You've already seen them, you know [he is referring to wailing in connection with a death]. (Do men cry like that, too?) No! Men only cry for a moment. . . .But women [cry] for a long time! They cry now and then a moment later, cry again. . . . They're always crying.

. . .(What about your wife? Does she cry, too?) Oh, yes she does! But not for extended periods. Because if we [are always] crying, we'll get sick.

Ambe'na Patu gives the impression that he believes that such gender differences in feeling and behaving are inborn, and that it would be better if women were more like men. Indo'na Rante's comments, on the other hand, reveal that some gender differences are culturally expected and even valued:

(Are boys or girls usually more mischievous?) Boys. Girls are only occasionally mischievous [pause]. But when boys are mischievous, it's good. When girls are mischievous, it's not good. It's the same if boys steal—it is somewhat good. But if girls [steal], it's really not good. It's the same when [children] talk. If boys brag/gossip, it suits them to a certain extent. But if girls do that, it's really not good.

Finally, there is a tendency among respondents to assume that life is somewhat easier for members of the opposite gender. Nene'na Tandi(m) comments:

Among people here, women have happier lives [than men]. Because women here are well cared for. They [really] work only once a year [in the fields], when they plant the rice seedlings. Men work every day—work in the rice fields, work in the gardens, all of that. But women here indeed are cared for. They are made happy so that they perform their household duties. Women only have to do kitchen work here. They don't help with the rice fields. Only men [do that kind of hard, physical work]. But when we [men] go [to work in the fields], [they] take good care of us [by providing meals, etc.].

Women, on the other hand, generally believe that the hardships of pregnancy and childbirth make their lives more difficult and painful than men's. For instance, Indo'na Rante, when asked if she has ever thought that it would have been better to have been born a man, replies,

Yes, indeed, I've thought that before. . . . The first time I was pregnant I thought, "Let a man try to do what we women do" [laughing]. . . . Nothing in a man's [experience] beats that.

INDIVIDUAL DIFFERENCES AND FAMILY RESEMBLANCES

Not only do Toraja recognize identities based on membership in certain subgroups, but they also recognize, and find interesting, individual differences in behavioral characteristics and tendencies. People comment on how individuals differ, for example, in terms of their tendency to steal, to be successful, to anger easily, or to be quiet and reserved. One explanation frequently offered for such individual differences is that they are due to fate, which is determined by the timing of the individual's birth.

Another common explanation is that individual behavior patterns are characteristic of certain families. While there is general agreement about the existence of such family resemblances, there is less agreement about how such behavior patterns are transmitted from generation to generation. Some people talk as if there were a genetic or biological basis to these patterns, though such ideas remain vague. When Indo'na Tiku is asked whether foster children differ from children one has given birth to, she replies:

> Yes, there often is a difference [she pauses]. If I compare Sampe with my "womb" children, I think that child [Sampe] often displays his parent's characteristics. . . . Because . . . his mother angers easily. If the slightest thing is wrong, [she] becomes angry. . . . When I look at Sampe, indeed he has his parent's characteristics. . . . Because . . . it doesn't matter how [one] instructs him, he doesn't pay any attention. [He believes that] whatever he says, that is what is right . . . none of my five children have the same character as Sampe.

Similarly, when To Minaa Sattu attempts to explain why occasionally there are adults who continue to act in childish ways, he says:

> It [childish behavior] is blood bones [inherited]! . . . (Meaning?) Meaning that it is usual/normal for the person. . . . For example, she/he might steal as a child. As an adult, she/he does not give that up.

Others suggest that behavior patterns characteristic of certain families are learned through modeling. For example, Indo'na Rante says that she is like her parents because

> I used to watch my mother [and think], "Oh, my parent is like this. People like her." Everyone used [to say], "Your mother is a

very good person." So I was [good], too, because I had my
mother as an example. [Conversely], if the parents aren't good,
their children will be that way, too. Because the parents serve as
an example! For example, if the parents are thieves, then of
course the children will be thieves, too! Because their parents are
their example. . . . (What about the attitudes/characteristics of
your older and younger siblings? Are they the same as or different
from yours?) The same! . . . Because if I had a younger sibling
who had an attitude/characteristic that wasn't good, I would
reprimand him/her. [I would say], "Why are you acting differently? Our parents are good." If they [younger siblings] stray too
far, [we say], "Don't do that."

Later she adds that if one sibling "is obstinate, then all [of the siblings]
will be. If one is good, then they're all good."

Similarly, Nene'na Limbong says:

If the parents are thieves or tricksters, then they [their children]
will be, too. If a person is a gambler, his/her children will also be
gamblers. . . .If we act like our fathers, indeed [it's because] we
were instructed to act like that from our fathers.

PRESENTATION OF SELF

In chapter 1, we examined Toraja notions of the moral person—that
is, beliefs about the morally proper way for people to think, act, and
feel. In chapter 2, we briefly discussed a style of self-presentation that
involves portraying the self as needy in the course of making "appeals"
of others. In this chapter, we focus on other aspects of self and self-
awareness.

It is a truism among villagers that one cannot judge a person's
wealth or social standing solely on the basis of his or her dress. Even
wealthy individuals wear their finer clothes only on special occasions
or store them away to use as mortuary dress. While this "dressing-
down" on a day-to-day basis reflects, in part, the economic realities of
peasant life, it also stems from a desire to appear poorer and more
humble than one may actually be, thus minimizing the chance that
others will be envious of one's successes, or that they will make potentially burdensome requests for assistance.

While quality of clothing is not a critical aspect of the presentation
of self, cleanliness of clothing and body is. The importance of cleanliness is reflected not only in the amount of time devoted to washing and

bathing activities, but also in people's self-conscious attitudes about their skin and clothes. To have smooth, clean, and fair skin is considered aesthetically important.

Bodily coordination and physical grace also are important to one's self-presentation. Those who slip or stumble along a mountain path, no matter how treacherous the weather conditions, or who spill food or drink at rituals (especially during the serving of guests) are openly ridiculed. Grace, balance, and coordination are taken for granted; those who display a lack of such grace, or worse, obvious awkwardness, are considered lacking in social competence.

In some instances, ideas about the proper presentation of self vary considerably according to context. Differences in "frontstage" versus "backstage" behavior are recognized by the Toraja as well as by the outside observer (cf. Errington 1979). Nene'na Tandi(f), for example, is very much aware that her behavior with her husband varies according to the situation. In public, she and Nene'na Tandi(m) remain somewhat aloof from one another, but at night, in the privacy of their own house, she says that they joke with and tease one another, and play cards together (see also the section on "Drinking Behavior" in chapter 4).

SENSE OF VULNERABILITY

One commonly shared aspect of the self among Toraja villagers appears to be a sense of being vulnerable to, or acted upon by other humans or outside forces. Though high status and wealthy people obviously have more economic and political control over their lives than poorer, lower status people, even higher status individuals often seem to view themselves as subject to the varying and unpredictable demands of family and community members (see Hollan 1989:174), and at the whim of more powerful spiritual forces.

That a sense of relative powerlessness and vulnerability is widely shared at some "deep" level is suggested by the prevalence of dream imagery containing such themes. Respondents report dreams, for example, of being slaughtered and cut up or of helplessly standing by as someone else is slaughtered, of being chased, and of experiencing spirit attacks (see chapters 4 and 6).

The extent to which villagers view themselves as the pawns of more powerful forces also is suggested by Ambe'na Toding's comments when he compares the relationship between humans and God to that between children and parents:

If we want to order children to be angry, we don't give [them] anything. So [whether children are angry or not] depends on the parents' [behavior]. If . . . when children ask for something . . . [they] are given it [and this happens repeatedly] . . . they won't be angry. . . . [The same is true] with us humans. If often when we ask for something [from God, but we] aren't given it, [anger] rises in our heart! . . . I don't know if it is from God or what, but indeed it arises in the heart. Yes, indeed it's from God, because it's from God if, for example, we become rich [that is, God controls our destinies]."

Ways of speaking that attribute autonomy and volition to various parts of the body also serve to deemphasize the self as a central locus of personal experience, will, and responsibility. As we discuss elsewhere, many emotion terms refer to a specific part of the person rather than the "self," and when looking for mistakes that an ill or misfortunate person may have committed, Toraja talk about mistakes committed by particular parts of the body—the hands, legs, eyes, mouth, and so forth. The following comments from Ambe'na Toding provide an illustration:

[Consider] for example, if a person kills a buffalo [because the buffalo has eaten his or her garden plants]. . . . Because his/her blood was hot, or high, or his/her heart was hot, he/she killed [the buffalo]. Because it [the killing] was medicine for the heart . . . it wasn't a mistake [of the self-conscious person], rather it was due to his/her high blood [pressure] or because [his/her heart] was hot like fire. Look at his/her hands [which committed the deed]. . . . [A person who is very angry] isn't aware of him/her self.

In a later interview, Ambe'na Toding elaborates on these ideas: In reply to a question about whether people regret their "mistakes," he says:

They usually regret them. Because indeed, as I said, [they] didn't intentionally act rashly. But yes, if we go too far, later we must regret it. But it wasn't committed intentionally; it comes from high blood [pressure]. People aren't conscious/aware when they are angry. Once they are conscious/aware, they pull back their rashness. No one can say, "I am always conscious/aware." No. Heat [anger] comes often. . . .Once we are conscious/aware, we admit [our mistakes, we] say, "If I have committed any mistakes, from my legs to my hair, I indeed [acknowledge them]." But what can one do, because we didn't intentionally [become angry] . . . or act rashly.

Ambe'na Toding is unusual in the extent to which he suggests that individuals are not responsible for their emotional reactions, or the mistakes they commit;[12] but villagers on the whole do view intense emotional experiences as involving a loss of "consciousness" and self-awareness, as we discuss further in the next chapter.

There also are certain times when individuals report feeling as if their body parts did act of their own accord, such as when people are possessed, or when they undergo intense emotional experiences (see chapter 4). To Minaa Sattu, for example, reports that in the past when he would hear the chanting of the *ma'maro* ceremony, his arms and legs would begin to jump and twitch of their own accord and he would feel that he had no choice but to become possessed by the visiting *deata*.

The sense of being vulnerable to, or acted upon by outside forces probably results from several factors. Beliefs about the spiritual world undoubtedly contribute to the perception that one is surrounded by, and occasionally at the mercy of, more powerful beings. Outside political and economic forces also probably contribute to a sense of being the pawn of others. And enculturative experiences are likely important contributing factors as well. Bateson and Mead (1942) and Bateson (1976), for instance, have discussed several enculturative practices among the Balinese that they believe contribute to the habit of surrendering autonomy in favor of accommodating to the movements and cues of others (Bateson and Mead 1942:14–15), and to the perception that body parts are only loosely attached and may be "independently animated" (Bateson and Mead 1942:25–26). These practices include forms of children's play as well as methods of instructing children in such areas as language and motor skills, some of which are characteristic of the Toraja as well.[13]

SELF-ASSERTION

While the sense of being "acted-upon" appears to be an important and perduring aspect of the self, there are contexts in which people behave and apparently feel more powerful and self-assertive. One such context involves occasional resistance to requests for aid and assistance. On the one hand, villagers are fond of saying that maturity and proper "understanding" necessarily eventuate in cooperative, compliant behavior. Yet several of the respondents at various times stated that others should not take their cooperation and compliance for granted, and some imagined themselves responding to a request for assistance with a resounding, "I don't want to!" While such a direct response to a request probably rarely occurs among adults, such statements indicate how important it is to people that their efforts to be cooperative be viewed as based on choice and not coercion.

In mostly private contexts, villagers also occasionally engage in self-inflation or assume a more self-assertive stance vis-à-vis others. For example, several people said to us, "Everyone knows who I am!" or "I know everything!" (about religion, politics, customs, magic, etc.). In part such claims may have been stimulated by people's desires to convince themselves, as well as us, that the attention being devoted to them was justified. However, it seems more likely to us that such statements are means by which individuals seek to assert their personal importance and seek to demonstrate how they can use their knowledge of the forces and relationships surrounding them to satisfy their own personal needs and desires. Some men, for example, claim that their possession of special knowledge about amulets or astronomy enables them to manipulate the life-enhancing powers of spiritual beings to insure the success of their crops. On at least some occasions, then, people feel *in* control and not just *under* control (cf. Heelas 1981; Lock 1981).

In dreams, too, one also occasionally finds expression of a desire to excel or stand out in some way, in contrast to the more usual cultural emphasis on cooperation, unity of purpose and identity, etc. Nene'na Limbong, for example, reports two such dreams. In one, "I climbed up the mountain [above Paku Asu]. . . .[At the top] of the mountain, in my dream, it was flat! Flat. But I knew that it was [the mountain above Paku Asu]. . ." When Nene'na Limbong stretched out his arms, he discovered that his fingertips reached several miles in each direction, from Makale in the south to Baruppu' in the north.[14]

In the second dream, Nene'na Limbong is in the midst of a large gathering of people. An important government official arrives and then selects several individuals, one by one, to climb to the top of a tall pole, but each declines. The official then sees Nene'na Limbong, who has been hiding in the crowd, and he selects him to climb the pole. Nene'na Limbong does so successfully and when he reaches the top, "I yell out, 'Everyone here: If there is something I tell [you to do]. . .you all must obey!' Ah, everyone said 'Yes!'. . .What was the meaning of that [dream]?

Oh! It wasn't [longer than] two or three years later that I became head [of the village]. That's the meaning!"

While some such dreams are "culture pattern" dreams (Lincoln 1935) in the sense that they may be a prerequisite for the assumption of certain roles and responsibilities, it seems to us, based on our knowledge of our respondents, that such dreams also are a clear expression of the individual dreamer's strivings to occasionally stand apart from, and dominate, others.

SELF-EVALUATION AND CHANGES IN THE SELF

Another characteristic of our respondents relating to aspects of "self" is that many find it difficult to make abstract evaluations of their own behavior. Indo'na Sapan, for example, seems to doubt that critical self evaluation is possible: "(How would you compare your character when you were still small to the character of your parents?) I'm not sure. How can one know one's self? I feel that they [her character and that of her parents] are identical/similar. [That's] how I feel, but someone else—I don't know [what they would say]."

When Ambe'na Patu is asked what part of his character or behavior he would change if he could, he laughs and replies:

> It depends on other people. If other people want us to change, we can change. . . . We may feel that our behavior/attitudes are good, but if other people don't like them, they may say, "Don't act like that.". . . How are we ourselves to know how to change? Only other people can know that, right? So if other people don't like us [our attitudes and behavior], we can try to change. We can try to change whatever attitude/behavior is not liked.

Although, as we have noted, the Toraja recognize that there are individual differences in character or behavior, there also is a tendency to assume that people's motivations are generally similar; that is, given situation X, people assume that others will generally want or feel Y (cf. F. Errington 1984; Wikan 1991). People also tend to assume that certain ways of feeling and behaving are characteristic of different stages of life, and that one's attitudes and character develop and unfold in certain predictable ways. Perhaps because of these assumptions, respondents often found it difficult to respond to requests that they discuss their regrets, unfulfilled aspirations, or desires for change in themselves. Although some respondents say that it is fairly easy to change one's behavior (unlike one's appearance), there also is a sense that the self is not something that one changes of one's own volition; rather, it simply is what it is at any given stage in life (cf. Levy 1973:222). Thus speculation about what might have been or what could be is considered pointless to a certain extent. Nene'na Tandi(m), for example, is genuinely saddened by the fact that he angered and alienated his parents in his youth, yet he consoles himself with the thought that his defiant, irresponsible behavior was not atypical of adolescents, and so in some sense the falling out he had with his parents could not be helped. Most of the respondents, then, do not judge themselves harshly or seek to change themselves in significant ways, though as we noted above, they are sensitive to the opinions and criticisms of others.

IDENTIFICATION OF THE SELF WITH OTHERS

We also have noted that Toraja cultural beliefs and values encourage a strong identification between self and family members and members of one's community. Our interview material indicates that on an experiential level, there often is a close association between self and others. Once, when we were casually interviewing one man about something that had happened to him some years ago, a companion confidently spoke on the man's behalf, as if he had personally experienced the events himself. Of course, when individuals are born and live in the same village throughout the course of their adult lives, the degree to which they share the same or similar experiences with others is much greater than in other settings.

4

MENTAL STATES AND PROCESSES

NOTIONS OF SPIRIT OR SOUL

Traditional notions of the spiritual and psychological components of a person are complex. According to van der Veen (1966:9), a missionary and linguist who lived among the Toraja for several years,

> the Sa'dan Toradja concept of a human being's spiritual nature is that he has a *sunga'* = life force, in the sense of span of life, and a *sumanga'* = life force, spirit, in the sense of his consciousness. In addition, they also speak of a man's *deata* = his vital force and his more or less personal spirit, his *alter ego*. Furthermore, a man also has a *bombo* = personal spirit, though usually this term is given to his personal spirit after his death.[1]

Van der Veen does not specify the degree to which these concepts and terms were personally salient for rural villagers at the time of his research. Thus we do not know whether they represent the esoteric knowledge of a relatively small group of religious experts or more widely shared understandings. Our research indicates that currently such concepts are vague—at least in the Paku Asu area, and among nonspecialists. While many villagers believe that the span of one's life is predetermined (see Hollan and Wellenkamp n.d.), that some part of the self (referred to as *deatan* by some, and as *bombo* by others) may wander away from the body during dreams, and that after death the spirit or soul leaves the body and travels to the afterworld, these ideas are not articulated with much precision or clarity. Of the terms mentioned by van der Veen, *bombo* is the one used most frequently by Paku Asu residents.

DREAMS AND DREAMING

Dreams, in general, are of much interest to Toraja, and people commonly report dreams to family members or friends.[2] Sometimes important decisions (regarding, for example, one's religious affiliation, one's work or travel) are based on dreams. In this section, we discuss general understandings of dreams and their meanings, and present examples of certain dream experiences. However, we also use dream material throughout the book to illustrate common psychological themes or preoccupations.

Paku Asu villagers make a rough distinction between three types of dream experiences: those that occur frequently, are recalled only in fragments, and usually have something to do with the previous day's activities; those that occur rather infrequently and include both "spirit attacks" and "nightmares"; and those that are easy to recall and extremely vivid, but occur rather infrequently. Only the latter are considered true "dreams" (*tindo*).

The first type of experience seems to be viewed as a form of nocturnal cogitation in which the mind continues to mull over the day's events. Such dream experiences, which usually carry little affect, are not considered to be especially significant and are not given much thought. Ambe'na Patu describes such dreams as "left-over thoughts that did not finish themselves during the day."[3]

The second type of dream experience is called *tauan*. *Tauan* are thought to arise from two different sources or circumstances. One, they may be the reliving of a particularly unpleasant or frightening moment in the dreamer's life, not infrequently an experience from the previous day. Such *tauan* are characterized by the dreamer's fitful sleep and nonsensical utterances as he or she attempts to cry out or flee from shocking or fearful events experienced in the dream. While *tauan* are similar to the first type of dream experience in that they may concern the previous day's activities, their distinguishing characteristic is the intensity of the negative emotion accompanying them.

Two, *tauan* also may result from a spirit attack. Respondents' accounts of *tauan* attributed to attacks by malicious spirits closely resemble the "incubus" dreams described by Jones (1951). Such experiences often include a sense of motor and verbal paralysis (experienced as the spirit's attempt to restrain the dreamer's movements), a feeling of suffocation, and an overwhelming sense of dread and anxiety. (In chapter 6, we comment further on both sorts of *tauan* experiences, as well as other disturbing dreams.)

True "dreams" (*tindo*), like spirit attack *tauan*, are thought to be "real" experiences in which the dreamer's mind or spirit communicates with the wandering spirits of other sleeping humans (as in dreams of a sexual or romantic nature), or with spiritual beings. As mentioned earlier, the Toraja believe that the world is populated with many beings besides humans. Although most of these entities are thought to be invisible in normal waking life, humans may communicate with them in dreams, when a part of the self temporarily leaves the body and travels to the haunts of other beings,[4] or when other beings come to visit the dreamer in sleep. Such encounters during dreams are considered "real" experiences (which, in fact, validate the existence of spiritual beings)[5] and yet the Toraja clearly distinguish them from normal, waking states of consciousness.

Tindo are of special interest to the Toraja because some of them are thought to be predictive of future events. All major events in one's life are thought to be foreshadowed in dreams: Nene'na Limbong once remarked, "Everything that we do or attain, we dream of first"; similarly, Nene'na Tandi(f) comments, "Whether it's suffering or contentment, we must dream of it first before we traverse it." Both Nene'na Limbong and Ambe'na Toding suggested to us that we must have dreamed of our trip to Indonesia before we left home.[6]

People say that one cannot be absolutely certain whether or not a given dream is prophetic; many times one can only wait and see whether the future will bear out the events that are represented in a dream. But generally speaking, villagers are more likely to consider a dream prophetic if its content is easily understood using conventional, "dreambook" interpretations (see below), or if it has an unusual and/ or intense (either positive or negative) emotional tone.

Villagers believe that prophetic dreams may have either auspicious or inauspicious meanings. The meaning of some dreams can be readily identified by laypeople using interpretations that are widely known and shared; dreams that cannot be readily intepreted in this manner can be analyzed by a dream interpretation expert. In both instances, however, interpretations of the same dream may vary, or there may be more than one legitimate interpretation. This is because there is some inherent ambiguity in Toraja dream intepretation. For example, dream events are believed to have at times literal, and at times symbolic, meanings or referents—the presence of gold in a dream may literally represent a piece of gold jewelry or it may represent one's future rice harvest, while a water buffalo may represent itself or one's children.[7] In many interpretations, seemingly disturbing events are interpreted as having positive or nonthreatening outcomes. Here are some examples of dreams recognized as having good or bad portents.

"Good" Dreams
to receive a bird or fowl = to have a child
to carry pork or buffalo meat = to have a good rice harvest
to have objects thrown at the dreamer = rain will fall
to have one's body butchered = to slaughter livestock
to stand on a mountain top = to become a leader
to hold an umbrella over people = to become a leader
to strike a gong = to become a *to minaa*
to steal objects = to receive those objects; become wealthy
to swim in a lake or ocean = to receive wealth
to jump over or cross water = to become wise or clever
to be followed by monkeys, cats, or dogs = to receive buffalo
to be gored by a buffalo = to buy a buffalo
to hold the moon = to become wealthy

"Bad" Dreams
buffalo enter the rice fields = rats will eat the rice harvest
to be naked = to become ill
to lose a tooth = someone in one's family will die
to enter a burial tomb = to die
to be carried off by a deceased person = to die
to fall into water up to one's neck = someone will die
to have objects stolen, lost, or carried away = to lose those
    objects, or to lose one's children
to have one's house burn or be destroyed = to lose wealth

Among the most common dreams that are presumed to be portentous are those involving communication with deceased relatives. Most of our respondents have had such dreams, and many such dreams reportedly are vivid. Ambe'na Patu, when asked if he has had dreams of his deceased grandmother and mother, replies:

Yes, I have. I've seen my grandmother and my mother and other people who have died. . . . (Did you speak to them?) Some I spoke to and some I didn't, I just saw them. Do Americans dream? (Yes.) About their mothers? (Yes. About various things. And here?) Various things. All the different kinds of work, we must "get" in dreams [first]. . . . (What does your grandmother say [in dreams]?) She talks. Sometimes she talks, sometimes she doesn't. But [in the dream] I think that she's still alive. When I awake, [I think], "Wah, what did I see in my dream?"

In many dreams, deceased relatives bring gifts (e.g., vegetables, cloth, medicine) or convey special talents or powers (such as the ability to heal or knowledge of amulets); such dreams are considered auspicious in nature. Indo'na Rante says,

> When we dream like that [of one's deceased parent], often they are true. . . .if we dream he/she comes carrying vegetables for the pigs, [that means] our pigs will thrive. . . . .Also usually if we're sick, and then we dream that the dead person comes bringing us water, we quickly recover! Or for example, if he/she comes, bringing us a letter, we will receive money. . . . Yes, several times I have had dreams like those examples.

In other dreams, deceased relatives may offer the dreamer advice, either of a general nature (e.g., "Take good care of your children"), or containing specific instructions. Indo'na Rante and her family changed residences, for instance, after Indo'na Rante dreamed that her husband's deceased mother told her she should move next to the mother-in-law's former home.[8] Nene'na Tandi(m) converted to Christianity (for the second time) when he was very ill and his wife's aunt dreamed that he would die if he were to remain Alukta:

> The night before she had a dream and early in the morning she came to tell me [about it]. She herself sent [someone] to go find the minister. . . . I didn't know anything about it. Not until the minister arrived did she tell me, "It's like this. I called for the minister and the church elders . . . so that you would be returned to being a Christian." I said, "Why, mama?" She said, "Last night I dreamed a person wearing white clothes came, a very old person. He/She told me, 'If Nene'na Tandi remains Aluk To Dolo, we will have to take his spirit.' ". . . Then I said [to her], "Thank you" [for telling him]. . . . People prayed and right after they said, "Amen," I asked for rice porridge! . . . After a week, I could walk [and then] I went to the church in Laka [the nearest church at the time].

Before Nene'na Tandi(m) converted, however, he had to convince his Alukta parents to agree to it. They eventually were persuaded, he says, because he asked them if they would be happy if he were to die as the dream predicted, and because they thought that if they "forced" him to remain Alukta, he might become insane.[9]

Ambe'na Patu once had a dream of his deceased mother, who told him that he should go ahead with his plans to build a house, even though he thought that he still did not have the necessary resources. "My mother came [in the dream and said], 'Gather together the bamboo.' [I said], 'Ah, there isn't enough rice yet [to feed the villagers who would assist him with the labor] . . . she said, 'The point is, just do it.' Wah, I woke up and I thought and thought about it. [I thought], 'Where am I going to get this rice?'" Ambe'na Patu says that he was able to obtain the rice from a variety of sources and build his house, and thus the dream was "indeed true." What is noteworthy about such experiences is not only the importance villagers attach to dreams, but also the psychological support that dreams provide.[10]

Dreams in which deceased relatives request that they be given, or openly confiscate, valued persons or property—which are thought to be inauspicious—also are common, though among our respondents they appear less frequent than dreams of receiving gifts or advice. Indo'na Rante reports one such dream:

> One time I dreamed that my mother came and asked for a chicken, which I gave her. Suddenly, one of my children died. Yes, she/he died, [and] I called the to minaa [who explained], that's the way it is. If a dead person comes [in a dream] and [takes] a chicken, pig, or buffalo, that represents our children. Or it may even represent ourselves.

Elsewhere, we describe other dreams of deceased relatives reported by our respondents.

Dreams during adolescence and young adulthood that are taken to be prophetic of one's future role—as a ritual specialist, a healer, etc.—or one's future accomplishments also are common, among both our respondents and other villagers. Ambe'na Patu, for example, dreamed in his youth that he was leading a large group of children. At first he thought the dream predicted that he would become a teacher and yet he did not end up completing his education; now he believes that the dream foretold that he would become a religious leader. Twice before taking exams in school, Indo'na Tiku had dreams that she says foretold her success: in the first dream she crossed a narrow bridge without falling, and in the second she climbed to the top of a mountain. Ambe'na Tangke is the only respondent who says that while he had such dreams in his youth, he has not experienced the good fortune the dreams supposedly foretold.

Although, as noted above, Toraja say that one cannot be certain if a given dream will later prove to be prophetic, there are ritual means one can use to influence the prophecy of a dream. To increase the possibility that good portents will occur, the dream can be "dammed-up" or "blocked" (*disapan*) by making an offering to the ancestors involved. However, there is some risk entailed in sharing a good dream with ritual specialists and others since they may attempt to "steal" the good portents. To Minaa Sattu, for instance, claimed that an unscrupulous *to minaa* had stolen a dream portent from a man who had asked the specialist to interpret his dream. After interpreting the dream as auspicious, the *to minaa* quickly sacrificed a chicken before the person who dreamed the dream had a chance to make his own sacrifice. According to To Minaa Sattu, the specialist, through his actions, was able to appropriate the good portents for himself. For this reason, people often are reluctant to discuss their "good" dreams outside of a circle of close friends and family until the dream "comes true." Nene'na Tandi(m) offers the following advice: "If you dream, pay attention to it. But you may not tell other people, [don't say], 'Last night I dreamed like this.' . . . Don't [tell others]. Even an American, moreover Indonesians, [who] are very knowledgeable [regarding dreams]."

When a dream appears to be inauspicious, the bad portents can be averted by having the dream reinterpreted, or more literally "explicated," "limited," or "set a boundary around" (*dibori, dilebang*) by a dream specialist. The specialist—who provides an alternate, and more favorable interpretation of the dream—may be given money (one informant referred to the money as a "ransom" payment), and a sacrifice may also be required. In this way, the dream's original, ominous meaning is neutralized or reversed (see chapter 6 for an example provided by Nene'na Limbong).[11]

Other common themes in dreams reported by respondents (that in some instances were thought to be prophetic and in some not) are dreams with a sexual or romantic content; dreams of being chased, for example, by a water buffalo, snake, or person; dreams with violent images, such as of humans being shot, bombed, or cut up; and dreams in which the dreamer excels or stands out in some way from his or her cohorts. One person—Nene'na Tandi(f)—reported flying dreams. Nene'na Limbong related the greatest number of dreams (over 10) and, of the respondents, he clearly is the most interested in, and concerned about, his dreams. Many of his dreams are described in other chapters.

SENSE PERCEPTION

Tactile experiences involved in touching and holding others are important to the Toraja. Parents often mention the importance of holding an infant during his or her first year (see Hollan and Wellenkamp n.d.), and bodily contact through grooming, sitting close to, and embracing, others occurs throughout life (only among adults of the same gender, however, in public settings). At death, a dying person should be held in someone's lap, and during the *ma'nene'* ritual, the bodies of the deceased may be removed from burial tombs and held again.

Also of particular importance are the senses of sight and smell. Nene'na Tandi(m) calls sight a "heavenly" sense because, he says, visual information is concrete and unambiguous in a way that other sense data are not. Partly because of this belief, eyewitness accounts presented during dispute resolutions are considered much superior to other forms of evidence.[12] People also believe that the reason a few villagers can see *bombo* while most others cannot has something to do with their eyes, which are presumed to be different from most people's.

Smells also receive a great deal of attention. Spirits and *bombo* are said to be attracted by particular smells (e.g., the pleasant fragrance emitted by a pregnant woman, the smell of a decaying body), and people say that one symptom of poisoning is that one's body smells badly. People often comment on odors, especially those found to be offensive, which include odors from human feces or intestinal gas, and dank, musty burial caves. Indo'na Tiku, when describing an earthquake that had occurred about seven years previously, remarked that the earthquake produced bad odors and that in some areas, the residents couldn't tolerate it. People commonly cover their faces and withdraw from what for us were mildly offensive smells.

THINKING AND FEELING

Local Terminology

The Toraja language contains several terms relating to mental experiences or states. A term with the general meaning of "to experience" or "to feel" is *sa'ding* (e.g., *kadake kusa'ding,* "I feel bad"). "To think" (also "to trick/deceive") is *ma'tangnga',* and "to desire" or "like" is *porai.* There is no general term for "emotions" analogous to *perasaan* in Indonesian.

Two central components of several terms relating to mental states or processes are *penaa* and *inaa.* Tammu and van der Veen's (1972) Toraja-Indonesian dictionary translates *penaa* as: 1) *hati,* literally "liver" but figuratively "heart" or "mind" and *pikiran,* "thought" or "opinion;" 2) *napas,* "breath;" and 3) *jiwa* or *roh,* "soul" or "spirit." [13] *Inaa* is a similar concept having such meanings as "heart," "mind," "interest," "thought," and "insight."

Just as many Indonesian emotion terms center around the term *hati* (such as *senang hati,* "happy/content;" and *sedih hati,* "sad"), so too *inaa* and especially *penaa* are integral to many Toraja emotion terms (for example, *kapua penaa,* literally, "big breath" but figuratively, "happy/proud"; *malassu penaa,* literally, "hot breath" but figuratively, "upset/angry"; *tu'pe inaa,* "sad/dejected"; *ma'inaa-naa,* "to think of/ yearn for"). [14]

Ara', "chest/breast"; *tambuk,* [15] "stomach/womb"; and *ulu,* "head" are components of some other terms referring to mental experience (e.g., *re'de ara'ku,* "my chest/breast is bubbling/boiling," meaning, "I'm very angry"). While many terms involve a particular part of the person (breath, chest/breast, stomach/womb, etc.), others do not, for example, *mataku',* "afraid"; *sengke,* "angry"; *masussa,* "distressed"; and *topo,* "hungry." [16]

Relationship Between Thinking and Feeling

As the above terms suggest, the Toraja do not draw sharp conceptual distinctions between different mental states and processes, [17] including thought and emotion (cf. Wikan 1991:35–36; Howell 1981:139). Rather, there is a tendency to see thinking and emotions as inextricably linked. Indo'na Tiku, for example, physically shuddered as she recounted the events surrounding the earthquake that had occurred some years earlier. She said that merely thinking about the earthquake led her to reexperience the fear she felt at the time. Similarly, To Minaa Sattu's eyes once filled with tears as he watched the arrival of his neighbors' visiting relatives and was reminded of his own long-absent daughter. He later reported that once the image of his daughter had entered his mind, he could not contain his longing for her.

While many villagers say or imply that there is a close connection between thought and emotions, there is less consensus regarding how precisely the two phenomena are related. One person said that the cognitive evaluation of a situation occurs before the experience of emotion—for example, the awareness that one is in danger precedes the experience of fear. But an equally thoughtful informant claimed the opposite: that the experience of emotion *leads one* to cognitively evaluate a situation. Using the same example: it is only after experiencing fear that one is led to think about the kind of danger that one is in. Both maintained, however, that thought or cognition of some sort usually precedes action.[18]

Despite the importance attributed to cognition in guiding behavior, it is the emotional end of what are perceived of as closely related processes that our respondents tend to talk about, and our discussion below reflects this local emphasis on emotions. However, we begin with some remarks concerning thinking and cognition.

Thinking and Cognition

Clear, rational thought is highly valued by the Toraja, both as an impediment to impulsive behavior and as a prelude to correct action. Some indication of this is given by an expression which likens sound, wise counsel to a clearing in the brush (see van der Veen 1966:30). The appreciation of rational, logical thought also is reflected in the respect shown to those, especially leaders and adjudicators, who exhibit clear thinking,[19] and is consonant with a more general cultural emphasis on order and control.

Another indication of the importance of thinking and cognitive abilities is the traditional pasttime of sharing riddles (*karume*),[20] and the emphasis placed on craftiness and the use of strategy (discussed in chapter 5). A "cognitive" emphasis also is reflected in the extensive terminology that exists regarding architectural features and other objects, and the efforts of people to teach us numerous words relating to parts of the body, the house, etc.

There is also a notion that one's experiences can be materially affected by one's thoughts and beliefs. It is freqently said, for example, that if one does not believe in spirits, traditional taboos, or dream prophecies, then none of these can affect one's life. Conversely, if one does believe in them, then one must be concerned with them.

While villagers value reason, rationality, and cleverness, there is also a belief that people can be "too" intelligent and "think too much" about things. Obsessive thinking or rumination—which appears to be not uncommon (see chapter 6)—is associated with both physical and mental illness.

Levy (1973:261) notes in his discussion of thinking in Tahiti that Tahitians tend to provide either brief, generalized responses to certain questions (e.g., "What were your parents like?" "They were good") or "a detailed, often dramatic re-creation" of events. The same could be said of many of our respondents and other Paku Asu villagers, who similarly respond briefly and globally to "questions calling for evaluation and summary" (Levy 1973:261), but who provide a step-by-step recreation when recounting an event.

General Aspects of Emotions

Many people say that emotions are felt in the chest and stomach areas. Some also say that feelings rise upward from one's trunk. One man, who was interviewed regarding his bereavement experiences, cupped his hands below his ribcage and then moved his arms upward to indicate the flow of his feelings. Another person said that a feeling is felt in the chest and stomach area, then it rises, and then there is movement, for example in one's face. He went on to say, however, that often feelings remain inside, hidden from view.

Toraja assume that there are both individual and gender differences regarding emotions. Some individuals are said to be more calm and patient (*sa'bara', rapa' penaa*) and less easily upset than others. Women, in contrast to men, are viewed, in general, as more susceptible to feelings of sadness, compassion, and, according to some informants, anger and irritation. Developmental differences also are recognized: Children are said to be "not yet conscious," meaning that they have less control over, and are therefore less responsible for, their emotional lives than adults, and some say that in old age, people become more emotional.

People talk about emotions as if they were highly contagious and as if, given the appropriate eliciting stimulus, they are difficult to avoid.[21] Yet, informants and respondents also often imply that emotional responses do not arise without specific triggering stimuli. For instance, Nene'na Limbong says that he is no longer angry at a man who tricked him because he has not seen him since the incident occurred. Similarly, those who have had a relative die say that once the body of the deceased is removed from the house, they are less distressed than when the body is in sight.

In the Toraja view of emotions, the experience of strong feelings is accompanied by a diminution in consciousness. Under normal circumstances, adults are said to be "conscious" (*mengkilala*), meaning both that one is alert and that one is aware of the implications of one's actions. But when one is very excited or upset (or inebriated, "crazy," or possessed), one becomes confused and dizzy and no longer "conscious," no longer aware of one's actions. In extreme cases, a person may be so overwhelmed with emotion, he or she may faint (*ma'ipu*).

In most daily contexts, spontaneous, dramatic expressions of emotion are rare.[22] While the expression of strong "positive" feelings such as passionate desire and exhiliaration is largely absent from everyday life,[23] it is the open expression of "negative" feelings such as "anger" and "sadness" that is actively guarded against.[24] There are several reasons for this, some of which depend on the particular emotions involved.

Elsewhere Hollan (1988a) has characterized the Toraja as nonviolent. In the following sections, we discuss attitudes and beliefs concerning anger and aggression and common sources of conflict, before discussing sadness and grief.

Aggression and the Expression of Anger

In most circumstances, angry outbursts in any form, including physical violence, as well as shouting, quarreling, angry gestures, and the like, are considered disgraceful. The negative evaluation of angry behavior is reflected in the reluctance of some of our respondents to discuss times that they have been angry. In an early interview with Nene'na Tandi(f), for example, she said that she never got angry; in later interviews, however, she claimed that while she has never become angry since becoming a Christian, she *used* to get angry often. The importance that is attached to not getting angry also is reflected in the fact that whether or not a person is prone to getting angry (*to sengkean, to arasan*) is considered to be a salient aspect of his or her character.

As we discussed in chapter 1, angry outbursts and quarreling are condemned because of their disruptive effect on social relationships and community unity. Angry behavior and interpersonal conflict also are considered morally wrong and capable of causing widespread misfortune in life. Despite the strong negative evaluation of expressions of anger in daily contexts, however, there are some occasions when it is considered legitimate and appropriate for someone to be angry (e.g., when a funeral is performed without the knowledge and consent of the deceased's absent children; when a person is tricked or shamed), but one's anger ideally should be expressed in subtle, indirect ways. For example, one can signal one's dissatisfaction with another person by avoiding his or her presence, or, if that is not possible, by refusing to speak with him or her. Indo'na Sapan, for example, did not speak to her parents for a week when they "forced" her to marry a man against her will. Other measures also can be taken: one can refuse to attend a ritual the offending person is sponsoring; one can request that a village council be convened to hear one's complaint; and a complaint can be registered with local police officials.

During our stay in Paku Asu, all of the above measures were used by villagers. But outbursts of anger, outside of specially designated contexts, were very rare, despite the occurrence of events that certainly tried people's patience—as when two boys started a fire that rapidly spread out of control and destroyed several gardens and coffee trees and came close to destroying some burial tombs.[25]

Stereotypical displays of anger do occur, however. For example, parents may shake their fists, point their fingers, or make threatening grimaces in feigned or at least controlled gestures of anger directed at children (which children usually disregard). On three occasions, we witnessed incidents of interpersonal violence, but the extent of the violence was extremely minor. In one case, a man pulled another man's hair and pushed his face to one side in a dispute over a tube of palm wine. In the second, one teenager bit a second teenager's hand and the second retaliated by kicking the first. In the third, a police official beat some unruly children with a branch.[26]

This is not to say that interpersonal violence on a greater magnitude does not occur. There seems to be more violence in private settings. Reportedly, police occasionally beat criminals, husbands beat wives, and teachers and parents beat children. There also are occasional cases of homicide and incidents of violence on the part of mentally distraught individuals (see below). But informal accounts, police crime statistics, and hospital records indicate that outright violence is uncommon.[27] Verbal altercations also are infrequent. For the most part, in daily life, there is relatively little overt expression of anger and hostility.[28]

Common Sources of Conflict

During the course of our interviews, and after months of behavioral observations, it became apparent to us that while angry feelings occasionally are expressed either overtly or covertly, there are many more times when they are consciously experienced yet remain unexpressed.[29] Later we discuss strategies people employ to manage conscious feelings

Typical Toraja landscape: lush, terraced ricefields and bamboo forests.

Women planting rice seedlings.

Village scene: houses (on left) facing rice barns

Front view of ancestral house *(tongkonan)* with split bamboo roof and carved and painted exterior.

Toraja children: (above) two girls; (below) a group of boys.

Toraja adults: (above) men with roosters; (below) women attending a ritual.

Temporary bamboo effigies of the dead *(tatau)* constructed for Alukta funerals: a ritual specialist *(to mebalun)* constructs a *tatau* (above) for a woman, (below) for a man.

Men in a circle performing a funeral chant *(ma'badong)*.

Slaughtering a water buffalo: (above) the buffalo has just been struck under the neck with a machete; (below) a platform from which the meat will be distributed.

The deceased's body is carefully attended to: (above) girls inside a house beside a wrapped body; (below) mourners wailing over a coffin near the burial grounds.

Burial: (above) a coffin is hauled into a burial vault; (below) a body is removed during a form of secondary burial *(ma'nene')*.

View of limestone burial vaults at Lemo (near Makale), with wooden *tatau* on balconies.

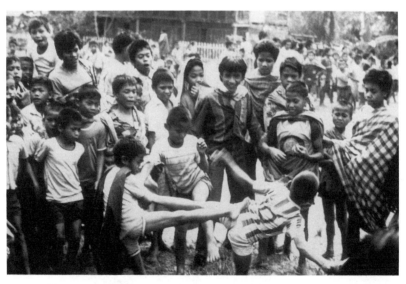

Pairs of boys engaged in a kickfight *(sisemba')*.

Scenes from a *ma'maro* ritual: (above) costumed girls dancing; (below) in the background, a group of people chant, while in the foreground, a woman (center) enters possession trance.

Feats performed during possession trance: (above) a man striking his left forearm with a fistful of branches; a woman walking on burning wood.

An act of healing: a sick boy is lifted and swung during a *ma'maro* ritual.

Close-up view of wooden effigies *(tatau)* of the dead.

of anger, disappointment, and so forth (see chapter 7). Here, we discuss some occasions when conflict typically arises, when sometimes there may be more direct display of anger and perhaps violence.

One such occasion is the division of meat at rituals. It is during the division of meat that one's social status is most clearly and publicly defined (see Volkman 1985). Because even the most fair-minded, well-intentioned meat divider cannot simultaneously satisfy the status aspirations of all of those in the community, it is inevitable that some people will be dissatisfied and feel shamed by their allotment. In this special context, the expression of anger is considered acceptable, although any anger expressed during a meat division should not be carried over into daily life.

During meat divisions, some people do openly express anger and appear genuinely upset, but participants also sometimes use the expression of anger in a strategic way to influence the division of meat. For instance, a person waiting to receive some meat may angrily assert his prominence in the community and recite his past slaughtering history *before* the division takes place, hoping to "force" the dividers into giving him a larger piece of meat.[30] Nene'na Tandi(m) explains:

> If, for example, [a man] is angry for a moment, and then angry again, and then again, he is looking for meat. He's just looking for meat. . . .He is scared his piece of meat will be small, so before the meat is divided, he acts angry so that the dividers must take notice of him. The dividers may give him a big piece just so he won't bother them.

People also may reject pieces of meat that they feel are incommensurate with their status, thereby attempting to shame the meat dividers. Or, those who feel slighted may temporarily hold their peace, but at the next ritual will slaughter a large, fine animal. Nene'na Tandi(m) elaborates:

> If, for example, we are refined, we cannot respond to anger with anger, [we must be] refined. Later at the next celebration. . .we will look for a large pig and slaughter it. We order the people who didn't give to us [at the previous celebration] to attend. They are shamed.

The dividers, on the other hand, may use the expression of anger to maintain control of the division and to dissuade people from pursuing their own self-interest at the expense of the community. How are we to equitably distribute meat, they ask, if certain people are constantly demanding more than their fair share? By angrily denouncing such behavior, they hope to shame or "scare" people into silence and passivity. Nene'na Tandi(m) explains that such anger is a "normal" part of the meat division:

> If people [dividers] get angry during the meat division, it's directed at those who keep asking for meat, so that those who divide the meat are happy [doing their job] and those who ask for meat are scared. So that is just a normal part [of the meat division].

Nene'na Limbong and Ambe'na Kondo, both of whom are meat dividers, offer similar accounts. Nene'na Limbong comments:

> It is usual for me to get angry at a meat division. For example. . .there's this man, he asks for meat two or three times, very often I will get angry. Because he is asking for himself alone. But I have to divide according to the rules. So that's why I get angry if someone asks for meat three times. He asks for meat several times or just takes it to give to his friends. That's when I get angry. Because I have to organize the division so that everybody gets a piece. So that at the end there isn't someone who didn't get a piece. That's why I get angry.

Ambe'na Kondo distinguishes this managerial anger from "real" anger: "Very often [I am angry at the meat division]. But I'm not really angry. It's only anger of the mouth! If we are angry at the mouth, that's so that people won't bother the distribution [of meat]."

Because the expression of anger during meat divisions is anticipated and relatively controlled—it occurs only in the context of a ritual and often is theatrical and purposeful—it is considered a "normal" problem. More disturbing to villagers, but equally expected, are openly angry responses to other incidents in which one feels publicly shamed, such as when sexual matters are discussed in front of close relatives of the opposite gender, or when curse words referring to sex between relatives are used. Indo'na Rante, for example, says that if someone were to say "motherfucker," that person "could be killed! People would fight until she/he were dead, if she/he spoke like that. 'We felt *masiri'* [ashamed],' people would say." Nene'na Tandi(m) says: "people [men] are angry here if [in the presence of one's daughter] someone says *taibaro* [semen]. Ah, we're ashamed. Or if. . .*kendumo* [had sexual intercourse] is said. . . .If someone. . .uttered words like that, I could exchange blows with them! Because I would be ashamed, because my child was present."

Although we did not witness any incidents of such a nature, To Minaa Sattu mentions one occasion on which he responded angrily when he felt publicly shamed. He only hesitantly discloses this when he is asked about times when he has been angry:

(Can you remember [a time] when you were the most angry?) I haven't yet [been really angry]. (No?) No [softly, in a low voice]. [long pause] Yes, you know when there was the celebration at X? My—you know Ambe'na Kondo? He was angry at me! And I returned it. Because [I thought]..."He is my child [nephew]. ...Why was I shamed in front of the community?" Of course, I returned his anger....Because someone told me to come [sit down and participate in the proceedings]... I sat down. And [then he] came [and said], "Leave!" [31]

The notion that a shamed person may lash out at those considered responsible for his or her humiliation figures prominently in an account told about a man named Busa' who was supposed to have lived in a village near the town of Rantepao in the late 1920s. According to one version of the story, Busa' was a good man who was greatly shamed when he witnessed his sister being beaten and stripped of her clothing by a married woman (who suspected the sister of having an affair with her husband). Busa' was very ashamed and wanted to die, but first he wanted to take revenge against the husband of the woman who had shamed him. He waited for the right opportunity, and then tried to kill the man with a knife, but the man ran off. Then Busa' 's, anger began to "boil over" even more, and his eyes went "dark," and he began to attack anyone who crossed his path, including children and a pregnant woman. In a short time, he had killed or wounded several victims and people were afraid to apprehend him. Eventually a driver disarmed him, but even after he had been jailed, he continued to struggle, throwing urine and feces at his captors. Busa' then was completely tied up and later died, much to the relief of local residents who on one occasion had been greatly frightened by a rumor that Busa' had escaped.

Whether or not the Busa' story has any factual basis, it seems to accurately reflect a potential for anger and fantasies of retaliation among people who have been shamed, although violent responses of the magnitude of Busa' 's appear to be very rare—which is why the story stands out in people's minds. [32] The Busa' story not only reflects certain tendencies of those who have been shamed, but in its retelling it also serves the purpose of clearly illustrating for villagers the possible dangers involved in shaming others.

We have noted that the sexual and emotional components of the marital relationship are de-emphasized in Toraja, and divorce is often described as a casual matter. At the same time, however, a spouse's unfaithfulness may evoke feelings of intense shame and anger and possibly lead to violence. Suicidal feelings also are recognized as a possibility in such situations. One of our neighbors claimed that he knew a man who had decapitated his wife's lover, and a couple of the eleven physical assaults recorded in police records for Tana Toraja during 1982 had to do with men fighting over women (we do not know the details of the cases). However, our sense is that fantasies and talk about violence in connection with adultery are much more common than actual occurrences.

Most of the violence that does occur in Toraja appears to be the culmination of a protracted dispute over resources,[33] especially land. Waterson (1981:342, 366–71) reports that a large percentage of formal civil suits have to do with disputes over land, and our own court research corroborates her findings. This in itself suggests the volatile nature of such disputes since, generally speaking, Toraja villagers would prefer to settle their disagreements at the village or district level. A large percentage of criminal cases also has to do with disputes over land. Of the single murder and eleven assaults recorded for 1982, the murder and a majority of the assaults involved land disputes.

The seriousness of disputes over land is indicated by Ambe'na Kondo when he explains the difference between "anger of the mouth"—angry words meant to intimidate—and "real" anger:

(You say that anger of the mouth is different from real anger, but how is it different? Can you remember a time when you were really angry?) If we are really angry, there must be problem. (A problem like what?) For example, if we have a rice field and someone tries to take it. . . . If there is property that is stolen. For example, if I work a rice field and someone tries to take it, that's when we are really angry. We can die in the rice field [fighting over it]. (Have you ever quarreled like that?) Yes, I have, but the elders in the village repaired [the matter].

Sadness, Grief, and Crying

Alukta rules explicitly regulate crying, wailing, and the expression of sadness. It is taboo (*pemali*), for instance, for an adult to audibly cry at any time except in connection with death or with attempts to conceive a child (see Waterson 1981:261). When Indo'na Rante is asked which of the numerous prohibitions she considers the most important to observe, she refers to those against adultery, cursing someone, and crying: "Crying," she says, "cannot be done just anytime." Similarly, sitting with one's chin cupped in one's hand (*ma'sakkun are*), a gesture interpreted as expressing intense feelings of sorrow and distress, is taboo. Children's crying is subject to far fewer restrictions, but even children should not cry at certain times and places, such as in the rice fields during harvesting. Singing funeral chants and wearing black clothing—both traditional expressions of grief—also are restricted to specific times and places.[34]

Despite such restrictions, people still do cry occasionally when they are not supposed to. When this happens—for example, when a wife cries during a quarrel with her husband, or when someone cries at the departure of a close relative or friend—according to Alukta tradition, a sacrificial offering should be made to atone for the transgression in order to avoid later misfortune.

Many of the prohibitions regulating crying and the expression of sadness are based on the belief that by performing actions normally associated with death and the smoke-descending ritual sphere one is inviting death to happen. One woman (the daughter of a Toraja woman and Chinese man) said that when her parents left by boat for a visit to China, her mother's relatives cried vigorously. She believes that the reason her mother has never returned and is presumed dead is because people cried for her as they normally only do for a person who has died. Similarly, Indo'na Sapan reports that her mother becomes angry when boys sing funeral chants in idle moments around the village and that she reproaches them saying, "Do you want to bring misfortune on us?"

Although the taboo against crying is currently disregarded by Pentecostal church members, for whom crying (in a manner very similar to traditional wailing) is an integral part of receiving the Holy Spirit, many villagers find this practice disturbing. For Ambe'na Patu, the Protestant minister, the fact that Pentecostals engage in crying was the major obstacle preventing him from joining the Pentecostal Church when he was younger.

While not taboo, even having one's eyes fill with tears is considered unseemly for adults. Indo'na Tiku cries only at night in bed when she is certain that no one will discover that she has been crying. Otherwise, if she has been crying and "I hear someone coming, quickly I make my tears disappear [she laughs]. So that no one knows." As with anger, open spontaneous expressions of sadness outside of special contexts (described below) are uncommon, although stereotypical displays of sadness do occur as when older women look especially sad when recollecting life's hardships and asking for the listener's sympathy and compassion.

Emotional Restraint

The Toraja, then, as many other central and western Indonesian groups (as well as other Austronesian groups), value emotional restraint and equanimity in daily life. And yet in comparison to some groups such as the Bugis of Luwu and the Javanese, Toraja standards do not seem to require the same degree of control over emotional expression. For example, Toraja appreciate wit and often engage in laughing and joking, and both men and women enjoy drinking limited amounts of alcoholic beverages.

There also are subtle differences between Toraja views of emotions and those of the Javanese and Bugis. The major concern of the Toraja in regards to their emotional lives is the avoidance of emotional upset, that is, feelings of anger, grief, distress, disappointment, and the like. The avoidance of these feelings includes not only proscriptions against their outward expression but also extends to attempts to limit the inner experience of such feelings. Toraja believe that one should not dwell on or be preoccupied with upsetting thoughts and that one should attempt to remain "conscious" (*mengkilala*) and to keep oneself from becoming emotionally upset. In contrast to the Javanese, however, the Toraja do not emphasize the desirability of avoiding emotional highs (in addition to emotional lows) and of maintaining a flatness of affect (*iklas,* in Javanese) (Geertz 1976:53, 240–41). Although the Toraja do not talk about the dangers of allowing oneself to feel happy, neither do they talk much about ways of attaining happiness. Mostly, they talk of how to avoid distress.

Also, Toraja ideas differ from those of the priyayi Javanese and the Bugis regarding the positive benefits of remaining conscious and of retaining a calm composure. Both the priyayi Javanese and the Bugis strive to maintain a calm composure (for example, by meditating) as a means of increasing one's spiritual potency and outward power (Geertz 1976; Keeler 1987; Errington 1983, 1989). In contrast, Paku Asu villagers seem more interested in pursuing calmness and consciousness as a means of avoiding emotional upheaval rather than as an end in itself or as something leading to a positive end. The exception to this statement is the way in which anger and interpersonal discord are viewed. The Toraja believe that if one avoids getting angry and does not engage in quarrels with others, this will bring one general fortune (*dalle'*) in life.

Consequences of Becoming Emotionally Upset

One reason that emotional turbulence or distress is avoided is because its expression is disturbing to others and is disruptive to the maintenance of smooth social relations. As noted above, those who become visibly and openly upset may be the object of shameful ostracism, ridicule, and gossip. When a visitor to the village became angry at a local market, for example, the incident became a lively topic of conversation as people criticized the visitor's behavior. In another instance, a boy about 10 years of age started crying in the midst of a group of people, whereupon several adults tried to get him to stop by wiping away his tears, swiping at his back, and talking to him, while one older boy threw a dirt clod near him in seeming disgust.

Another reason that emotional turbulence is avoided is because, as discussed above, the expression of certain emotions is curtailed by traditional prohibitions.

Finally, emotional upset is avoided because of beliefs about its adverse effects on one's health. Like the Javanese (Geertz 1961:134), Balinese (Wikan 1991), and other Austronesian groups (see, for example, Watson-Gegeo and White 1990), Toraja believe that illness can be caused by negative emotional experiences.[35] For example, Indo'na Tiku attributes her poor eyesight to the occasional times that she has cried at night while lying in bed, an act which she says is known to cause clouding of one's vision. More severe, prolonged emotional and cognitive distress is believed to be capable of causing more serious health problems such as weight loss, stomach and heart ailments, tuberculosis, and premature death.[36] Prolonged distress also is considered to be a major cause of insanity (see chapter 6).

Beliefs about the harmful aspects of negative emotional experiences are related to the idea that strongly felt emotions are associated with "heat," which under normal circumstances is considered to be antithetical to the "coolness" of health (see Wellenkamp 1988a, 1988b).[37] The injurious effects of being upset are believed to result even if one refrains from outwardly expressing one's feelings; and according to some, "storing" one's unexpressed feelings inside oneself is especially dangerous. Thus, for a number of reasons, one should attempt to avoid altogether becoming emotionally upset (except on certain special occasions discussed below). In later chapters, we discuss what typically causes villagers anxiety and distress, and we describe common techniques that people use to help prevent themselves and others from becoming upset. These include avoiding potentially upsetting situations, attempting to remain calm and "conscious" when such events are unavoidable, and trying to not talk or think about distressing events.

Expression of Emotion in Special Contexts

Although villagers generally attempt to avoid experiencing and expressing intense emotions, there are special occasions when it is considered appropriate and even beneficial to do so. While the expression of intense emotion on these occasions is restricted to certain times, places, and forms,[38] it is nevertheless in dramatic contrast to everyday behavior.

Kickfights, *sisemba'*, are one occasion on which aggressive, violent behavior, normally condemned, is allowed and even encouraged. In the Paku Asu area, kickfights are held annually during a period of about a month at the beginning of the agricultural season, when the rice seeds are sowed; they also may be held at *ma'maro* rituals. Kickfights involve pairs of boys (sometimes as young as five or six years of age) followed later by adolescent males and then adult men,[39] who team up on one side of a field to compete against pairs on the opposing side.[40] One person in a pair kicks at his opponent, while the second uses his weight to support his partner's defensive or offensive movements. Fights between pairs occur simultaneously and in a fairly unstructured way, as partners exchange positions and engage different opponents. The result is a general melee, with teams surging back and forth across the field. When one side has been run competely off the field, the kickfight ends. Interestingly, people ask about which side of an engagement was *defeated,* rather than which side won: the emphasis is less on winning than on avoiding defeat.

The behavior and ethos of kickfights is very different from the tenor of everyday life: people yell and taunt one another and move en masse with much energy (cf. Siegel 1966). Injuries are expected and those that occur are compared to injuries caused by being stepped on by a water buffalo (*nalese tedong*)—that is, those who inflict injuries during the course of a kickfight are free from blame or legal prosecution. Although we never saw anyone seriously injured during a kickfight, powerful blows may be delivered and contestants' (particularly younger boys') faces often look intense. Two of our male respondents claim that their present physical ailments are the result of wounds received years ago in kickfights.[41]

While several of our older respondents are proud of their past kickfighting abilities, and while most participants and spectators appear to consider kickfights enjoyable and exciting, there is some ambivalence about participating as well. For example, several people say they are frightened to participate in large-scale kickfights, especially those between groups who are only distantly related to one another, because, they say, the nature of *sisemba'* has changed in recent years. Now, reportedly, people play with anger in their hearts, disregard the rules, or use magic against their opponents in an effort to inflict serious harm. As a result, some people are hesitant to enter a kickfight unless they themselves have some way of magically protecting themselves against injury.

During the kickfights we observed, there was much bluffing, and apparently some reluctance on the part of many participants to engage others in serious fighting. It was not uncommon for only a handful of boys and men of each age group to actively engage their opponents in intense competition. Some older, experienced men, apparently frustrated by the reluctance of some of the youths, stood in the field, aggressively urging the youths into contact with the opposition. A "defensive" approach to kickfighting is evident in the way in which one team may be chased nearly off the field before it turns to engage the opposition.

Kickfights provide men and boys the opportunity to observe, express, and experiment with aggressive behaviors usually proscribed in nonritual contexts. As such, they provide socialization for a minimal amount of aggression (primarily defensive in nature), which in former times was needed in connection with warfare and headhunting.

A link between kickfights and aggressive warfare is readily made by Toraja villagers. Many people say that kickfights are "like a war."[42] In some ways, such statements seem to exaggerate the amount of violence involved in kickfights, while at the same time they imply that kickfights serve as outlets for hostile feelings. The Bugis, one man said, have no sport. They use knives and kill each other. But we Toraja *sisemba'* (and thus express hostility in a "safe" way). Some people also explicitly suggest that kickfights in former times helped prepare males for warfare, although they point out that kickfights only prepared males in a general way for fighting, since traditional warfare involved the use of blowpipes and spears, not bodily contact.

Other occasions on which violent behavior is expected and encouraged are certain smoke-ascending rituals such as the *ma'maro,* during which both male and female participants are possessed by *deata* (spirits), and following their instructions, thrash, cut, and stab themselves and others (see section below on "Losses of Consciousness").[43]

Following a death and during death rituals, wailing and crying (*umbating, tumangi'*) often occurs. Crying and wailing in connection with death are encouraged for several reasons, including the belief that some expression of sadness and distress is beneficial for those close to the deceased (see below).[44]

Many people say they cannot remember what words they utter when they wail because they are not "conscious." The out-of-the-ordinary and affecting nature of wailing is reflected in comments made by some villagers. Nene'na Tandi(f), for example, says that her skin prickles when she hears someone wailing, and another woman, Indo'na Sumpu, says that when she hears wailing, "why, my soul almost floats. My body almost flies. . . . I don't know if I'm sitting or if I'm standing or what." In addition to crying and wailing, mournful flute music may be played at funerals and there may be funeral chanting and songs.

The expression of strong emotion (which may involve loss of "consciousness" and later amnesia) or violent actions on such specially designated occasions often are associated with personal and community well-being. For instance, while excessive crying following a death is thought to be harmful, occasional periods of crying and wailing are said to bring relief by allowing the release of heavy, hot feelings. In fact, those who do *not* cry are said to be susceptible to illness. As Allo, a young man, says, "If we don't cry, we feel dizzy. It gives us a headache. Thus, it's better to just cry. Usually if a person does not cry, various types of illness will arise within the person." Another informant, Indo'na Sumpu, says that those who are too shy to wail "will quickly become ill. Because within his/her heart there are feelings that are fluttering that he/she wants to release. (Thus, it is better to release them?) Yes, it is better to release them because those who cry, all of the contents of their heart is said. Thus, when they have stopped, although

usually they are still sad, they are quiet. But if one does not cry, usually
. . . one is attacked by thoughts."

Positive benefits also are associated with kickfights and possession
trance. People claim that the more blood that is shed and bones that
are broken during kickfights, the higher the subsequent yield of the rice
harvest and the quicker the recovery of the ill.[45] Those who become
possessed by the *deata* during *ma'maro* rituals may acquire temporary
healing powers, which they use to minister to the sick. *Non*participation in these events can bring harmful consequences: It is said that
those who are possessed and yet fail to follow the instructions of the
spirits will fall ill or become insane, and boys and men who watch the
kickfights from the sidelines are said to experience a shaking of their
legs that compels them to join in the activity.[46]

LOSSES AND TRANSFORMATIONS OF CONSCIOUSNESS

We have noted that villagers are generally fearful of experiences that
involve the loss of self-control and self-awareness. And yet there are
special contexts in which such experiences are sought or at least are
not avoided. Here, we examine some of these. We also discuss incidents
of losses of consciousness that occur spontaneously, outside of a special
context.

Possession Trance

Ma'maro and *ma'bugi'* ceremonies are occasions when a temporary
loss of normal consciousness among some people is anticipated and
culturally encouraged. While we witnessed two *ma'maro* ceremonies,
we did not observe a *ma'bugi'* ritual,[47] and for this reason, the following discussion focuses on the *ma'maro*, although the *ma'bugi'* is very
similar (see Nooy-Palm 1986:139–44 and Crystal and Yamashita
1987).

Previously, *ma'maro* ceremonies were held regularly, perhaps annually (if there were no deceased persons in the village awaiting funerals); since the introduction of Christianity, however, both *ma'maro*
and *ma'bugi'* (along with other smoke-ascending rituals) have de-
creased in frequency (see Wellenkamp 1988a).[48] *Ma'maro* ceremonies
are held for a number of reasons, including as a prelude or denouement
to other types of rituals (Hollan 1984:244; Nooy-Palm 1986:121–51),
but in general they are concerned with healing, prosperity, and transformation. In keeping with this emphasis (see Wellenkamp 1988a),

images of heat and fire and of dissolution and disorder are prominent in the *ma'maro,* followed by "cooling" and transformation. Some of the feats reportedly performed by ritual specialists involve crushing eggs and crabs that then become whole again, and chickens that are killed and eaten but from the pile of bones are brought back to life. According to Zerner (1981:112), "the course of events in the maro follows a thermal progression from cool to hot to coolness again, a process through which things, as well as persons, are considered blessed and transformed." The actions of those who are possessed by spirits called from afar to enter the village is a central part of the disorder and "heat" that characterize the ritual.

Like most Toraja rituals, the *ma'maro* ceremony consists of a number of steps and activities spread out over hours and days; in the following, however, we discuss only those aspects directly related to the gathering in and manifestation of the spirit world. (For a more complete description of the *ma'maro,* see Nooy-Palm 1986:121–39; Coville 1988; Zerner 1981.)

One of the central activities in the *ma'maro* ceremony in the Paku Asu area is the construction of a tall trident-shaped banner called a *bate*. Made of bamboo poles and decorated with the red leaves of the *tabang* plant (Cordyline terminalis) and with heirlooms, including swords and cloths thought to possess special powers,[49] the *bate* could be said to be used like a lightening rod to attract and hold the attention of the spirit world during the ceremony.[50] The *bate* is first erected in the hosts' courtyard and then later moved to an open ritual field; in both places, participants become possessed, in conjunction with the rhythmic chanting of paired verses called *gelong*.

When *gelong* are performed as a prelude to the arrival of the spirits,[51] they are accompanied by the driving beat of a drum and are performed while a group of participants hold hands and dance, initially circling slowly but then increasing the tempo of their movements as the tempo of the singing increases.[52] The *gelong* call upon the *deata* of the heavens, earth, and underworld to gather together at the site of the ceremony, promising them submission if they do:

> Spirits here in this village
> Lord (*puang*) here in this village
> Ruler (*datu*) at the edge of the house
> Come here, let us be together jumping,
> Spirits surround/cover my body
> Lord at the edge of my outside

Do not go far from the jumpers
I follow the custom of the ancestors
Exemplar guarding the earth
Does not want to be left behind
Returns to be remembered   (Zerner 1981:106–107).

Whatever you desire
Whatever you wish in your heart
Go there and take me
Even if only for one night
Make visible your world
Whatever you desire from my heart
Go there and take me
Go and take it from me
Even if only for one night   (Zerner 1981:107).

You must possess me,
Press on as I feel faint,
Awareness is ending,
You drive me quivering to earth
                (Crystal and Yamashita 1987:54).

Other verses describe the ritual ground as "truly red, surely on fire" (Zerner 1981:106) and speak of monumental changes in the earth's surface: mountains are pressed down and valleys are lifted up (Zerner 1981:106) while rivers reverse direction (Nooy-Palm 1969:182). Zerner (1981:106) observes: "the cataclysmic geophysical imagery . . . is both a sign of the powers of the arriving spirits and the turmoil, movement, and agitation which follow as people invite and are taken by the spirits."

Once participants are "with" (sisola) or "taken by" (diala) the deata, the deata are said to order them to perform specific behaviors, including beating others and themselves with sticks and branches, cutting or poking the skin with knives and swords, walking on fire or burning embers, and behaving or moving in ways that appear sexually provocative (e.g., for women, the loosening of the hair).[53] Such behaviors are viewed as strange and extraordinary and as evidence of the presence and power of the spirits.

Should a possessed person refuse to obey a deata's request, people say that he or she will become seriously ill, crazy, or die. According to To Minaa Sattu:

[Once] our stomach starts going like this [he breathes very shallowly and rapidly, forcing his stomach to expand and contract slightly] . . . and our breath becomes rapid. . .if we were not to obey . . . we would become crazy. . .and sick. That's why . . . those who don't [obey] . . . have thin bodies. Yes, they have thin bodies . . . and they become permanently sick inside. . . . And that is the worst sickness of all! So those who don't [obey] . . . age very quickly. That [to not become possessed] is called *ditantang* [divorced, let go].

One wealthy, high status man said that for some time he has tried to persuade his wife not to participate in the *ma'maro*, fearing that she would eventually be hurt while beating herself with branches. His wife, however, he said, fears that it would be far more dangerous for her to disobey the commands of the *deata* than to continue to participate. Another person reported that the *deata* who possessed her had once told her that they would kill anyone who tried to interrupt or prevent her participation. The cultural message of spirit possession clearly is one of compliance: one must submit to the powerful forces of the *deata*, and in return the community will receive health and prosperity.[54]

While the feats and behaviors performed by the possessed (*to kandeatan*) during a *ma'maro* ceremony vary, many involve aggressive acts directed against either the self or others. During one of the ceremonies we witnessed, for example, the first person to be possessed was an older woman who ran through the audience kicking people. In other instances, *to kandeatan* chase after people with branches and sticks. One person said that he often tries to engage others in kickfights when he is possessed, and another man reported that he puts on a pair of buffalo horns and charges at people.

Acts of autoaggression, however, are especially prominent. Many participants beat themselves on the forearms or the back of the legs with sticks or branches, or press the blades of machetes or ancient swords into the flesh of their forearms, their stomachs, or their calves. Others lean over and press their stomachs into the blade of a sword held horizontally at waist height either in front of the possessed person, or behind him or her. Still others use small knives to prick wounds in their foreheads or slash cuts in their tongues. (The blood which flows from the head and tongue cutting is then smeared on the leaves of the *tabang* plant and used to treat sick villagers.) One woman we observed walked repeatedly over a small fire, eventually putting it out by stamping on it.

Based on observations and interviews, it appears to us that *ma'maro* participants generally experience a temporary state of psychological "dissociation," defined as a state "in which ongoing behavior is not subject to recall when the actor emerges from that state" and in which "the actor behaves, but his behavior is closed to his conscious level of awareness" (Spiro 1978:159). To Minaa Sattu, for example, reports: "[We] feel our bodies go like this [jump of their own accord]. . . . When we are possessed, we are just like a crazy person! We don't recognize anyone. [We think], 'Who is this?' [when looking at others]. . . . Only after the *gelong* are recited [the verses that serve to end the possession trance] do we begin to remember a little."

While most people claim to have amnesia for the period that they are possessed, in a few instances participants report visualizing the *deata*. To Minaa Sattu says, for example, that during some *ma'maro* celebrations he has seen the *deata:*

> (So when the *deata* came, could you see them?) Yes, I could see them! They looked like humans. But they had very small bodies. And their hair was blue. . . . [They] were like shadows. . . . (Male or female?) A mixture, just like humans. Many came. . . . (So the *deata* that entered you, was it male or female?) A mixture! (So there were more than one?) Yes, lots!

A similar vision was reported by another man who claimed that he, too, had seen very tiny humanlike figures (no larger than the end joint of his smallest finger), though in his case the *deata* appeared to have blonde hair.

It is important to note that only a small minority of the people present at a *ma'maro* become possessed,[55] often those who have both a personal and family history of such involvement. To Minaa Sattu is the only one of our eleven respondents who has experienced possession trance,[56] and his mother (when she was still alive) had similar experiences, as does his older sister. Other respondents, however, have family members who have become possessed, such as Ambe'na Toding, whose younger brother regularly becomes possessed at *ma'maro* rituals, as does Indo'na Sapan's mother and Ambe'na Tangke's mother-in-law.[57]

Though it is often said that the possessed have no choice over the acts that the *deata* ask them to perform,[58] individuals tend to "specialize" in certain kinds of feats, performing them consistently over the years, and some individuals are renowned for performing particular behaviors. There also appears to be considerable individual variation with regard to the intensity with which the *to kandeatan* attack themselves. Some people hit themselves hard enough to raise welts on the skin, while others handle the blades or branches delicately, leaving no physical marks.[59] The following excerpt from fieldnotes (taken by Hollan) describes several feats performed by a young man who exhibited especially intense and violent behavior:

> He cracked himself repeatedly over the head with hard bamboo stalks—hitting himself hard enough to crack and splinter the bamboo. Then he used a bundle of small branches (which are used to sweep the house and yard) to whip himself on his forearms and the backs of his legs. Next he used a long knife, pressing it into his forearms, his legs, the back of his neck, and his stomach. He then propped the knife, blade up, in a shallow slit in the ground and stood on it in his bare feet. Then he repeatedly rolled on his back over the blade. Next, several men held a sword on the ground with the tip of the blade pointed up and he leaned over the sword and placed his entire body weight on its tip, drawing his feet completely off the ground. Finally, he lay down under a mat on the ground while some men placed large stones in a pile at least two feet deep on top of him. After he was completely buried, he attempted to break free of the rocks, but their weight caused him to stumble and he struggled to his feet. He then repeated the "burial and resurrection" sequence three times.

Except for those who intentionally drew blood from their foreheads or tongues to use for healing purposes, we witnessed only one man who injured himself during a *ma'maro* ritual by stumbling and hitting his shin. Though his injury was minor, he appeared to be alarmed by the sight of his blood and some people commented that the *deata* probably were angry at him for his failure to follow their orders or for his lack of faith in their powers.

From the point of view of Alukta adherents, the lack of injuries at most *ma'maro* ceremonies is explained by the fact that although the *deata* order villagers to perform apparently dangerous acts, they also use their powers to protect the possessed from serious injury—a protection that is contingent upon the possessed person's faith and obedience, as well as that of spectators.[60] Also, it is thought that whatever wounds occur during the course of a possession ceremony can be cured through the healing powers of the *tabang* plant, the leaves of which are rubbed and massaged on the *to kandeatan*'s body.

How does the audience view possession behavior? First, most people, Christian and Alukta alike, appear to accept the authenticity of spirit possession. Christians sometimes say that possession behavior is foolish or silly and they sometimes compare the *deata*'s powers unfavorably to those of God, but they do not, for the most part, doubt that possessed people are under the influence of special forces or that their ritual behavior is beyond their personal control. Many villagers are impressed by the apparently miraculous feats performed during the course of a *ma'maro* ceremony. Ambe'na Kondo remarks, for example: "If we who do not *ma'deata* [become possessed] tried to [do what those who are possessed do]. . .we would surely die!"

Many people also are frightened by the sight of those possessed. Indo'na Tiku, who enjoys watching kickfights, feels differently about watching people who are possessed:

> I [only] go for awhile to watch, and then I return home. Because in my view those *maro* people are like. . .crazy people. . . . They jump up and down. Have you seen them? (Yes.) They are . . . exactly like crazy people. [Later when asked what she feels if she watches someone who is possessed]: I am afraid to watch. Especially if they use knives or a machete [to apparently cut themselves], eeh, I am very frightened to see that.

Similarly, when Indo'na Sapan is asked what she feels when she watches people who are possessed, she replies: "We feel frightened, because they don't feel anything." And Ambe'na Kondo remarks: "People who are possessed, they aren't conscious anymore. . . .They don't feel anything. If we look at them, we are frightened." Later he continues: "[They] don't remember anything. They are like [he pauses to think] an angry person."

For these respondents, their fear of watching possessed people apparently is connected to the realization that the possessed are no longer in "conscious" control of their behavior and are temporarily "crazy" (*maro-maro*).[61] The behavior of the possessed clearly illustrates for spectators what people are capable of if they lose their self-control, and it likely suggests to spectators that they, too, may have bizarre or unacceptable parts of the self that are normally hidden from view.

Interestingly, despite the fact that the possessed are not held accountable for their behavior during a *ma'maro* ceremony since ostensibly they act only in accordance with the wishes and demands of the *deata*, several people who have experienced possession are somewhat embarrassed or ashamed by their ritual behavior (which is described to them later by their relatives and neighbors). This illustrates, we believe, how deeply internalized is the general cultural devaluation of lapses of self-awareness and self-control, a devaluation that has increased in recent years as a result of modernizing and Protestant Christian influences (see Wellenkamp 1988a).[62] To Minaa Sattu, for instance, reports:

> When we are in the middle of lots of people [acting out the *deata*'s wishes], we aren't ashamed! Because we have been seized by the *deata*. But after we have recovered, we feel ashamed a little bit! (Really?) Yes, really [laughing with embarrassment]. (Why do you feel ashamed?) Because we [pause]. Because we . . . remember/are conscious. [We think], "Oh, how come I was the one who . . . the *deata* [possessed]?" Lots of other people weren't seized [by the *deata*]. That's why we feel a bit ashamed. Because everyone has been watching us. That's why feelings of shame begin to arise a little bit. . . . All possessed people feel a little bit ashamed after they have begun to recover! But what can one do? It is not we [the *to kandeatan*] who are in control. Indeed, it is not we who are in control. It is the *deata* who are in control. [It is they] who seize us and have us enter into the midst of people. What is one to do?

While To Minaa Sattu reiterates the standard cultural doctrine that people who become possessed are not responsible for their actions, he himself became so discomforted by his ritual behavior over the years that he began to drink magical water which, he claims, prevents him from becoming possessed. At the time of the interviews, it had been ten years since To Minaa Sattu had last become possessed.[63]

Although cases of spirit possession that occur spontaneously outside of a ritual context are found in Java (Geertz 1976:19–21; Keeler 1987:116–18) and elsewhere in the Pacific, we know of no such cases in Toraja, with the exception of Ambe'na Tangke, who has not spontaneously experienced possession in the traditional sense, but who has been possessed by the Holy Spirit.

Possession by the Holy Spirit

While all Christian groups in the Paku Asu area discourage Christian participation in *ma'bugi'* and *ma'maro* ceremonies, the small Pentecostal congregation encourages periodic possession by the "Holy Spirit." Such experiences usually occur in the context of church services, when participants call upon the Holy Spirit to enter them, although Ambe'na Tangke reports that he has had private experiences of possession. Like those who are possessed by the *deata,* those who are "filled" by the Holy Spirit appear to undergo temporary transformations of normal consciousness, which may involve dissociation and amnesia. But there are also significant differences between traditional possession experiences and possession by the Holy Spirit. During one Pentecostal church service we attended, many of the participants, rather than being "animated" by their possession and displaying aggressive or "crazy" behaviors as in the *ma'maro* ritual, openly cried in a manner similar to traditional wailing. Like wailing, such crying is interpreted as a way of eliciting spiritual blessings (see Wellenkamp 1992), and may also serve as a form of cathartic release, as the passages below suggest. Also in contrast to traditional possession states, participants generally emphasize the euphoric effects of the experience, not its disorienting or shame-producing aspects.

Ambe'na Tangke is the only one of our respondents who has experienced possession by the Holy Spirit, though Ambe'na Toding also is a Pentecostal and has witnessed others become possessed. According to Ambe'na Toding,

> when someone experiences fulfillment [by the Holy Spirit], he/she usually cries. . . (Have you ever experienced that?) Not yet. Many who have say, "Even if I were stabbed in the eye I would not cry. . . . But once I have experienced fulfillment [been possessed] I cry, I don't feel anything" [am not fully "conscious"]. . . . Often also . . . it makes one happy/content. . . . (So people say they are happier/more content?) Yes . . . [they feel] *penaa masallo'* [generous/willing].

Ambe'na Tangke's first possession experience occurred spontaneously during a period of illness. It was this experience which eventually led to his joining the Pentecostal Church:

> I was . . . in Ujung Pandang . . . and had been sick for a week. And it happened that the Spirit came! Like in the Pentecostal Church. I cried. It was extraordinary how the Spirit came and instructed me. I believed/trusted It more than any human! . . . I was completely convinced [of the spirit's reality and presence]. . . . It didn't say anything, but Its presence enlightened me. There was no voice, but the Spirit instructed my heart with clarity. And then I cried.

Ambe'na Tangke goes on to describe how he asked a relative to call for a Pentecostal minister but the relative declined to do so:

She/He said, "As for me [I believe] that this child has an illness.
. . . Maybe he's dizzy/confused." I said several times, "Bring me a
Pentecostal minister." She/He didn't want to. Then she/he took
me to the hospital! I got better a little and I was taken to the
village. [But] my illness continued. Then I got a Bible and I fasted
each night. . . . Finally, the Spirit came [again]. At that time I
hadn't yet become a Pentecostal. [But] I got better so I didn't
need to call the Pentecostal minister. Later when I met Indo'na
Tangke [his wife], she happened to be Pentecostal, and then I
became one, [too].

When asked if he can see the spirit when it comes, or if he only feels
its presence, Ambe'na Tangke replies,

I can't see it clearly, with my eyes. . .the Spirit is inside my body.
. . . The Spirit comes whether our eyes are open, or whether they
are closed. The point is, the Spirit comes . . . and explains to me
all of the bad deeds in this world. And not just . . . my bad deeds,
my sins [but everyone's]. . . . Consequently, I cry continuously
[feeling regretful/remorseful]. And [I] pray. . . . (And does the
spirit still come [to you] now?) Yes, at our church. . . . If we truly
call/beckon [to the Spirit], the Spirit [comes]. . . . (So about how
often has the spirit come to you since the first time in Ujung
Pandang? Is it often, or just occasionally?) Just two times. . . .
Usually I know/feel it before [the Spirit] comes to the church
gathering. . . . [After the Spirit comes] we feel refreshed!

Trance

According to Bourguignon (1979:233–69), possession trance and trance
typically occur in different sorts of societies. However, in Toraja, both
are found. One healer in Paku Asu, who has matted locks (see chapter
7), occasionally seeks trance experiences through isolation and fasting.

Wailing

As briefly noted earlier, people also report that they are not fully
conscious when they engage in wailing, and some people actually faint
(see section below on "Reactions to Extreme Emotional Experiences
and Unexpected Events"). People also report feelings of release and
relief following periods of wailing (see Wellenkamp 1988b:495–96).

Drinking Behavior

The drinking of alcoholic beverages is another occasion when "consciousness" may be temporarily diminished. The Toraja have long consumed palm wine (*tuak*) made from the *induk* (sugar palm) tree. Nowadays, villagers (those who can afford it) also have access to bottled beer and distilled liquors sold in Makale and Rantepao and in smaller, local markets throughout the region. Drinking in the Paku Asu area—which is primarily limited to the consumption of palm wine—is most conspicuous, especially among men, at large rituals, where it is considered a sign of status. But drinking also occurs, to a much lesser degree, at "weekly" (every six days) local markets, and occasionally in the home. Generally speaking, moderate, controlled drinking is thought to have some positive benefits (e.g., it is thought to promote physical well-being for women who have recently given birth).

With a few exceptions (which we discuss below), most villagers who drink—some do not because of physical ailments or personal preference—drink moderately. During many rituals, trips to the market, and a few private drinking sessions, we observed only a few men who were obviously intoxicated (*malango*). Partly this is due to a desire to remain "conscious" and to avoid feelings of disorientation, and partly it can be traced to the fact that most villagers do not have ready access to alcoholic beverages. Indo'na Tiku says that she used to drink palm wine regularly when she lived near a relative who on a daily basis gave her and her family palm wine. For the most part, however, alcoholic beverages are considered a luxury item that is consumed only on special occasions.

Some respondents remember a time when they or family members have drunk to excess. Ambe'na Kondo, when asked if he has ever been drunk, replies, "Yes, I have. When we're drunk, we go right to sleep. If we can't tolerate it, we vomit. (Have you ever done that?) Yes. (Does one feel content when drunk?) Ah, it's not that [one] is content, but if [one] surpasses [a certain amount, then one will get sick]! [pause] Like at X, five of us drank three bamboo containers [of palm wine]. We finished them [he laughs]."

Indo'na Tiku reports that her former husband once became very sick from drinking *tuak* at a local market on an empty stomach. "Fortunately," she says, "Ambe'na Tiku returned from . . . the market before he . . . [vomited] at the house." As Indo'na Tiku's comments suggest, even more than the physical discomfort and psychological disorienta-

tion that intoxication can cause, villagers fear being shamed and ridiculed should they become drunk. Disdain for those who lose control of
themselves and their actions is clearly evident in Ambe'na Kondo's
evaluation of an intoxicated man's behavior: "We must measure [our
drinking], because if we surpass [a measured amount], it isn't good.
You remember X, right? . . . He once drank until he was vomiting and
defecating! He wasn't ashamed. Many people saw him like that. . . .
His clothes were covered with filth [he laughs loudly and disdainfully].
Everything came out! [still laughing] He was no longer 'conscious.' "

Nene'na Tandi(m) also makes clear that villagers fear being shamed
and ridiculed should they drink to excess:

> (You said that people who become possessed are like crazy people
> or people who are drunk. Do people like to get drunk?) No!
> Ordinarily, out of 100 people, only two or three drink until
> they're drunk. We call those people greedy. We aren't like other
> people who drink until they're drunk, like the Bugis. They [the
> Bugis] drink and don't feel anything until they're drunk. But we
> Toraja don't do that. We only drink a little. Because we feel, if
> you're going to drink until you get drunk, it should be in your
> own house. But if you drink at the market or at a celebration,
> you must guard your reputation and honor. We can't drink in
> places like that until we are drunk. People would think that we
> didn't know how to behave correctly. We would feel ashamed.
> That is what we must guard against. Because our self worth must
> be guarded. No one would respect us if they looked at us and
> said, "Oh, that person is not good. He/She isn't ashamed."
>
> (But if you were to stay in your own house?) That would be
> okay. When I was younger and still liked to drink, if I bought
> some *tuak* at the market, I would carry it here to the house. After
> I finished drinking, I'd go straight to sleep. Like that. . . . I didn't
> [drink until drunk at the market], no! . . . And if I went to a
> celebration, if I started feeling dizzy [from drinking too much], I
> went straight home! I didn't say a word to anyone. I went home
> alone. (And if someone does become drunk, they feel what?)
> Ashamed! Ashamed. They feel ashamed. People always warn/
> reprimand others: "You [act like you] don't feel anything. You're
> drunk." So we would feel ashamed![64]

If most villagers drink only occasionally and in moderation, why do
a few engage more regularly in drinking? Ambe'na Kondo stands out
among our respondents and informants as someone who has an un-

usually strong interest in drinking: he often encouraged us to buy and share *tuak* at celebrations and he sometimes appeared inebriated. He also is identified by other villagers as a person who likes to drink, and he is one of the few people we observed whose demeanor changed after consuming alchohol. He became more jovial and talkative, in keeping with the prevailing public ethos, and less sullen and uncommunicative—his more typical, though somewhat deviant, interpersonal style. Although he does not say this himself, it seems that drinking allows him to overcome feelings of shyness and self-consciousness that keep him somewhat isolated from other villagers on a day-to-day basis. His relatively heavy drinking, then, appears to be both a response to feelings of stress and anxiety and the result of his efforts to become more smoothly integrated into the community.

Reactions to Extreme Emotional Experiences and Unexpected Events

Sometimes losses of consciousness are neither voluntarily induced nor culturally encouraged. At least six of our eleven respondents have experienced fainting spells or feelings of disorientation in the wake of disturbing or unexpected events. Such reactions are infrequent, but when they occur, they appear to occur in situations of interpersonal loss or intense grief, and in contexts of extreme fear, shame, or frustration.

The situation in which fainting (*ma'ipu, malippang*) is most culturally expected (other than in connection with illness) is when wailing at a death.[65] According to Indo'na Rante, people often faint when "someone whom we love *very* much [dies]." Such fainting is presumed to be the result of intense feelings of sorrow and pain. Some people imply that it is the intensity of one's feelings that leads one to faint, while others say that it is one's inability to fully express one's feelings that leads to fainting. Indo'na Rante, for instance, says that people faint when "our hearts are not satisfied [pause]. Our desire is just to cry, and then our voices are gone [one becomes hoarse] [and we] faint."

Although none of our respondents report that they have fainted while wailing at a death, on two occasions we observed men (from other villages) who fainted at their fathers' funerals. In the first instance, a man about 40 years of age fainted while wailing and helping to carry his father's body to a burial cave. A companion of ours said at the time that it is understandable for a child who loses a parent to be very upset (and thus to faint) because your parents have taken care of you and they have passed on their knowledge to you. He added that he should know about such matters because both of his parents and five of his children had died. In the second incident, a younger man fainted while wailing in the yard of his deceased father's house.[66]

Indo'na Rante reports that she fainted once following her sister's death, apparently because she felt very surprised and frustrated when her sister was unexpectedly buried without Indo'na Rante's knowledge. When her younger sister died some years ago, Indo'na Rante traveled hastily to the coastal city of Ujung Pandang (where her sister had been living) to attend the funeral. By the time that she arrived, however, her sister had already been buried. This surprised her considerably since her relatives had sent for her to come, and because the cultural expectation is that a funeral should be delayed if possible so that absent relatives who wish to attend are given time to arrive. When Indo'na Rante was informed that she had missed the funeral, she collapsed and remained in bed for several hours: "I didn't say anything, I went straight into the house, people [later] said, and lay down/slept through the night. I didn't breathe. . . . I fainted because I was startled. I was called to come and yet unexpectedly when I arrived [she] had already been buried. That was the difficulty."

Nene'na Limbong reports that he fainted once when someone reportedly attempted to poison him (see chapter 5) and Ambe'na Patu fainted once while in a distant village for a school competition. To Minaa Sattu fainted once when he reportedly was hit by a *bombo* (see chapter 1), and he experienced uncomfortable feelings of disorientation after a dispute with a merchant in a faraway village (see chapter 5).[67]

Unlike losses of "consciousness" during possession trance, which is associated with personal and community well-being, those that occur spontaneously and unintentionally often are a cause for concern.[68]

MORALITY AND CONSCIENCE

Among the deeds most frequently mentioned when villagers are asked to comment on troublesome behavior are stealing, incest, adultery, trickery,[69] spreading false rumors, and quarreling with others. Nene'na Limbong remarks: "For example, they [troublemaking people] steal. For example, they trick/deceive. For example, they long for their neighbors' property. For example, they like to commit adultery. For example, they like to steal other people's belongings—their wives." And Ambe'na Kondo comments: "Regarding mistakes . . . for example, someone is a thief; someone commits adultery; someone gossips/slanders. Those are mistakes."

When respondents are asked about matters relating to "conscience," and whether they have had the desire to do something considered wrong, many say that while they may be tempted to steal, etc., they are dissuaded by their fear of being seen by others.

As in many small, face-to-face communities, fear of public censure is a major form of social control in rural villages in Toraja. The general lack of privacy and the not unfounded belief that "someone is always watching" put pressure on people to adhere to community standards of proper behavior. Indo'na Tiku says:

It's like this. If someone steals something . . . that person thinks that no one has seen him/her. But [people who do wrong] are always seen by someone! . . . [someone thinks], "Where is that person from?" and unexpectedly he/she will spy [on the wrongdoer], [thinking], "Oh, who is that?" Because . . . maybe a person is going to enter [a field] to steal some corn, for example, and he/she is seen by someone [who thinks], "Wah, maybe that person isn't the owner of the corn. Why is she/he stealing?" And then he/she [the watchful observer] will really spy [on the person].[70]

Later in the interview, the discussion continues:

(What if there is no chance that the person will be seen? Might he/she then go ahead and. . .?) We always know if someone does something [wrong]. If, for example, he/she steals, or if, for example, we steal something, right? We steal something out of someone's garden or field or whatever, even if we aren't seen right there, maybe as we leave, we'll be seen by one of our neighbors! Or if not a neighbor, then very often a child within [one's own] house will talk to other children [about the theft]. . . . So it will always be found out if someone takes something. For example, if school children . . . take someone's sweet potatoes or corn . . . for example, if there are two children. One says—the one who has just taken [the food says to the other]. . . "Don't tell the teacher or anyone about it [the theft]." But after a while, because someone at a distance saw them or the owner hears that schoolchildren took [his/her food] we look for [the thieves] at school. Even if we don't know who [the culprits are], we ask, "Who stole someone else's sweet potatoes?" Then of course the one who [was present] but did not take [the food] will say, "Here's the one who did it." . . . So truly, our criminal deeds are always found out. Yes, it's just like the proverb: "No matter how well something is wrapped, if it is rotten it is going to smell." So whatever is indeed rotten, no matter how many layers it is wrapped in, its odor will come out. So what that means is even if it has been several years since we did something that others don't know about, in the end it will be found out. . . . Indeed I can attest to that, not personally but when I look at other people's misdeeds, indeed it's true.

Similarly, To Minaa Sattu tries to imagine a situation in which it would be possible to commit adultery without being detected, but concludes: "Even if no one saw; if we did it [committed adultery] . . .by the second night [afterwards], surely by the third night, everyone would know!"

According to respondents, even if it were possible to avoid the watchful eye of fellow villagers, one cannot escape being seen by the gods and ancestors, or for Christians, by God, and such spiritual beings insure that someone will witness the misdeed or find out about it in some way. To Minaa Sattu, for example, says: "A thief might say, 'I wasn't seen by anyone.' . . . [But] later someone will say, A is a thief or B stole something. Because . . . there are some [the gods and ancestors] who are responsible for insuring that he/she [the thief] is seen."

Villagers also believe that "evidence" of one's misdeeds inevitably will surface in incidents of illness or misfortune. To Minaa Sattu says:

If we men were to do something bad like that [commit adultery], people would know! They would look at our livestock, you know, our pigs, buffalo [and] there would be signs [e.g., they would be sickly or deformed]. They would gather together [and say], "This person's behavior isn't good. He has committed adultery.". . . If people do something that isn't good, they will certainly have a difficult time making a living. And their children . . . will always be thin. [And they] won't be healthy. That's how we know!

According to Indo'na Rante, when a young woman from another village sent home some money she earned through prostitution in the city,

There was "evidence" [of her misdeeds]. When [the money] was put into [acquiring a new] ricefield, a huge rain came [and] ruined it. . . . She sent money here [and her relatives] bought a water

buffalo and it died. . . . Those were the signs [of her misdeeds].
. . . [The district officer] told her, "Don't send money like that to
the village. You are sending hardship/distress to your parents."

Even Ambe'na Patu, the minister, says: "Those who sin will feel sick
or their children will die. They'll get sick or lose all their wealth. That's
the way it is if [one] sins." [71]

As the above comments indicate, while the Toraja believe that misfortune in some form is inevitable following a transgression, it is also
believed that the timing and target of the misfortune may vary. That is,
if a person does something wrong, it may be his or her children or
descendants or the community as a whole who suffer in some way. The
possibility that those other than the wrongdoer may suffer because of
the wrongdoer's behavior has the effect of drawing people into each
other's affairs and insures that villagers pay close attention to their
neighbors' and family members' conduct.

Also, an occasion of disaster or misfortune may prompt (at least
among Alukta villagers) not only individual mistake-searching (see
chapter 7), but a community-wide search for wrongdoing as well.
Ambe'na Toding provides an example:

> If the rice is being eaten by rats, the elders will gather together.
> They'll think, "Oh, probably close relatives [third cousins or
> closer] have had sex together." Then they'll start looking for first
> or second cousins [who have had sex together].

Similarly, Nene'na Tandi says:

> For example, if you and Belo were close relatives and you had sex
> together, the evidence [of your "mistake"] may not be closely tied
> to you and Belo! It [misfortune] might hit another family, or the
> entire community. But then the people in the village will think,
> "Maybe there are some close relatives who have had sex to-
> gether." They'll look and look and look until they find out who
> did it. As soon as they find out [and the mistake is acknowl-
> edged], all the plants will become healthy and grow again.

To Minaa Sattu suggests that at such community gatherings, it is
obvious who the guilty parties are. Speaking again about illicit sex, To
Minaa Sattu says: "That sort of thing is not done during the day, it's
done at night. That's why it's not seen. But . . . [the gods and ancestors]
see it, and thus everyone will know about it! . . . When we hold the
gathering/meeting [to determine who has committed a wrong], the

[guilty] person will come, and his/her face will be red. . . . And then everyone will know!"

In addition to fear of public censure and anxiety about later misfortune, a few respondents also emphasize that there are negative consequences in the afterlife for engaging in wrongdoing.[72] Nene'na Tandi(f), for example, maintains:

> Whatever [wrong] things that we do . . . later we'll regret/repent them. Because this world here, we only spend the night in. [Whereas] later, we'll stay permanently there [in the next world]. So whatever we do in this world, another day we will do there [in the afterlife], too [that is, one's time on earth is short in comparison with the afterlife, and the nature of one's present life has repercusions for the next].

Similarly, Nene'na Limbong, when asked what he feels when he thinks about death, replies:

> Whether [a person is] a Christian, an Aluk, a Hong Kong person, an American, a Muslim—there will come a time when they will be examined/investigated, each one individually. I know that. So later the path we took when we were living will be examined . . . if we were honest, if we tricked [people]. . . . [We will be examined] when we die.

For Alukta adherents, the comprehensive nature of the traditional prohibitions serves, on the one hand, to provide very clear, detailed instructions on how to behave (and thus avoid disaster and misfortune), while at the same time making it inevitable that infractions or "mistakes" (*sala*) will occur. Ambe'na Toding comments: "Humans must make as many mistakes as they have hair [on their heads]. That's the way it is. None of us can say that we haven't made mistakes. Each day all people make mistakes."

Even Ambe'na Patu, the Protestant minister, implies that wrongdoing occurs frequently. After listing several things that one should not do (have more than one wife, murder, steal, lie) he says:

> All of those things, lots [of people do them]. . . . Like me . . . didn't I lie earlier? Like when I promise you [I will come for an interview] and then I don't come, I've lied. Right [laughing]? Several times [I] have promised [to come] but I didn't. So, I've already lied. But indeed it wasn't intentional. Suddenly [something arises] . . . and I don't come. . . .But according to God, [one] can't do that, [one] must come.

While Ambe'na Patu and other respondents maintain that misdeeds are inevitable, they also say that those who err often are unaware of their mistakes, or require someone else to identify them.[73] Ambe'na Kondo remarks: "I would say [right now] that I don't have any mistakes/sins. But that's not possible. I must have some." Ambe'na Patu similarly says: "There are mistakes that we make [and yet] indeed [when we commit them] we think that this is good, but God's choice/view is that it isn't good." Later he continues: "I don't yet know what my mistakes are. Indeed they are selected by others. When we do something [wrong], indeed we don't know our own mistakes. . .other people are the ones who say, 'That's wrong.' "

For both Alukta and Christian villagers, making a mistake involves violating a rule, knowingly or unknowingly, which should have kept one out of trouble. One's intentions are irrelevant in determining whether or not a mistake has been committed; what matters is one's overt behavior, not one's internal thoughts, feelings, or assessments. Indo'na Rante's account of what happened to a woman who was raped provides a clear example:

> Once . . . near here . . . there was [a man] who grabbed [a woman]. . . . She immediately screamed, [but] he held his knife [next to her and said], "If you scream, I'll cut you." So she was forced to remain quiet, what a pity. . . . So she was quiet while he did it [raped her], but this woman already had a husband [she clears her throat]. . . . not two months later [after the rape], her child died. . . . Then she had a pig that died [speaking very quietly], and then a buffalo died [she clears her throat again]. Eh, because of that—because she was already "dizzy," you know [upset by the deaths]—she herself admitted [that she had had sex with another man]. [She said], "Indeed I did something [wrong] but . . . I was forced [to do it].". . . [She] was told to slaughter a pig and admit her mistake. Because she had already had one child die!

This sense of morality and wrongdoing, one found elsewhere in the Pacific (cf. Levy 1973), is very different from the Western, especially Protestant, concept of "sin." The emphasis is not on one's hidden desires and personal intentions, but rather on obeying the rules and staying out of trouble.

In Paku Asu, both Christian and Alukta villagers tend to view moral behavior as the avoidance of "mistakes" and "errors" that trigger community disapproval or spiritual retribution. That is, the introduction of Christianity into Paku Asu does not yet seem to have greatly altered aspects of "conscience," nor significantly changed the sanctions against improper behavior.

In chapter 7, we discuss the options available to Alukta and Christian villagers for correcting "errors" once they have been committed.

PART II
Suffering

Once when we were visiting an acquaintance in another village, a man asked us, "Did you come to study our way of life?" Before one of us could offer a reply, our host said, "No, they have come to study the way of our suffering." Suffering is a pervasive theme in both informal conversations and in our interview material. Some examples follow.

NENE'NA TANDI(M): When you return [to America] . . . [what you have learned of Toraja] you may not lose, nor forget, nor ignore/ waste. All of it must be held onto firmly. There is a big possibility that . . . with God's help, you will have one or two children [and] this will become history [you will pass on]: "During this year, on this date, I went to Indonesia, straight to a village . . . in a mountain area and there I acquired knowledge. . . . [I saw] the life of people who have misery, who are poor, who suffer.". . .[You will tell Americans] that it's really true that the people live on the slope of a mountain that seems like it's in the sky . . . [that] the people . . . live on vegetables and sweet potatoes. That nothing has to be bought, but that indeed, everything is more expensive than if it is paid for. Why? Because of the difficulties . . . On the slope of the mountains, indeed there are a hundred difficulties. . . . If you look at the lives of all the people in Paku Asu, indeed, everything is very difficult. Compared with other people. . .[we] are isolated/desolate. . . . It can't be said that all of Indonesia is prosperous. There are many difficulties for those who live in the mountains.

AMBE'NA TODING: It's empty talk [nonsense] if people tell you they've been happy since birth. *All* people suffer. [In the next interview he picks up this point again]: From the day I was born, all I've done is work. I haven't rested. Because if we sufferers were to rest for even one day, we might not eat for a month. Even if we're sick, we must work. That's why many Toraja are sick: they work too hard. . . . Just call us Toraja the sufferers. It has been that way since the time of our ancestors. From early in the morning, we're in the fields or gardens, just like a work horse. So indeed, we are sufferers.

TO MINAA SATTU: We have many difficulties. Many. And only a little happiness. . . . We must make a living, which is difficult. We must earn money, which is difficult. For most people here, it's hard to make a living. For example, right now we have begun to plant rice. But how many months must we suffer before it is ready [for harvest]? So there are many difficulties. For example, we may not have the money to buy clothes. . . . Most of the people here aren't happy. They all have difficulties.

In part, talk of suffering and hardship is intentionally exaggerated to evoke compassion and elicit the aid of others; it also serves to deflect other people's envy and resentment on occasions when one prospers (see discussion of vertical relationships in chapter 2). There is, then, what might be called a rhetoric of suffering (cf. Gaines and Farmer 1986). When we first moved to Paku Asu one of our neighbors told us repeatedly of the hardship she and her husband and their several children have had to endure. In telling us about such hardship experiences, she was probably hoping to make us sympathetic to any future requests she and her family might make of us. After the first several weeks, however, she no longer talked of her and her family's hardships, probably because she had surmised, correctly, that we had been informed by other villagers of the family's considerable wealth relative to other residents.

While some people exaggerate the extent of their suffering, others who talk about suffering and hardship seem to be merely repeating a cultural cliche. Ambe'na Tangke's wife remarked one day that farming was a very difficult way of making a living and that village life in general was full of suffering. Her tone of voice, however, was cheerful and when asked why she and her husband had returned to the village after living for awhile outside of Tana Toraja, she indicated that, in fact, village life was not unagreeable to her or at least was preferable to city life.

For many, however, talk of hardship and suffering seems genuine, reflecting both personal experience and philosophical belief. While some respondents say that they have experienced both happiness and suffering in their lives, and that life in general involves both, others claim that periods of hardship and suffering have been more numerous than experiences of happiness and contentment. Ambe'na Patu, the minister, says, for example: "The problem is, there is no happiness.

Even the Bible states that once we enter this world, there is no happiness. So things are always difficult. We always think/worry. . . . We think/worry about making a living each day, we think/worry about all kinds of things. So there is no happiness in life."

For many villagers, happiness and contentment could best be defined as the occasional and fleeting *absence* of suffering and hardship. Thus when Indon'na Sapan is asked when are people joyful or cheerful, she replies, "When we feel happy/content, you know. Like when—[pause] I'm not sure [pause]. . . . Like when there is some difficulty and then something makes the difficulty disappear, that's when I feel cheerful."

In this section, we examine the nature and sources of Paku Asu villagers' discontent and suffering. Although economic difficulties are perhaps the most salient source of people's discontent, there are other things that also worry and disturb villagers and that contribute to the perception that life is full of suffering. In chapter 5, we discuss prevalent interpersonal concerns and anxieties, and in chapter 6, aspects of disorder and dysphoria. Finally, in chapter 7, we discuss prevalent ways of coping with suffering and misfortune.

5

PREVALENT INTERPERSONAL CONCERNS AND ANXIETIES

While villagers value and encourage polite, respectful behavior, they are aware that etiquette and other forms of social convention may obscure, rather than illuminate, other people's true thoughts, feelings, and intentions. There is a concern that surface appearances cannot be trusted and that people may not be what they appear, as the following quotations illustrate:

INDO'NA TIKU: Many . . . talk with us, but we know that their inner contents are not the same as their words. So we must pay attention to their behavior. Is this a good person? Yes, we must see. . . . So we must be cautious . . . if we don't know them well. We must study their behavior. . . . Do the words of these people match their hearts?

NENE'NA TANDI(M): Here we don't know people's hearts. Everyone has sweet mouths [words], but underneath, we don't know. So we must be cautious.

AMBE'NA TODING: Don't trust/believe. Don't trust/believe just anyone. (Then how do you know who to trust/believe?) We don't know who [can be trusted/believed]. We don't know people's hearts. So don't trust/believe just anyone. The point is, you must have evidence [of someone's honesty or dishonesty, etc.].

Among our respondents and informants, there is a pervasive sense of cautiousness about others. In what follows, we discuss more specifically the fears and concerns that people have of one another.[1]

BEING ROBBED

One of us once asked a Bugis woman who worked at a health clinic near Paku Asu what she considered to be important differences between the Toraja and the lowland Bugis and Makassar. She replied that she was impressed by the absence of theft among the Toraja. In the highlands, she said, unlike in the coastal areas, even a single woman could travel freely without fear of theft or banditry. Theft is considered a serious infraction among the Toraja, and our interviews with government officials as well as official crime statistics suggest that theft is not a common occurrence in Tana Toraja, especially outside of the town areas in the central valley.[2]

Paku Asu residents, like government and police officials, also often comment on the absence of theft in the village. People often say that Paku Asu is completely "safe." One local official once pointed out some tools that had been left in a field over night, indicating, he said, villagers' confidence that they would not be stolen. Nene'na Tandi(m) proudly claimed that despite his status as a relative "outsider," having moved to Paku Asu after he married Nene'na Tandi(f), he had yet to experience a theft during his many years in the village.

There do, however, appear to be a few minor incidents of Toraja villagers stealing or taking things that do not properly belong to them. For example, children sometimes take food while herding buffalo (although such actions are not clearly labeled as "theft"). Also, during a severe drought during our stay, some Paku Asu residents hoarded water from nearby springs even though they knew that by so doing, they were making life more difficult for their neighbors. We also were told that there were a small number of petty thieves (those who grow up in a family of thieves or who are chronic gamblers who engage in petty theft to pay off debts). Occasionally, too, family heirlooms (carved wooden bowls, cloths, swords, etc.) are sold to tourists and other outsiders.

Still, outright theft by all indications occurs rarely, and yet villagers nevertheless worry about the possibility of someone stealing from them or others, even though the lack of privacy in the village would seem to make theft difficult. We ourselves were frequently warned to guard against thieves (*to boko*). We were told, for example, never to leave our house unattended, or at the very least, to make certain that it was securely locked while we were away. Some people suggested that we acquire a watchdog to warn us of approaching strangers and to scare off thieves.[3] Nene'na Tandi(m) advised us never to tell strangers where we lived. He reminded us that in Tana Toraja, as elsewhere in Indonesia, it is common for passersby to ask one another "Where are you going?" or "Where are you coming from?" Since thieves may use this information to find houses to rob, he counseled us to reply to such questions with some vague statement such as, "We're from over the last hill," or better yet, to say that we were from a village far from Paku Asu. To further discourage potential thieves, it was also suggested that we arrange for an escort whenever we left the village.

The precautions urged upon us probably were based on villagers' assessment that we—in contrast to other residents—were more likely targets of theft, given our status as relatively "wealthy" outsiders.[4] However, there are other indications that people are concerned about possible thieves. For example, there is often a presumption that missing items have been stolen. Thus when a neighbor discovered one of his chickens missing he stated (without any apparent evidence) that it had been stolen; and when a water buffalo apparently knocked down some rice stalks piled up in a field, many people at first assumed that a thief had taken the rice.[5]

Dreams of theft also are common. People dream both about stealing things from others (which is considered a "good" dream foretelling that the dreamer will eventually acquire the object or whatever the object represents) and about having things or people stolen from them (considered a "bad" dream indicating the dreamer will eventually lose something or someone of value).

Not only the content of such dreams, but also people's responses to them indicate the importance of theft in fantasy. For example, one of us once asked Nene'na Limbong what it would mean to dream that one had been robbed. Apparently thinking that one of us must have had such a dream, he warned us to keep our doors locked at night and then mentioned that if thieves were somehow able to gain access to the house, we would be justified in attacking them with our machete. The anticipation of a violent defense against intrusive thieves was shared by others. A neighbor, for example, was worried that she might be attacked by a thief or rapist in the night and that she might need to defend herself with a weapon.

Such fantasies seem exaggerated relative to the likelihood that a villager would ever be assaulted or robbed, and yet being robbed is something villagers clearly worry about. Such worries seem to reflect a general sense of being vulnerable to outside (and unknown) forces, and a sense that one's economic security in life is precarious; concerns about being robbed also can be partly attributed to other experiences in which people feel they have been taken advantage of in some way.

BEING TRICKED AND DECEIVED

One of the Toraja's most renowned local heroes is Pong Tiku, a man who led a spirited resistance against the Dutch in 1906. Some of Pong Tiku's skirmishes with the Dutch occurred in the vicinity of Paku Asu and several of our informants gave us lively accounts of the events surrounding Pong Tiku's resistance and his eventual capture and execution. One of the most striking elements of these oral histories is the claim that Pong Tiku was not defeated on the battlefield, but was captured through trickery and deceit.[6] One version of the events maintains that Pong Tiku surrendered his arms only after the Dutch had promised to share military and political power. In subsequent negotiations, the Dutch reneged on their promises and captured Pong Tiku. In a second version, Pong Tiku requests and is granted a ceasefire so that he may give a proper funeral to his recently deceased parent. The Dutch then seize him. In a third version, Pong Tiku is betrayed by a brother who schemes to have Pong Tiku's wife for himself. The brother enters into a nefarious deal with the Dutch that requires him to lead Pong Tiku into an ambush; in exchange he gains his own freedom and the opportunity to marry his sister-in-law.

The use of treacherous tactics not only is attributed to the Dutch in legends about Pong Tiku but also to the Bugis. According to some informants, among the more insidious ploys the Bugis have used in their repeated attempts to achieve domination and control of Tana Toraja was the fostering of gambling. Toraja have traditionally engaged in gambling at cockfights held at the funerals of high status people and on market days, but prior to Bugis meddling, some people say, such gambling was well-limited. However, Bugis merchants, supposedly desirous of Toraja land and realizing that gamblers can be easily manipulated and exploited, encouraged more frequent gambling and introduced new opportunities for gambling such as card games. Though Bugis designs were eventually foiled by the Dutch, gambling remains, some villagers say, a troubling preoccupation among some people—a present-day legacy of earlier Bugis intrigue.

Claims about being tricked and deceived (*pakena*) by outside groups partly serve as a ready explanation for defeat and domination, but they also reflect people's ongoing concerns about being victimized by others. Clever thinking and the use of deception are viewed ambivalently: in some sense they are admired as means of defeating enemies, of acquiring what one desires (but does not yet possess), and of defending morally questionable actions; and yet such tactics also are condemned, particularly when used with relatives and fellow residents.

Nene'na Limbong, whose public demeanor is that of a refined gentleman, relates with obvious satisfaction several incidents in which he cleverly manipulates outsiders to his advantage. For example:

> In direct violation of Dutch policy, Nene'na Limbong once cut down a rare species of hardwood tree that he needed to build a rice barn. His deed was discovered and he was detained by the Dutch for questioning. His strategy was to "play dumb." He claimed that he was a farmer, not a man of the forest, and did not know that he was cutting down an endangered tree. When the Dutch pointed out that the tree had been specially marked for easy identification, he responded that he was a poor, ignorant peasant who could not distinguish one mark from another. The Dutch then released him and allowed him to keep the wood.

> Japanese occupation forces during World War II placed Nene'na Limbong in charge of planning and executing some construction projects. According to Nene'na Limbong, the Japanese decided to test his loyalty by deliberately overpaying him for materials and supplies. Seeing through their ploy, Nene'na Limbong returned the surplus funds. The Japanese then began to trust him, a turn of events that he used to his advantage by requesting precious goods (soap, salt, cloth) that he had been denied before.

> When the Dutch reoccupied Tana Toraja after World War II, they began to confiscate buildings and material left behind by the Japanese. Nene'na Limbong was ordered to remove the roof from one building and carry it to another construction site. After complying, Nene'na Limbong and his fellow villagers immediately demolished and carried away what was left of the roofless build-

ing. When confronted by the Dutch over the "theft," Nene'na Limbong maintained that the confiscation order mentioned only the roof of the building. He and the villagers had not "stolen" anything; they had merely assumed that the rest of the building had been "thrown away." The Dutch conceded the technical point and allowed the villagers to keep the goods.

More recently, Nene'na Limbong led the district officer into believing that one of the ballot boxes had disappeared and needed to be replaced before an upcoming election. The officer gave Nene'na Limbong a new box, which he then used as a container for family heirlooms.

When Nene'na Limbong was pressed for payment for road construction services provided to Paku Asu villagers by a wealthy townsperson, he accentuated his advanced years, knowing that the creditor—a younger man—could not easily be too demanding or angry with a respected elder.[7]

Cleverness and deception are used against outsiders (and occasionally insiders) both "offensively" to achieve desired goals, as well as "defensively" to rationalize and justify actions already taken, especially those of a morally ambiguous nature. In private, people often brag about their "clever" responses to accusations of wrongdoing, and they grudgingly admire this ability in others. Indo'na Tiku once described how she had deftly handled the charge of government officials that the house she was building in another village was located too close to the road and had to be moved. Indon'na Tiku said that her first response was to ask why the road itself could not be moved, since this would be easier to accomplish than the movement or demolition of her half-completed house. She was told that to do so would violate the property rights of the church across the road. Suspecting that the officials were merely *assuming* that members of the church would object to a widening of the road, Indo'na Tiku soon discovered that in fact, the church had no such objection, and knowing this, she continued to build. When the officials again demanded that she move the house, she told them first, that there was no good reason why the road could not be moved away from her house since the church did not object to the use of its property, and second, that the government was being inconsistent in its directives to the community: on the one hand it encourages villagers to "develop" and improve their property, and on the other hand, it prosecuted those who tried! Indo'na Tiku claimed that the officials were so impressed by her "clever" response, that they ceased their opposition and allowed construction of the house to continue.

In interactions with fellow residents and family members, the use of cleverness and deception is publicly condemned and yet sometimes privately admired. Following the forest fire set by two village boys (described in chapter 4), one of our neighbors, Ambe'na Sumpu, made some critical comments about one of the boys because he had failed to produce a "clever" explanation for his behavior. According to Ambe'na Sumpu, instead of admitting that he and his companion had been lighting small fires as a pasttime, he could have said, for example, that he had been cooking sweet potatoes and that his cooking fire had accidentally gotten out of control. The fact that the boy failed to produce a "clever" response indicated to Ambe'na Sumpu that he was rather slow-witted. In contrast, the boy's parents had attempted to avoid responsibility for their son's actions by claiming that they had not "ordered" the boy to start the fire—a "clever" response, from Ambe'na Sumpu's point of view.[8]

The ambivalence with which the Toraja regard the use of strategy and clever thinking—particularly when used among close associates— is evident in their reactions to the exploits of Dana', the trickster figure of Toraja folktales. Dana' never works if he can avoid it, preferring to "trick" others (including family members and fellow villagers) into providing for his needs and pleasures. When Dana' 's mother dies, for example, Dana', due to his past laziness, has no water buffalo to provide for his mother's funeral celebration. But he comes up with a solution to his predicament by placing his mother's body on a buffalo path where it is trampled upon by water buffalo. Angrily claiming that the villagers' buffalo have killed his mother, Dana' persuades the other villagers to provide a lavish celebration for this mother. Among Dana' 's other outrageous exploits are the following:

> One day Dana' challenges his father to see which of them can catch the most eels in a day. As they discuss the rules of the contest, Dana' reminds his father that a murderer known for smearing himself with mud has recently been seen in the area. The next day, Dana' and his father set out to hunt eels. While Dana' 's father works hard to catch as many eels as he can, Dana' hides in the brush and watches his father's progress. After Dana' 's father has caught several eels, Dana' covers himself in mud and runs toward his father, screaming and shouting. Dana' 's father, thinking that the murderer is upon him, turns and runs for his

life, leaving his eels behind. Dana' retrieves his father's eels, washes the mud off himself, and declares himself the winner of the contest.

One year Dana' decides to build a rice barn just as the harvest begins. Each day as Dana' 's neighbors return from the fields with their freshly cut rice, they ridicule Dana' 's efforts, knowing that he has been too lazy to plant rice himself, and so will have no food to put in his barn. Despite these taunts, Dana' continues to work. Once the barn is complete, however, Dana' acknowledges that it is senseless to have an empty barn and so announces his intention to burn it to the ground. This news alarms the village, since Dana' has strategically placed his barn amongst those of his neighbors. If he decides to burn his own barn down, he will very likely destroy his neighbors' as well. After tense negotiations, the neighbors agree to fill Dana' 's barn with rice so that he will not be tempted to burn it down.

One day Dana' 's eye is caught by the wealth of a certain noble. He decides to visit the noble's estate, claiming to have important business to discuss. The noble agrees to meet with Dana', but Dana' refuses to speak until he and the noble have reached the privacy of the estate's buffalo pastures. Once there, Dana' points to a white buffalo and mentions to the noble that as a young man, he once had sex with such a buffalo and that it had been the most satisfying sexual experience of his life. Having successfully aroused the noble's curiosity and desire, Dana' then suggests that the noble experience such pleasures for himself. The noble agrees, and that night, with Dana' standing guard, he has sex with the white buffalo. The next day, however, Dana' threatens to tell others about the incident unless the noble pays him a large sum of gold and silver. Fearing for his reputation, the noble agrees to Dana' 's demands.

While villagers find Dana' stories very amusing and entertaining, people's ambivalence about trickery and deceit becomes clear when discussing Dana' 's character. One man felt it necessary to point out that Dana' is not actually a criminal: he is merely a "clever" person who takes advantage of other people's ignorance. A second man agreed, but then laughed and said that even so, it would be hard to find parents who would name a child Dana'.

While the most blatant attempts to trick and deceive others occur in interactions with relative outsiders, attempts to take advantage of others do occur among close associates,[9] and the possibility of being tricked or deceived is something villagers often worry about. Much of the daily concern about being tricked and deceived has to do with sharing and exchanging resources and services. People fear either that others will make illegitimate requests of them—asking for something when there is no genuine need—or that they will "borrow" something and never return or repay it. Villagers also fear that when they make a legitimate request of others, they may be turned down by fellow residents who falsely claim that they do not have the resources to fulfill the request. The ultimate trickster is the person who not only conceals his or her own wealth but who also makes illegitimate requests of others. According to Ambe'na Toding, for example:

> There are people whose rice, after harvest, never leaves their barn. They go about coaxing, eating at other people's houses. How are they going to finish their own rice [if they are constantly eating others']?

Although Ambe'na Toding worries about being taken advantage of by such unscrupulous individuals, he also views them dispassionately as clever people who manage to accumulate wealth by consuming other people's resources instead of their own:

> If we are smart/clever managing [our resources], [and] go about to other people's houses to eat, we don't have to cook ourselves. . . . Wherever you find a smart/clever person, there also you will find buffalo [an indication of wealth].

When Nene'na Limbong is asked how he knows whether or not someone can be trusted, he replies:

> Who can be trusted? We look at the person. If she/he doesn't trick/deceive, and if she/he doesn't lie, that's the person we trust. . . . But if someone tricks/deceives, if they ask for things and are lazy [to return them], those people disappoint us. They borrow people's things, and after they've gotten a lot, they run! Run to some other place. That's the way it is with debtors. I've seen many like that.

Ambe'na Toding complains that he is often coaxed into lending things with the expectation that the borrower will eventually repay him with similar favors, only to discover sometime later that his requests go unheeded:

> Many times people come to me asking to borrow something. [I say], "Here, take it! Take it. No matter." That's right. "Take it. No matter." Shovels, tools, other things. I give them as long as the other person needs them. If someone asks for money, I give it to them. [I just] give it to them. But after that, they disappoint me. . . . When I was building [a house], I asked for tools, but they weren't given. . . . Many people are like that now. They disappoint [others] . . .if they are short of anything they come and coax us to give, but once they are given, they don't [reciprocate].

Ambe'na Toding mentions that people attempt to coax (*ma'sede*) him into giving. As noted in chapter 2, requests to others that take the form of "appeals" are especially difficult for people to deny.

Several other respondents also report that they have, at one time or another, been tricked or deceived. Indo'na Rante, for instance, says that she once lent some money to a man who has never repaid her and that when she thinks of the incident, she feels like she wants to beat him (see chapter 4, note 31). She says she has refrained from seeking the return of her money, however, for fear that he might "poison" her (see below).

Incidents of trickery and deceit concerning the sharing of resources and services are made possible by a relatively flexible exchange system (which, for example, allows payments for loaned items to be delayed for several months or years),[10] by moral ideas about the importance of helping others in need (see Wellenkamp 1984, 1992), by norms of etiquette, which do not allow one to demand repayment of a loan, and by fears of magical retaliation. One constraint that works to limit the amount of trickery and deceit in the village is the fact that once someone is perceived as untrustworthy, others will no longer lend to them. When Nene'na Limbong is asked why some people have so much suffering in their lives while others, like himself, remain relatively prosperous, he replies:

> It is the people who trick/deceive who always have difficulties! Because people don't give them anything. Because they are trick-sters/deceivers. That's why they always have [difficulties]. For example, if there is a death in the family and I ask for [borrow] pigs or ask for buffalo and then repay them when the time comes, that is not trickery/deceit. So we must be trustworthy, so that people will believe/trust us. Those who are always having difficulties, they are tricksters/deceivers! . . . They want to borrow things, but people don't lend to them anymore.

Still, this constraint does not affect the more prosperous villagers as much as it does the poorer ones. Nene'na Limbong, referring to a recent Christian celebration, once commented that only the relatively poorer members of the congregation contributed livestock for the feast. He concluded that the wealthier people had "tricked" the other members of the congregation. Nene'na Limbong, himself a wealthy person, maintained that "trickery" on the part of wealthier people is not unusual. He claimed that wealthier people, who are less often in need of help, have less to lose by acquiring a reputation for deceit, since they can more easily survive without the help of others. Thus they can risk deceiving people where a less prosperous person cannot for fear of being labeled a "trickster."

Villagers' concerns and anxieties about others withholding resources and goods and about having their own resources taken away unjustly in part are realistically based in that Paku Asu residents do tend to closely guard their own self interests. This tendency is exacerbated by the ethic of sharing and the cultural notion that if one is lacking in some way, one only has to request whatever it is one needs from those who are more affluent. That is, the more villagers exhort one another to share and to give, the more they tend to protectively guard their own interests. This in turn makes necessary an even greater emphasis on the public values of giving and sharing (cf. Knauft 1985 and Lindholm 1982).

BEING GOSSIPED ABOUT AND SLANDERED

When Indo'na Tiku is asked what is the worst feeling a person can have, she responds:

> The worst feeling? If we are always ridiculed by people. Yes, that is the feeling that we feel isn't pleasant. . . . Second . . . if we are talked about by others, even though we haven't done anything [wrong]. That also is a feeling that isn't good. [Later, when asked if she has ever been ridiculed she replies]: Mmm . . . for example, with children, if we say something, often they will repeat it. . . . As for adults ridiculing [me], I haven't experienced that yet. But as for words behind my back, talk about something . . . I haven't done, that has [happened to me].

Two respondents, during discussions of feelings of shame, bring up the topic of slander. Ambe'na Patu, for example, when asked to give an example of when someone feels shame, says: "If someone hasn't done anything, but [someone] is angry with him/her ... [and] tells [false] stories about him/her in public, he/she feels shame." In response to a similar question, Ambe'na Toding says: "There is much [shame] if someone slanders me. Very often I [want to] hit that person." Nene'na Limbong, who also reports being slandered by others, is more contemptuous of those who attempt to make his name "rotten." He calls such detractors "crazy" and "stupid."

Even though it is considered improper to gossip, rumors and slanderous remarks are common in Paku Asu.[11] When one of us mentioned to Nene'na Tandi(m) that the Toraja rarely physically aggress against one another, he agreed. But then he quickly added that, With words, we are always angry. More than once people warned us about other villagers—including our respondents—telling us, for example, that so-and-so used magic against others, or was lecherous, or tricked and deceived people. Often, rather than stating the negative information directly, people preface their remarks with phrases such as, "It is said that...," "Others say that...," or "If I'm not mistaken...." In part such linguistic maneuvers allow one to engage in gossip while limiting (to a certain extent) one's responsibility for spreading false rumors.

Being the target of slanderous remarks is upsetting to people because of the potentially damaging effects such remarks may have on their standing in the community. One's reputation not only is important in and of itself, but it also is intimately linked with one's ability to elicit assistance from others in times of need, since such help is based in part upon one's reputation for honesty and trustworthiness.

Slanderous remarks also are potentially very damaging to the social well-being of the community. Some people claim that the social consequences of engaging in gossip and slander are more serious than if someone were to commit an overtly violent act. According to one informant, Ambe'na Rempa, spreading false rumors is worse than murder: While murder is reprehensible, the number of individuals who are harmed by the incident is limited; in contrast, incidents of slander may pit the members of an entire community against each other. Another man said that if you murder or assault someone, it is possible to concretely assess the damage caused by the act in terms of lost labor or income. But the damage caused by slander—widespread feelings of anger, distrust, and resentment—is potentially extensive and long-lasting.[12]

People assume that slanderous remarks and malicious gossip are motivated by hostility and envy. Ambe'na Toding explains:

For example, I am hot or angry [with someone]. I say "Oh, that person is a thief. He goes around stealing things." When in fact, he is not a thief. Because we are upset with that person, there is anger. I say those [slanderous] things so that respect for that person will fall or so that his wealth will suffer. Many people do such things [slander others]!

Nene'na Tandi(m) also emphasizes the malicious intent of those who spread false rumors and the damaging effects that can result:

Suspicion destroys. It ruins our peace of mind. Sometimes, for example, Nene'na Tandi [his wife] gets suspicious. She thinks, "Maybe he [meaning himself] wants another woman or maybe another woman wants him." She comes to me and says that someone has told her [that he has been with another woman]. If we believed such things, it wouldn't be long before we were divorced. Those [rumors] are destructive. It is like poison, like poison. There are people, many people here, that, for example, if they wanted to destroy a marriage [would say], "Oh, Nene'na Tandi [his wife] always goes around with Sampe." I say, "How can that be? Sampe is my friend." Then I am angry with Nene'na Tandi . . . [and] the one who started it says, "Hopefully, they will divorce." Like that. That is like poisoning. That is called . . . rotten politics. It destroys households, destroys morale, destroys everything![13]

Villagers are at times very credulous, and at other times incredulous, of village rumors (cf. Schwartz 1973), depending on their relationship to the person who is the target of the gossip. Perhaps not surprisingly, villagers are more willing to believe negative remarks about someone of whom they are envious or with whom they are in competition. Thus, for example, Nene'na Tandi(m) allowed himself to become a co-plaintiff in a legal complaint against Nene'na Limbong, one of his chief social and political rivals, even though the case apparently was built almost entirely upon unsubstantiated rumor. Later, Nene'na Tandi(m) was rebuked by government officials for causing them to waste their time and energy on a frivolous case.

At other times, villagers emphasize the importance of having concrete "evidence" when making a determination about whether to believe slanderous remarks. Ambe'na Toding, when asked how he knows who he can trust, replies:

We don't know people's hearts, so we can't believe just anyone. The point is, you must have evidence. Because there are people who will say someone isn't honest, even though he is! So you must have evidence. [In another interview he says]: For example, if I go about and say you're a thief, even though you aren't— many people do such things [slander people]—other people will say, "Where's the evidence?" But if there isn't any evidence, many people will say that it's only empty talk, that it [the slanderous remark] is said only to make the person fall [in respect and prestige].... People must think like that, "Don't believe other people."

Nene'na Tandi(m), when explaining to his wife why she must not believe rumors that he has affairs with other women, tells her: "Don't believe someone's mouth. Don't believe the wind, if there is no evidence." [14]

UNFAITHFULNESS OF A SPOUSE

Nene'na Limbong, like many of the respondents, includes theft, trickery/deceit, and gossip/slander among the most socially disruptive acts a person can commit. But when pressed to identify the single worse "crime," "sin," or "mistake," he replies: "The biggest one? (Yes.) The worst sin is [he pauses] to commit adultery. Adultery. Do you understand adultery? That's when people prowl at night."

Others share this opinion. Ambe'na Kondo comments: "[Adultery] destroys the household, it destroys the attempt to make a living.... For us Toraja, if we are already married, and we go play [have sex] elsewhere, that is *pemali* [prohibited]." To Minaa Sattu says: "If we in Tana Toraja say a sin [has been committed], we mean adultery.... If someone's husband leaves ... [and] we go look, [and think], 'Oh! He has left.' Later that afternoon, we go to his house and commit adultery. That's when we commit a sin. That is a sin."

Although adultery is widely criticized,[15] some people talk as if it were a common occurrence. Nene'na Tandi(m) claims he felt relieved when we chose Paku Asu as our fieldsite as opposed to some of the surrounding villages: "Back then, when I first heard that you had visited X, I told people you wouldn't stay there long because all of the men there are scoundrels [adulterers]. The men in Y are the same."

Even within Paku Asu, Christians and Alukta adherents often accuse each other of committing adultery, the Christians claiming that Alukta adherents engage in illicit sex during their nighttime funeral ceremonies, and the Alukta adherents claiming that the Christians, who no longer are constrained by the traditional prohibitions, are more likely to commit adultery. Because of the presumption that something untoward might occur, or that others might have suspicions about one's behavior, it is considered inappropriate for married men and women who are not closely related or married to one another to visit alone together in a house.[16]

Some people, however, suggest that extramarital sexual relations are acceptable under certain circumstances. Some villagers say that a childless married woman may legitimately have sexual relations with another man in the hopes of conceiving a child. Ambe'na Tangke believes that it is acceptable or at least understandable for husbands to engage in sexual relations with other women during times when their wives should not, or do not desire to, engage in sex. Referring to the postpartum sex taboo,[17] Ambe'na Tangke says: "There are some who can tolerate it, wait a year before they do it [have sex with their wife]. But there are many [alternative] ways of seeking [it]. If we [husbands] go to Laka, wah! There are women there. If we go to Rantepao, there are women there, too. So [some] give a year to their wife. They don't bother her. They give her a year [by going to another woman]. When the wife wants to do it again [have sex], when the man arrives, she'll pull him to her [laughing]. [Then] there's lots of desire!"

Some men also talk in a bemused way about the supposed extramarital affairs of prominent, high status men. Our neighbor, Ambe'na Sumpu, once related how he had been sleeping soundly one night in a nearby village when he was awakened by the screams of a neighbor woman. Fearing that the neighbor was being assaulted, he armed himself with a large stick and ran to the trail leading to her house. He then heard the intruder running toward him and quickly hid in the bushes beside the trail; when the intruder approached, he tripped him with his stick. Ambe'na Sumpu claimed that he was just about to grab the intruder when he discovered, much to his chagrin, that the man he had tripped was Ne' Kadang, one of the wealthiest men in the community and the father of a government official.

The bemused tone in which Ambe'na Sumpu told this story is noteworthy given that, in other contexts, he criticized adulterers as the worst kind of scoundrels. That Ambe'na Sumpu could so readily accept Ne' Kadang's behavior while claiming, in principle, that extramarital sexual liaisons are a grave violation of community and religious values suggests that high status may confer a certain degree of license in such matters.[18] On the other hand, To Minaa Sattu and Nene'na Limbong both claim that high status individuals are held to higher standards of conduct than lower status individuals.

Though none of our respondents reported being involved in extra-marital affairs at the time of the interviews, many said that suspicions of adultery had at one time or another caused quarrels between them-selves and their spouses and were an important source of friction in many marriages, particularly during the early years of a marriage. When Ambe'na Toding is asked, for example, about quarrels with his wife over suspicions of infidelity, he replies: "Oh, many times. . . . It's quite normal. I am often accused, whether it's true or not."[19]

The couple, Nene'na Tandi(m) and Nene'na Tandi(f), also individually report that feelings of jealousy and suspicions of adultery have occurred during their marriage. Nene'na Tandi(m) counsels that a husband must be careful to explain to his wife how he spends his money since there may be a presumption on the wife's part that it is spent on another woman: "For example, if I have 10,000 rupiahs and I take 5,000 rupiahs and spend it on food and drink for my friends in the market, Nene'na Tandi [his wife], sitting at home might think, 'Maybe Nene'na Tandi has another wife somewhere on whom he is spending that money.' " He also reports that his wife has said that she would commit suicide if he were to leave her for another woman. Nene'na Tandi(f), on the other hand, claims that it is her husband who was jealous during the early years of their marriage: "Before, Nene'na Tandi was like that. If I went somewhere alone, he would be angry. . . . Eh, once I crushed/struck him [because] I was angry [because he was jealous]. I said, 'Leave! Don't stay here, leave!' But now, no. [He] has changed!"

Indo'na Rante says that early in her marriage she suspected that her husband was involved with other women when several of their children died,[20] but that now she feels that she would know if he had sexual relations with another woman: "No matter where he would go to 'mix' [have an affair], I would have a feeling, if he did it. For example, if I were to stay at the house and he left, for example, if there was a dead person [a funeral], and he spent several nights [there]. Before he did anything, the point is, before he even talked to another woman, I would have a feeling about it."

Indo'na Sapan reports that she is hated by "the wife of that man who is always coming around here [a married man who unsuccessfully courted her]. . . . So that now that woman won't even talk to me" because she assumes Indo'na Sapan has had an affair with her husband.

Indo'na Sapan also says disapprovingly that one village woman "as soon as her man goes out [of the house] she starts screaming. Angrily [because she is suspicious about where he is going]. . . . And yet that woman, her body is *thin*. That's why I say, 'Whose loss is it?' " Finally, Nene'na Limbong admits that he is so suspicious of the intentions of other males in the village, that he orders his wife never to leave the yard of their house unless accompanied by one of their children.

Given that there is much concern about adultery, how common is it? According to both Indo'na Tiku and Indo'na Rante, adultery is not very common, and yet it is one of the main reasons for divorce. Of our eleven respondents, at least five and possibly six have divorced either to marry someone else, or because their spouse left to marry another person. The extent to which adultery occurs but does not lead to divorce is difficult to judge.[21]

When adultery does occur in Toraja, reactions to it may be intense. Although divorce itself is often described publicly as a rather casual affair, privately some people claim that to discover that one's spouse has been unfaithful is the single most shameful and painful experience a person can endure.[22] A neighbor once said that he would rather die than live with the humiliation of such an incident. Another informant said that there are two ways a husband can respond to avoid shame when his wife has been with another man: he can kill his wife's lover,[23] or he can immediately seek a divorce. If he is a "patient" person, however, he will make peace with his wife; if they are Christian, they will pray, and if they are Alukta, they will sacrifice a pig.

Indo'na Sapan, in explaining why she refused to reconcile with a husband who had committed adultery, says: "Two times [he] returned [here] crying, wanting to take me back [with him]. But I didn't want [to go]. Because his deed . . . hadn't disappeared from my heart." In another interview, she says, "That is the worst pain, if a man [commits adultery]." When asked whether up to the present, she hasn't yet wanted to remarry, she says, "That's right! Because I think, maybe later I would be made [ashamed] again [by a husband's unfaithfulness]."

Ambe'na Toding also comments on the pain that a spouse's infidelity can cause: "[One asks], 'Why does she make me ashamed like that?'. . .Upset/hurt. . . . If he loves the woman, he might kill himself. . . . If he loves his wife. . . . Indeed humans must have such [painful] feelings [under such circumstances]. . . . Women or men . . . the point is, all humans [feel that way]!"

A spouse's infidelity may also provoke intense anger. Indo'na Sapan, for example, recalls how she reacted when the woman with whom her husband was having an affair came to their home one day:

> Once I threw a knife. At Ambe'na Sapan. Because we were sitting on the top of the house, right? . . .It was midday. The older sibling [her husband's brother] was sleeping in the bedroom. . . . I was sitting here, the table was here. Ambe'na Sapan was sitting here. And then she came, that woman, to call him. Eh, my heart became hot, you know. I— the ashtray on top of the table, I threw it. After that, I went to find a knife. I wanted— Because I, I couldn't tolerate it anymore. Because it had been placed [in my] face. If it had been somewhere else, I wouldn't have acted that way. But she came to the house, you know? . . .[When she called to him], he was quiet. I said, "Eh, why are you pretending [not to hear her], why don't you respond? Go! Go with her." I went to find a knife. . . . My heart was *very* hot. I didn't feel anything. I said, "Us humans, we are born once and we die once [she was ready to die].". . .I said, "That's enough." I said to Ambe'na Sapan, "It's enough, now that I've had to see it myself."

Indo'na Tiku also was upset by her husband's affair and their subsequent separation. According to Indo'na Tiku, the affair began when Ambe'na Tiku took a government job in Randan, a nearby village. One day a week Ambe'na Tiku returned home to Paku Asu, but the rest of the time he lived in Randan. Eventually, Ambe'na Tiku became involved with a neighbor, a woman who was married to a much older man. When the woman's husband left the village, Indo'na Tiku, who had suspected that her husband was having an affair, realized that this woman was probably her husband's lover, and she went to Randan to confirm her suspicions. Indo'na Tiku says that after she confronted her husband and he admitted that he was involved with the woman,

> I was always angry then. I no longer presented a good heart [her attitude was no longer charitable]. To the contrary, I gave words that indeed . . . can't be repeated, *because* my heart was already *hot* [angry]. . . . When he left . . . I didn't want to give him his clothes. . . . But after a long while [she pauses], [he] would come to the house [and say], "I ask for your help. Give me just *one* [set] of my office clothes.". . .[I told him], "I want to sell them. . . . If I can't [sell them], I'll give them to your children.". . . But when he came, I felt sad seeing him again because [she laughs] he

didn't have any clothes. . . . I was forced to give him one . . . shirt, [and] one pair of pants.

Indo'na Tiku says that by refusing to let Ambe'na Tiku have his clothes, "in that way, I . . . let out/got rid of my painful feelings. . . . Actually *what* use did I have for a man's clothes? But it served as medicine for my heart. After a long, long time [before a year had passed], I returned all of the clothes!"

Prior to her separation from Ambe'na Tiku, Indo'na Tiku says that people used to tell her that her husband had been consorting with other women at funerals, and she would sometimes cry at night, wondering "if I had been insulted/humiliated." Indo'na Tiku says that she preferred to be left by her husband than to continue

> to suffer inwardly/mentally. Because deeds like that indeed they wound our hearts very much. . . . Indeed . . . my experience—I haven't had an illness that compares to that. . . . There's no medicine, if we don't know how to conduct ourselves, if we don't know how to console ourselves. . . . Like me! If . . . I had not been able to . . . console myself, maybe I would have become crazy or something. As a result of an emotional wound. When Ambe'na Tiku . . . took another woman, wah, I was counseled by my family to go hit that woman. But fortunately . . . I was able . . . to remember my office/place so that I responded, "Ah, it's not necessary. I can live without a husband.". . .Because I would have been ashamed. If I went to hit that person, maybe—certainly, there would have been words from behind [gossip] or ridicule that that person [meaning herself] does not want to be left. Moreover, I'm a government employee. Why would I want to follow a man if I have an office? Work, you know. . . . So that was my thinking then, and so I was just quiet. And people said, "Indeed we can attest to Indo'na Tiku's patience.". . . Because I remembered my office. I didn't want to ruin my name.

Indo'na Sapan and Indo'na Tiku both emphasize their feelings of shame and anger in response to their husbands becoming involved with other women. But Indo'na Tiku also says that after her husband left, she experienced feelings of sadness and longing that were to her somewhat inexplicable. Such feelings, she believes, were the result of having been the victim of love magic (see following section), which makes a woman want to follow a man "no matter where he goes. If we're given it, usually, when the man goes a far distance, the woman cries continuously, remembering him." To help her overcome her feelings of long-ing following her separation from her husband, Indo'na Tiku quickly found a healer who could treat her "so that I wouldn't always think of him."

BEING THE VICTIM OF MAGIC

Magical knowledge and power is said to be used for many beneficial purposes, but it may also be used to manipulate and seduce people, and to cause mischief and illness. One of the most common motives for the use of malicious magic, people say, is to embarrass the hosts of a large ritual. This is accomplished, for example, by magically preventing the cooking water from boiling so that guests cannot be readily served, or by casting a spell on the sacrificial buffalo so that rather than die quickly as soon as their throats are slashed, they run, wounded, from the ritual field.

Magic also is believed to be used in a more directly hostile fashion. Indo'na Rante explains that envy may motivate someone to attempt to destroy another person's happiness: "If, for example, we are content [if life runs smoothly and there is enough to eat] . . . for example, a husband and wife are content . . . very often someone will use magic [against them] . . . so that they will suffer and become sick." She later adds that arguments between people also may lead to the use of harm-ful magic: "For example, if someone has been in an argument and is angry, she/he may put magic into someone's [an opponent's] drink. Then, as soon as the drink is finished, that person suffers [the effects of the magic]. . . . Many Toraja have such magic."

Nene'na Tandi(m) provides another example:

If, for example, a *to minaa* is given his earlier pieces of meat [in the meat division at a ritual] and that's all; if he doesn't receive [his later pieces] . . . he won't take that meat home [the first portion he received]. Instead, he'll take it to the river and cast a spell on it. I don't know how he does it. He'll say, "This meat, this isn't just any meat, this is the meat of the dead person [the one whose funeral he just attended], and the person who divided this meat will follow you [into death] in three or four nights." Then he throws a piece to the west and a piece to the south [directions associated with the ancestors, the souls of the dead, and Puya, the Land of the Dead]. After he throws the meat, he goes home. Then, three nights later, the man who divided the meat will get sick and die![24]

The concern with magically induced illness is reflected in the classification of illnesses: *Saki biasa,* "ordinary illnesses," are those that
occur frequently but are usually not serious, for example boils or
headaches. *Saki deata,* "spirit illnesses," are those caused by the violation of *aluk* (prescriptions) and *pemali* (prohibitions). These illnesses
are typically more serious than *saki biasa* and the sick person must
acknowledge his or her "mistakes" and often make a sacrificial offering
before recovery is presumed to be assured. The third category of illness,
saki to lino, "human illnesses," comprises illnesses thought to be caused
by humans. Human-caused illnesses are said to result from "poisons"
(*rasun*)—which are introduced into someone's food or drink, placed on
the trail for someone to step on, or spoken into the wind—or from
magical spells (*doti*). The contents of these spells are a mystery to
people. Some informants say that the spell is unintelligible to anyone
but the poisoner; others say that the spells are potentially comprehensible, but that they are always spoken in a foreign tongue—Bugis, a
Western language, or the language of the *deata.* An illness that is of
sudden onset or is peculiar in some way, or one that has not responded
to other treatments is often presumed to be human-caused (Geertz
1976:109).

Several knowledgeable villagers believe that until thirty or so years
ago, human-caused illness was rare. Some people attribute the recent
increase in human-caused illness to the spread of education and literacy: now, they say, there are many clever, educated people who know
how to acquire magical knowledge from spiritual beings, or buy it
from traders to the west of Tana Toraja.[25]

Many illnesses and deaths are attributed to magical causes. For
example, Ambe'na Kondo's father, who had been unable to work for
several years because of what appeared to be a cancerous growth on
one of his feet, was said to be suffering from the effects of poison,
which someone who had argued with him reportedly put on the trail
for him to step on. This explanation of his ailment was widely accepted
even by a highly educated government official.

In another case, Indo'na Rante had a dream in which her deceased
mother told her that her sister's recent loss of vision in one eye was
magically caused:

> I often dream [of my mother]. . . . My older sibling, her eye is
> sick, you know? . . . I dreamed that she [her mother] came to the
> house. I said, "Oh, why are you sitting [below the ricebarn],
> mother?" She said, "Your older sister, her eye is sick." [She

pauses and then continues] I said, "Why is it sick?" She said, "Someone has pierced it." Someone used magic on her . . . even if we take her to the doctor, if [the sickness] is from magic, she can't [get well]. . . . I went there [to her sister] and said, "Your [sickness] is not from the gods, as some people say. Someone has pierced it."

Both Indo'na Sapan and To Minaa Sattu believe that their children have been poisoned before, and another villager said that when her father was dying, he claimed that he had been poisoned by someone who owed him some money.

While the belief in magically induced illness is widespread (only a few people such as Ambe'na Patu and To Minaa To Paa, a Paku Asu ritual specialist, said that there is no human-caused illness in the area), and while there appears to be some people who actually do attempt to use magical procedures against others (for example, Ambe'na Kondo's wife told Indo'na Sapan that a man from another village had asked her to slip a substance, a love potion of some kind, into Indo'na Sapan's drink), the extent to which villagers are personally worried about becoming the victim of magic varies. For instance, Nene'na Tandi(f), although she warned us not to drink or eat with strangers, says that she has never been poisoned and that she believes that God protects her from poisoning attempts: "If there is some food that he/she [a potential poisoner] puts some poison in, indeed within our hearts we would say [think to ourselves], 'Probably there's something in this.' So we wouldn't eat it. . . . God lets us know."

Other villagers have more anxiety about possibly being poisoned or becoming the victim of love magic, as reflected in their use of preventative measures and in their fear of reprisals when they happen to offend, outperform, or upset someone. In some instances, however, beliefs about poisoning and love magic serve as ready explanations for untoward or shameful events and thus are not so much a source of distress in people's lives, but a means of coping with distress.

Nene'na Tandi(m) is one person who says that he has been the victim of poisoning (see below) and he takes precautions against further incidents. For example, he will not make long journeys to the west of Paku Asu where extremely malevolent magic is purportedly practiced, and he has swallowed a substance designed to make him invulnerable to poisoning attacks. Other people attempt to protect themselves by drinking curative water or by wearing amulets and charmed bracelets. Some people claim that one may foil a poisoning attempt conveyed via a spell by immediately repeating the poisoner's spell. This reportedly reverses the effects of the spell so that the poisoner him or herself falls ill.

Situations in which people either fear that they will be poisoned, or report that they have been poisoned, often are those in which upsetting interactions have occurred with non-kin or distant kin while engaging in activities of a competitive nature. Such incidents occur most frequently when one is traveling away from home: in large markets, where strangers bargain over goods and prices; at large rituals, where affines or distantly related people engage in the competitive slaughter of livestock; at school, where children from different villages attend classes; and during the hearing of legal cases.

Four of our eleven respondents—Nene'na Tandi(m), Indo'na Rante, Nene'na Limbong, and To Minaa Sattu—believe that they have experienced magically induced illnesses at least once in their lives; their vivid recollections of these incidents illustrate that the threat of poisoning may arouse much fear and anxiety. Two other respondents—Indo'na Sapan and Indo'na Tiku—believe that they have been the actual or intended victims of love magic.

Nene'na Tandi(m) recalls the first time someone used magic against him:

> The first time I was poisoned, there was a divorce case. I was called to discuss the matter. As it turned out, the person from here won [did not have to pay a divorce fine], and the person from Batu lost. About a week later I went to the market. I bought some palm wine and was drinking it. I was drinking from a cup, and just as I was about to take a sip, this woman comes up. She grabbed [my arm] and said "How's the palm wine, is it good?" I said, "Yes, it's good. If you want some, here, take it." She was still holding [my arm] and must have put something in my cup. After I finished drinking I felt dizzy, my body felt weak, and I didn't feel well. I couldn't drink any more palm wine. I went straight home and went to sleep. Before I knew it, I had a fever. Nene'na Tandi [his wife] asked me how I got sick. I said, "I got sick at the market, from this woman. Go call Ne' Atu [a local healer]." Even before Ne' Atu entered the house, he knew the problem! He said, "Indeed, this man has been poisoned." He treated me and I recovered.

Nene'na Tandi(m) links his poisoning experience to the role he played in the divorce case. He implies that he was attacked by someone from Batu in retaliation for successfully defending the Paku Asu villager. He also reports that the poisoning occurred in the market, one of the places where non-kin, or only distantly related kin, come into close proximity.

Nene'na Tandi(m) says that he was the victim of magic on another occasion as well:

> The second time, I was returning from Rantepao where I had sent letters to my relatives telling them that my mother had just died. It was raining. I passed a man near Kayu [a village on the way home] who was sitting by the trail. Thinking he was a man from here [Paku Asu], I said, "Come on, let's go home." He immediately stood up, but didn't say anything. Then he must have blown at me [cast a spell]. But at the time he was behind me, and I didn't know what he had done. Shortly after, I started up the mountain and I began to feel hot, like fire. Then it started to rain again and continued raining until I got home, where I went straight to sleep. . . . A person examined me and said that I had been poisoned. . . . I was given special water [which had curative properties]. I drank it. After I drank it, chicken lice came out of my body [proof that someone had used magic against him]. After one week, I recovered.

Nene'na Tandi(m) says that he was so frightened by this incident that he began to avoid strangers:

> About a month later, there was a celebration here, but I didn't want to attend it! All the people around here looked for me. "Where is Nene'na Tandi? . . . Why doesn't he appear?" . . . They [fellow villagers] were sent to the south and to the north, looking for me. . . . Then Ne' Tanduk came here . . . and he asked me, "Why didn't you attend the celebration?" I said, "It's like this. I am frightened now. I am not frightened of the celebration, but I'm frightened of the humans [who might be there]. There are people who want to kill me." Ne' Tanduk said, "You are truly frightened of that?" And I said "Yes, I am truly frightened."

In this case, Nene'na Tandi(m) was able to identify the man who used magic against him—the stranger on the trail—but he did not know what the motive was for the attack. As a consequence, he began to fear all "distant" people and large, public events until he was given something to swallow that was designed to make him invulnerable to future attacks.

Like Nene'na Tandi(m), Indo'na Rante says that she has been the victim of magic on two occasions, and that lice also came out of her body during a treatment procedure:

(When you were given magic, were you sick then?) Yes, I was sick! . . . I felt like I was going to die. I was given water [to drink] by that old person [a healer]. All the lice came out from my eyes [pause]. (And then you recovered?) Yes [pause]. The person who has it [magic] is from here, [he] lives near the school [she believes he used magic against her because he was envious of her and her husband's success]. . . . That's why I don't pass by his house [when walking through the village].

Nene'na Limbong believes that he has been the victim of magic three times. Each instance occurred when Nene'na Limbong participated in the adjudication of a dispute. He describes the first case:

With a suddenness that startled me, someone [at the local market] came and threw a quid of tobacco at me. . . . Immediately my face began to swell, and [the rest of] my body. . . . I left the market and went home. My father was still sleeping. I told him I had been struck [by magic]. . . . My father put some water in a glass and then he spoke [over it] and gave it to me. I slept, [and when] I got up, I was already [cured]! . . . (Where was the person who gave you the poison from?) From over there. It's called— not "poison." The knowledge was "thrown" [at me] together with some words [a spell]. (Why did she/he give it to you?) Because he had a case that I [helped] to decide . . . and he lost . . . he was upset/disappointed. But the gods backed that decision because . . . after my father gave me water [I recovered].

In the second incident, Nene'na Limbong was called to settle a dispute in another village:

By the time I got there, there were already . . . over ten people present. We arrived at the house of the head of the village, but he wasn't there. So we spent the night. . . . Because when we arrived . . . [we were told] that the head of the village went to Rantepao . . . and wouldn't return until the next day. We were talking [to some people from the other village] and these people didn't yet know who I was. Then this man came up and started arguing the case [even before the headman had returned], ridiculing us. Then I responded. They had no answer to my speech because they knew that I spoke the truth and they knew that I could not be defeated. Indeed, I had a reputation for always winning. Then someone recognized me, one of the ones involved in the dispute. [He said], "Oh, this is Nene'na Limbong. Indeed, we've heard that no one wins against you." . . . Then he cast a spell on me . . . like blowing. . . . Immediately I "fainted."

To help himself regain full "consciousness," Nene'na Limbong invoked the mythic ancestors, calling upon them to protect him. With their help, Nene'na Limbong claims, he eventually recovered from the attack.

Nene'na Limbong includes the following as a third case of being victimized by malevolent magic. This instance differs from most in that it affects several people at once:

That time also involved a household [divorce] case. The woman [the wife of a man from Paku Asu] had gotten involved with another man. So I went there to ask for the *kapa'* [the divorce fine]. . . . We arrived there [and] we had started to talk about asking for the *kapa'*, [and] wah, the rice barn we were sitting on went like this [began to shake up and down]! Like this and this [he demonstrates by moving his body]! We were all scared. Because the barn was going like this . . . I was scared [he whispers]. . . . But a friend told me, "Don't be scared. These people around here do this sort of thing [use magic] all the time."

Again, Nene'na Limbong says that he only regained full "consciousness" after he had invoked the ancestors.

To Minaa Sattu also believes that he suffered from a magical attack in the aftermath of a dispute, though in this case a trade dispute. He and two companions had traveled to a village far to the west of Paku Asu to trade reed mats for chickens. To Minaa Sattu met a merchant there, set an exchange rate for his mats, and was then invited to the merchant's house for dinner. All went well until the actual exchange of goods took place, when the merchant tried to pawn off on To Minaa Sattu some small, diseased chickens in place of the healthy, fat ones that To Minaa Sattu was expecting. To Minaa Sattu protested the exchange, but when this failed to produce a more equitable arrangement, he demanded the return of his mats, canceled the transaction, and stormed out of the merchant's house.

As soon as he reached the road outside the merchant's house, To Minaa Sattu claims that he began to feel sick and disoriented, as if he had been physically turned upside down with his feet in the air and his head on the road. Fearing that he had been poisoned, he drank some curative water—which he carried with him whenever he left the village—and staggered back into town to meet his friends. When he arrived, his companions were so concerned by his appearance that they insisted he rest before trying to return home. That night, however, he had visions of chickens crawling over his body and he was unable to sleep. The next day, his illness grew worse: he was nauseated and vomiting, yet unable to defecate, and his body—from head to waist—felt swollen and puffy, as if he would float away. While describing these sensations, To Minaa Sattu held up an ashtray to demonstrate how his eyes had bulged out from his head, and he placed his arms out in front of his waist to indicate how distended his stomach had become.

Unable to walk, To Minaa Sattu was carried home by his companions and he remained in bed, feeling quite ill, for several weeks. Eventually he had a dream in which an ancestor confirmed what he had suspected: that he had been poisoned by the deceitful merchant. The ancestor then offered him a cure for his illness and from that point on, he says, his recovery was rapid and uneventful.

Indo'na Tiku believes that she was once the victim of love magic. She believes that the brother of her former husband used love magic against her to get her to marry Ambe'na Tiku:

[At first I felt] I would rather have my head cut off than marry him. Because actually, Ambe'na Tiku had a wife. But she ... didn't have any children. And Ambe'na Tiku said, "I want to have children." But I still rejected him. . . . If we don't want someone, it's not unusual to be given something in our food, so that we'll want him/her. (Oh, it's like that.) Yes! It's very common now! . . . Even if we don't want him, if he gives us something which attracks/pulls us, of course we'll want [him]. Because Ambe'na Tiku was already very old! But I was still young [he is about ten years older] [she pauses]. So that's how I ended up marrying him.

Now Indo'na Tiku counsels young women to be careful to reject suitors politely so that they do not themselves become the targets of love magic. Nene'na Tandi(m) similarly warns women about exchanging long glances with men:

[I say], "Don't turn your face [to a man] if he's looking at you because many people here will say words [utter a magic spell to seduce the woman]!" . . . Once [the spell] is said, the woman's heart will flutter, flutter, flutter, and she'll want to look at the man. (After the man says the spell?) Yes. So that by afternoon, the woman desires to meet with the man. She wants to be with him.

Indo'na Sapan believes that she, like Indo'na Tiku, has been the target of magic used by an older, married man (Ambe'na Payung) in an effort to win her affections, and yet in Indo'na Sapan's case, she was able to successfully resist his advances. According to Indo'na Sapan, the wife of Ambe'na Kondo told her that Ambe'na Payung had tried to enlist her help in his attempts to seduce Indo'na Sapan:

> Indo'na Kondo supposedly is always given magic [by Ambe'na Payung]. He says [to her], "Give this to her [Indo'na Sapan], so that she'll follow me." . . . He says to Indo'na Kondo, "Indo'na Sapan is always coming to your house. When you give her some-thing to drink, put this [the love magic] in it." . . . But Indo'na Kondo [says], "As soon as he leaves, I throw it out. Why would I want to do that to a relative?" I thanked her for that. If it had been someone else [other than Indo'na Kondo], certainly they would have given it to me. And I would be like a crazy person [running after him]!

Indo'na Sapan believes, however, that eventually she unknowingly stepped on something that Ambe'na Payung had placed in her path. But instead of falling madly in love with Ambe'na Payung, Indo'na Sapan became very "ill," suffering from symptoms of what would be called "depression" in the West (see chapter 6). When Indo'na Sapan sought treatment for her illness from a ritual specialist and healer, he informed her that Ambe'na Payung was using magic against her. In-do'na Sapan then came to believe that Ambe'na Payung was attempting to blackmail her into becoming involved with him. She reports that Ambe'na Payung even took credit for causing her illness and told people that he would cure her if she would go along with his wishes. (It is believed that those who use magic against others also have the power to heal them.) She steadfastly refused to do so, however, because she did not want to hurt his wife and because she feared that he would eventually turn his attentions to another woman.

Men are not the only ones who are believed to practice love magic. Indo'na Tiku, for example, claims that the only reason her husband left her was because his new wife seduced him through magical means:

Ambe'na Tiku . . . said that she would come to his room at night.
. . . Once there, she would urge/persuade him. And in the morning . . . she herself made the water [for coffee or tea]. . . . So it
would have been easy for her to put something in his drink [she
pauses]. In fact, Ambe'na Tiku himself says to people, "My heart
was indeed *heavy* when I left Indo'na Tiku because I remembered
her heart. . . . She can't return *anything* [any bad feelings]. Indeed, she is a good person. But [it happened] because of that [the
love magic]. I didn't intend for it [to happen]." That's what he
[Ambe'na Tiku] always says to his male friends.[26]

Respondents have sought somewhat different remedies for their
magically induced illnesses and experiences. When Nene'na Limbong
was struck by magic, on two occasions he formally invoked the mythic
ancestors and asked them to protect him. To Minaa Sattu, on the other
hand, dreamed that an ancestor came to him and offered him a cure.
He later expressed his thanks to the ancestor by sacrificing a pig at a
ma'nene' ceremony.

The other respondents—Indo'na Rante, Nene'na Tandi(m), Indo'na
Sapan, and Indo'na Tiku—turned to professional healers for help (see
chapters 6 and 7). Nene'na Tandi(m) was so frightened by his second
experience of magically induced illness that he would not go to large
public gatherings until he was given preventive medicine:

It was then that I got some poison "medicine" which I still have!
But what was given to me was put inside my body, not outside
[as an amulet would be worn]. . . . Then I tested it. There was
this person from X . . . I said [to him], "You better make some
medicine for me because there are many people who want to kill
me." . . . He took nine different substances. I was watching. He
cut them up, put them in some water, but none of them would
sink [into the water]! Then he immediately said to me, "I can't
beat you, sir. You have defeated me." I said, "Why?" He told me,
"You already have medicine that provides security against poison
in your body. . . . So it would be in vain for me to make [this
medicine]." Ah, that's when I knew that it was true, that it [the
medicine] was in my body!

— 6 —

DYSPHORIA AND DISORDER

RUMINATION, ANXIETY, AND DISTRESS

We mentioned in chapter 4 that Toraja value reason and rationality, and yet they also believe that people can be "too" intelligent and that they can think and worry too much about things. Excessive rumination, distress, and anxiety are thought to possibly lead to severe mental or physical disorder, and even premature death. Indo'na Tiku, for instance, says: "People who cannot limit their distress, eventually it will ruin their body. It will ruin their thinking. So if our thinking is ruined, it means we're no longer normal. . . . [If a person cannot be consoled/distracted], often he/she will die." Nene'na Tandi(m) claims that his first two wives died of grief and disappointment after he left them. The topic comes up when he is asked if he has ever thought about committing suicide. He replies;

> Oh, as for me, I haven't yet had a thought like that. . . . Because as long as I've been an adult, I haven't yet been divorced by a woman . . . I've always been the one to break things off. Think about this: . . . my first wife, after I divorced [her], died. The second one, I divorced, died. What was the cause? The cause was

that I have a good heart. It wasn't possessions that they desired but sweet words, a good heart. . . . [They thought], "where can I find a man like that?". . . Why did they die right away? . . . just because of thinking [too much]. (Just thinking?) Yes, just thinking.

Despite the recognized dangers of rumination, many of our respondents as well as other villagers report that they think too much (*ma-'tangnga'-tangnga'*, literally "to think and think") about certain problems in their lives. In addition to the interpersonal concerns discussed in the previous chapter, people commonly ruminate about such matters as the absence or loss of loved ones; economic concerns such as making a living, paying for ritual debts, and financing children's educations; "bad" dreams; health concerns; and legal disputes. People may even ruminate about how they ruminate too much. Ambe'na Toding comments:

> I . . . want to find happiness, but I don't find it. What about good fortune . . . ? I don't have any. . . . There are some people whose children are well educated [and find employment in the city], but none of my children are educated! So there are many things [I think about]. That's why I'm thin. [I think so much that] it is often midnight before I can fall asleep. . . . Thoughts like that make people sick. If someone is happy, he/she must be fat, [because] there's nothing that he/she thinks about. Indeed [he/she] thinks about things, but only about matters having to do with the next day. Not other [distressing] things. . . . (So it's often midnight before you can fall asleep?) It's often like that. . . . (What about after you've already fallen asleep, can you sleep until morning or do you wake up [before then]?) I wake up . . . if someone is making noise, I can't sleep. . . . Or I turn my body left to right [tosses and turns] because I don't feel comfortable. . . . I think . . . "Why aren't I a little prosperous?" . . . I am always praying, [asking] why. I throw away my energy, my health [in his pursuits to become prosperous]. Why don't I [find wealth]? . . . And yet there are people who sit in their chairs and they have many times the wealth [that I have].

Elsewhere Ambe'na Toding says:

> Thoughts/worries often arise in my heart. I want to free myself of them, I want to make myself conscious/aware, but they often come. What do I do? I don't know. The point is, it's common,

common when I feel distressed. . . . There's no use—it [only] causes problems in [our] body—if we think/ruminate like that. . . . But often [such thoughts] suddenly arise within [me].

When Indo'na Sapan is asked if she has experienced more happiness or hardship in her life, she pauses and then replies in a quiet, low tone of voice:

As for me, [there's been] more hardship than happiness. Because I think about everything, you know? Like my children and my parents. And I don't have any siblings [she is an only child]. . . . Moreover, I'm not together with my children [they live in urban areas]. . . . I just think . . . "When will we be together [again]?" [And yet] if I were to go with my children, what about my parents? . . . I'm only happy if we're all together. . . . (If [you] feel troubled, is there something that—) Can make it go away? [She pauses and then continues] Maybe there isn't. There is, but it only [helps] a little, you know? . . . if we talk to others. . . . There was someone next to us [a neighbor] . . . one of the children went to Manado, a girl. . . . when it was morning like this, her mother would already start crying [because the daughter was absent]. . . . I always told her . . . "Don't always remember/think of her." She would say, "Wah, I can't tolerate it. . . . Of several children, she's the only girl." . . . And then that person [the mother] died [from thinking about her absent daughter]! What a pity.

A little later in the interview, Indo'na Sapan says that when people are troubled, food does not taste good to them and they have difficulty sleeping "when [their thinking] . . . just keeps going. Yes! Indeed, I've already experienced all of that. . . . It's like our body feels sick/painful all over. It's like [we're] sick, weak, [and] can't move. Because of [our] distress."

Like Indo'na Sapan, Nene'na Tandi(m) comments on the potentially dangerous consequences of psychological distress:

If people . . . realize that someone has troubled thoughts . . . [they know] that person will soon die. All people like that die because of their thinking. . . . (Are there a lot of people like that, whose thinking is troubled and they can't be treated . . . ?) Ah, the dead person up [the trail] from here, [she died] from thinking, too! . . . because her primary wish was to become Christian, [she] wanted to be baptized. Her children promised to come, but they didn't and so her thinking . . . wandered and wandered . . . night and day . . . Until she died.

In another interview, Nene'na Tandi(m) gives another example of when people experience distress:

> According to people here, if we are given a lot of meat at celebrations [which must eventually be repaid], indeed, we can't sleep at night! We can't sleep! [We stay up] thinking, "How will I pay for all this meat?"

The period following a death is an especially distressing time for many Toraja individuals. Few Paku Asu villagers reach adulthood without experiencing the death of someone close to them. All of our respondents have lost at least one parent; Ambe'na Patu, Indo'na Rante, Nene'na Tandi(m), and To Minaa Sattu have all lost siblings; Nene'na Limbong lost his first wife; and Indo'na Sapan, Indo'na Tiku, Ambe'na Patu, and Ambe'na Kondo are the only ones who have *not* lost children. Such losses, especially those of parents and children, are acknowledged to be stressful and, as we noted earlier, the expression of grief through limited periods of crying and wailing is both expected and encouraged. At the same time, it is hoped that feelings of grief will have subsided with the entombment of the body and the completion of formal mourning practices (see Hollan and Wellenkamp n.d.).

The period during which the body is kept in the house is reported to be a trying one for the relatives of the deceased. With the exception of Indo'na Tiku, who says that some people do not mind having the deceased's body stored in the house because they feel "at least we are still together," most people consistently report that they and others they know find it burdensome. One source of stress is the smell of the decaying body. Although it is hoped that the preparation of the body will eliminate or at least reduce some of the odor, it is not always effective and we were told that some bodies smell intensely.[1] In addition to the odor, people must contend with the *bombo* of those near death, which are thought to be attracted to the houses where the deceased are located.

The presence of the deceased in the house is also burdensome because it serves constantly to remind people of their loss. Ambe'na Kondo's wife says that prior to her mother's funeral, she would sit and look at her mother's body and think, "Oh, what a pity, when my mother was alive [she would say] . . . 'Here's some hot water. Drink some.' " Many say that once the body is buried and thus no longer in constant view, one's grief is considerably lessened. Indo'na Sapan says that when the body is in the house, "we look at [the body]. Our sadness comes again. . . . But when [the body has been moved to] another place, even if we remember [the deceased], if we don't see him/her with our eyes, we don't remember as much."

People's anxiety following a death is said to be greatly exacerbated by the hardship involved in financing and preparing for the funeral. The sense of hardship is reflected in the parallel Nene'na Limbong draws between being "bombed" and the experience of having several relatives die. He interpreted a dream in which he had been hit by a bomb dropped from a plane as foretelling the deaths of several of his close family members: "I was struck by a bomb. [It meant that I] would be struck by the grief/hardship of death—the death of my mother, the death of my father, the death of my wife—and that the amount of the sacrifices [pigs and water buffalo required for the funerals] would be tremendous." It should be noted, however, that while providing for funerals is burdensome, many aspects of the funeral, such as providing tributes and memorials to the deceased, are viewed as a source of consolation and satisfaction (see Wellenkamp 1988b:489–90).

Although ideally feelings of grief have subsided by the time of the burial and the completion of the funeral, some people continue to be preoccupied by thoughts of their deceased relatives. One woman claims, "it's not possible that our grief will disappear, disappear completely, once we have experienced a death. When there are a lot of people around, yes, usually it disappears. But when there's another dead person, and we go there [to the house of someone who has died], grief arises in the heart again. Thus, we always remember." Indo'na Rante comments:

> [When someone dies] our thoughts are dizzy. It doesn't matter what people say to us, we don't pay any attention. How could we when we have such troubling thoughts? . . . Even food or drink, we aren't aware of/pay attention to. The point is, we just *stay* [sit] like that [thinking]. . . . (What about sleeping? Can [one] sleep?) Wah! No! . . . We can't sleep, Belo, if we're thinking. That's why . . . it's often 10:00 before I go to sleep. I'm forced to just [stay up] making mats. . . . It is useless for me to lie down if I'm not sleepy. Often my body hurts from turning over and over. . . . If it's 7:00 or 8:00 for example and [I] want to go to sleep, [I can't because] my thoughts will still be running. Because often I

remember my [deceased] younger sister [long pause]. Often I imagine her face. That's what I remember.

Elsewhere Indo'na Rante says that she has a weak heart and as a consequence, she cannot have sugar in her coffee, and she must be careful not to become anxious or distressed:

[I've had a weak heart] for five years. When my heart starts to pound/palpitate, I go again to the clinic [where] I'm injected [with medicine].... (Do you know why you have that condition?) Because that's what happens ... if we always are experiencing hardship. If we just think [ruminate] about things. For example, if we just sit like this and our thinking wanders/drifts. Later, we get heart illness. (What do you think about?) About difficulties! ... for example, about death. Because my [deceased] mother isn't here. My [deceased] siblings aren't here. My [deceased] children aren't here. That's what I think about. That's what causes illness.

In chapter 7, we examine some of the ways in which people cope with anxiety and distress.

SOMATIC COMPLAINTS

Like many populations that lack modern sewage facilities and reliable sources of clean water, Toraja adults and children experience a fair amount of gastrointestinal complaints, including diarrhea, nausea, and vomiting.[2] Respiratory illnesses also are common, which may be due in part to close living conditions, especially during large celebrations. By far the most common physical symptoms reported to health officers in the Paku Asu area during our stay were diarrhea and stomach ailments, coughs, and fever.

It appears that at least some common somatic complaints, however, are related to psychological stress, and it is these that we briefly discuss here.

Many adults, especially middle-aged men, complain of persistent ulcerlike symptoms. The distress is severe enough to cause people to change their diets significantly, by avoiding hot peppers, coffee, sugar, and palm wine and eating mostly bland foods, including rice porridge. One person, Ambe'na Rempa, said that he felt as if he had a "wound" in his stomach and that the pain was unlike stomachaches caused by worms, gas, hepatitis, overeating, undereating, or spoiled food. His own theory was that the wound had been caused by eating too infrequently, which caused the sides of his stomach to collapse and rub against one another. As a consequence, he tried to eat small amounts of food throughout the day to prevent his stomach from becoming empty. He also drank large amounts of cool water, which he said had both healing and pain-relieving effects. One Toraja psychiatrist in the town of Rantepao said that she often has given patients medicine for gastrointestinal complaints, but that the medicine proves ineffective; however, when she then gives them tranquilizers, their conditions improve.

Complaints about dizziness and headaches, disturbed sleep, and a lack of appetite also are quite common and are often explained by villagers as the result of "thinking too much" about one's problems and concerns.

High blood pressure and heart problems are also of concern to Paku Asu residents. As noted above, Indo'na Rante says that she has a weak heart, and both Nene'na Tandi(m) and Ambe'na Toding say that they suffer from high blood pressure. According to Nene'na Tandi(m), he was surprised when he was told that he had high blood pressure, because "if someone has high blood pressure, [it is due to] their always getting angry! But I don't! How many times have you been to the church and [have seen that] when I'm talking to people, they often are laughing [he laughs]?! But when someone has high blood pressure, when they talk, they are angry!"

DISTURBING DREAMS

Disturbing dreams have much personal significance for villagers. While people report many positive dream experiences, they also report many disturbing ones. Some dreams are disturbing in and of themselves, while others are disturbing because they are presumed to foretell a disasterous event. In many of the dreams, the dreamer feels powerless or under siege by some more powerful being, either human or spiritual; affectively, such dreams often are characterized by intense feelings of fear (*mataku'*). Other disturbing dreams reported by respondents have to do with death, and are characterized by intense sadness.

More than once Ambe'na Kondo has dreamed of being led away by a person who has died, a dream that is supposed to foretell the dreamer's death. Ambe'na Kondo is unusual among our respondents in that he says that he refuses to think about such dreams, although the reason he gives for this is that he believes that to dwell upon the inevitability of one's own death would be very unsettling:

[If we dream] of someone who has already died, and [in the dream] we follow him/her, [that means] we must [ourselves] die. . . . If we were to think about that, it would ruin/damage [our hearts]. (Have you ever had a dream like that?) Yes. But I don't think about them.

Ambe'na Kondo claims that in general, he ignores his dreams.

If someone asks me, "Have you had a dream?" I say, "No." I don't believe in dreams. . . . For example, if I dreamed of something last night, and when I thought about it [I decided] that it was bad [foretold disaster], then I would be afraid. And so I don't believe [in dreams]! If we were to think about them, they would ruin/damage our hearts.

While Ambe'na Kondo chooses to ignore inauspicious dreams, other villagers may have a disturbing dream reinterpreted. Nene'na Limbong, for example, asked a specialist to reinterpret a dream that, like the ones reported by Ambe'na Kondo, foretold his death. In the dream,

My [deceased] father came and tried to take me away! . . . My father wanted to take me. He said he wanted to take me, that my time was up and that I had to go. I said, "I don't want to go!" But he grabbed my arms and tried to take me! He said, "I must take you." But I said that I didn't want to go! "It's not time for me to follow you!" But he grabbed my arms again and tried to take me. I struggled with him and he tried to grab me. I was sitting at the front of the rice barn, but he dragged me away from the barn. But I continued to struggle. As he dragged me by the front of the house, I wrapped my legs around a stone and held on. Then I was able to pull my arms away and I ran! I didn't see my father again.

Nene'na Limbong's dream was reinterpreted (*dibori*) to mean that the soul of his dead father was hungry and thus, Nene'na Limbong immediately sacrificed a pig for him. In this way, he believes, he averted his own premature death.

While the "reinterpretation" of Nene'na Limbong's dream in some sense continues to recognize the aggressive aspects of the dream (Nene'na Limbong's father is still depicted as being desirous of something valuable belonging to Nene'na Limbong), in many other instances (as noted in chapter 4), dreams are interpreted in a way that ignores or denies any hostile or aggressive elements. Indo'na Rante, for example, offers a conventional interpretation of the following dream: "I dreamed that I saw people being cut down and shot, lots of them. Indeed I was frightened. . . . But if someone is frightened [by a dream like that], they'll ask someone, 'What's the meaning/reason?' [and they'll respond], 'Oh, later you will slaughter a buffalo.' "

Dreams in which the dreamer is "victimized" in some way appear to be common. Such imagery is especially striking in "sacrifice" dreams. Nene'na Limbong, for example, reports a dream in which he is slaughtered like a sacrificial animal:

> One time I dreamed that my throat had been cut! There was a man who cut my throat. I fell down dead! Dead! And I was very frightened. I woke up frightened [thinking], "I'm dead!" A man cut me with a sword and I fell dead and my eyes went dark. Then my body was chopped and chopped and chopped and distributed to A and B and C [he whispers in a low, frightened tone of voice]. [I thought], "Oh, this is my body being cut up!" But I could see it happen! I was cut up and distributed. I was very frightened.

This dream was interpreted in a conventional manner to mean that Nene'na Limbong would eventually slaughter many water buffalo.

The stark imagery of this dream, which is dominated by Nene'na Limbong's unconscious identification with a sacrificial animal, dramatically conveys a sense of being helpless and preyed upon by one's associates (see Hollan 1989 for a fuller interpretation of this dream).[3]

To Minaa Sattu also reports a "sacrifice" dream, but in his dream, rather than being a victim, he is a spectator to the killing:

> One time I dreamed that I went to the sky/upperworld and there were people there having a funeral. . . . People said [of one of the water buffalo waiting to be sacrificed], "This buffalo is Nene'na Datu [his older sister]." But her body was that of a beautiful buffalo! It was black and white, a *salego* [the most prized and expensive type]. . . . Then the buffalo was stabbed. [Some people] called me over and said, "Hey, To Minaa, look at this buffalo." And I went to look. [I thought to myself], "This is a human! She looks like a person!" . . . Before she died, she looked like a buffalo. But after she had been killed, she looked like a person. I cried and cried [and thought], "Why have you killed my elder sibling?" [Later he continues]: She was cut up, and her body was distributed! But her leg was like a human leg, her hand a human

hand! I saw it, you know? I sat myself and watched. . . . But I wasn't given anything! . . . (Why weren't you?) I don't know![4]

To Minaa Sattu claims that this dream accurately foretold the death of his sister, who was gravely ill at the time that he had the dream: "It wasn't long after I dreamed that that she died. . . . (She really died?) She really died!" To Minaa Sattu's interpretation of his "sacrifice" dream contrasts with that of Nene'na Limbong's in that it is quite literal: "If there is a celebration in the sky/upperworld, it's really true that humans are going to be slaughtered! (Humans will be?) Yes. If lots of small children die [here on earth], lots of [pigs and buffalo] have been slaughtered in the sky/upperworld." It is doubtful that other villagers would agree with To Minaa Sattu's claim that people die on earth as a consequence of feasting in the upperworld, but the notion that one's sorrows and privations result from the demands and needs of others appears widely shared, if not on a conscious level, then unconsciously.

Note that in the dream To Minaa Sattu stands by and watches as his sister is sacrificed. His indirect identification with those who conduct the killing—in stark contrast to Nene'na Limbong, who explicitly identifies with the victim of the sacrifice—seems atypical (see Hollan 1989 for further discussion of this dream).

Like To Minaa Sattu, Ambe'na Toding—whose mother died when he was young and who has had several children die—has had dreams in which he is crying:

(What are you dreaming about when you cry?) The central thing is [pause] something we don't like, you know [speaking in a subdued tone of voice]? What I mean is, for example, if there is something we prefer and it's not given to us [i.e., when one is unfairly treated]. Or . . . various things. Like if someone . . . dies, even though he/she [actually] hasn't [yet]. I have done that, too. (You've dreamed like that?) Yes, often. I've often cried, too. When I awaken, I have tears in my eyes. [I think], "Why did I cry last night?" Usually I report it to someone else. . . . Usually if someone dreams . . . like that . . . a chicken must be burned/ roasted [sacrificed to prevent later misfortune]. (What does it mean to dream about a death?) To get/experience a death [in a dream] can mean something good will happen, or, something bad/evil. For example, if someone's pig dies [in a dream] it can mean that his/her child will die. Or [it can mean] that he/she will slaughter [an animal at a celebration]. . . . But hopefully—what we request [from spiritual beings]—is to have good dreams."

Other disturbing dreams reported by respondents include dreams of being chased by someone or something. Indo'na Sapan, for instance, has often had frightening dreams of being chased:

> There's someone who wants me, you know? And I don't want [him]. And he chases me. That's what frightens me. (Yes.) Often *I* have had [such dreams]! (So there's a man chasing you?) Yes! (And you wake up suddenly and feel afraid?) Yes. I'm trembling! (So what do you do? Do you go back to sleep or maybe get up and drink something, or what?) I get up and drink something right away if I'm trembling. My heart feels like it's swaying. That's why I quickly get something to drink [she coughs]. Because if we don't drink [something], we feel like our head will break. Because we've been frightened."

Tauan comprise another category of disturbing dream experiences. As noted in chapter 4, *tauan* include experiences of spirit attack, as well as what English-speaking observers would call "nightmares," which the Toraja presume are stimulated by a particularly unpleasant or frightening moment in the dreamer's life, often an experience from the previous day. At least six of our respondents have experienced at least one sort of *tauan*.

Experiences of spirit-attack *tauan* vary some from dreamer to dreamer, but common to many is a feeling of paralysis. Ambe'na Tangke reports, for example:

> When it comes [the spirit], I can feel it! Usually I begin to struggle like this [he demonstrates by turning the trunk of his body back and forth while keeping his arms at his sides]. . . . I don't see it, usually I'm just sleeping, but I feel it! If the spirit comes, I can't speak and I can't move! (But you struggle? You try to speak but can't?) Yes! I try to move, but I can't!

Two respondents report that they have experienced a spirit attack when they were still awake with their eyes open. Such experiences appear to occur during states of semiconsciousness and appear similar to Levy's (1973:394–98) description of hypnoid hallucinations among Tahitians. To Minaa Sattu reports:

> I saw a person [come out of the ground]. My mouth was shut [so that he could not cry out] and my body was held. My legs were

also held. But I wasn't really asleep. My eyes were still open. Then it [the spirit] came out of the ground. . . . It had a long body. I thought, "Why is it like that [have such a long body]? Maybe it's not human." I saw it, but my mouth couldn't open, and my arms and legs were held.

Indo'na Sapan reports: "That *setang* [spirit], that *setang* tramples on us! We want to move, but we can't. We want to speak, but we can't. *Often* I experience that! Eh! Yes, it's like you want to breathe, but it [one's breath] disappears." Indo'na Sapan has heard that some people keep knives by their beds, to protect themselves from such spirits.

Most respondents do not provide detailed descriptions of the appearance of the spirit; rather, they emphasize the feeling of being restrained and smothered. A few say that the spirits are humanlike and have long bodies, but most cannot, for example, specify the gender of the spirit. One exception is Nene'na Limbong, who provides the following account:

I went to sleep about 10 p.m., but my eyes were still open! But my body was already asleep. But my eyes were still open and I could see. [I thought], "Oh, what is this?" Then it came. . . . It came and trampled on my stomach! Then it trampeled on my hands and legs. I wanted to say something, but I couldn't speak! I wanted to talk, but nothing would come out! Indeed, I could see everything. . . . My legs were trampeled on and my hands and arms were trampeled on and I was frightened! Indeed, I was frightened. And my heart inside was pounding [he speaks louder to convey his sense of fear and anxiety]. . . . So my heart was pounding, beating hard! . . . People die from experiences like that! (They can die?) Die! . . . [Because of] the restricted breathing. (And the spirit that jumped on you, was it male or female?) Female! . . . (And what did she look like?) Like a human, but her hair wasn't tied up [women usually keep their hair knotted in a bun during the day]! Indeed, it was very long! I was very frightened, frightened to see her, but I saw her with my own eyes! . . . I have seen many people die because of an experience like that, because they can't survive it [the spirit attack] and they can't fight it [the spirit] . . . until they are defeated!

Referring to the second type of *tauan* experience, Ambe'na Patu says: "People often have nightmares; when they talk [in their sleep] but don't know it. They have to do with what the person did during the day. For example, if they were startled or scared, that night [in their dreams] they are also startled or scared." Indo'na Rante says of her son's nightmares: "For example, if right now, he plays with his friends and they hit him or frighten him . . . later, during the night, he starts screaming." She continues later: "It's like he wants to run, and we hold onto him. That is what's called *tauan*."

Indo'na Rante herself once had a *tauan* experience, following the death of a relative in childbirth. At the time, Indo'na Rante had recently experienced childbirth herself. When her niece died unexpectedly, "that night I started screaming [in her sleep]. Because I was afraid." Indo'na Rante says that she was afraid of being attacked by her niece's spirit. As noted earlier, the spirits of women who die in childbirth (*lobang boko'*) are believed to be dangerous if certain ritual procedures are not carried out shortly after death. According to Indo'na Rante, "they will hit people. [And] those people will die. That's why . . . I *tauan* then."

Nene'na Tandi(m) also links nightmares to being startled, but he suggests that being startled often is the result of quarreling with someone:

> Those who have nightmares, they are startled. . . . They sleep and then the next moment they arise and start talking—like a crazy person. . . . [When someone] has a nightmare, whatever is said earlier, during the day, startles us and awakens us, like if I were talking to you, and I was angry with you, or you were angry with me, later when I'm asleep, I wake up! You came [in the dream] and were angry at me! That is the startle that [causes] what is called *tauan*. . . . In my opinion, those who have nightmares are those who . . . get angry with people. . . . But it is only after getting home that they remember, "Wah, earlier . . . my feelings had begun to flare up [get angry]." We go to sleep still angry and a moment later we arise startled, angry again![5]

Nene'na Tandi(m) goes on to warn that a person experiencing a nightmare is potentially dangerous. He or she may mistake other sleepers in the room for the person they are arguing with in the dream:

> Usually if the person having the nightmare is still talking and we come to tell them [to awaken them], they will hit us! Because they are angry, still angry with the person who is arguing with them [in the dream and] we come, [and] they mistake us for that

person. If they happen to be near a knife, they want to use it on us! That's one strict prohibition of the elders: Elders say, "Don't get close to someone who is having a nightmare. And don't try to talk to them. It's better to be quiet." But we are amazed [by the dreamer's behavior]. . . . Sometimes they will open the door and run off. . . . So if someone has a nightmare, we guard the door.

Again, what seems common to many of these disturbing dream experiences is a sense of being vulnerable and sometimes at the mercy of more powerful, aggressive beings and forces.

SUICIDE

Suicidal Feelings and Attitudes Toward Suicide

Both Christian and Alukta villagers believe that suicide—whether committed by hanging, as was common in former times, or by ingesting poisons and pesticides,[6] as is common today—is morally wrong. Nene'na Tandi(f), for instance, comments: "People . . . who kill themselves . . . they don't know that . . . God won't accept them [into Heaven]. . . . Because they force their own deaths, you know? God hasn't yet taken their [souls]. [So] God won't accept them."

When asked, our respondents say that they have never personally considered committing suicide. Indo'na Tiku, for example, says: "I feel it's very sinful [to commit suicide]. I would really add to my sins if . . . a thought arose like that [she coughs]. Because then we would be taking something that belongs to God. (So even when Ambe'na Tiku—) Left? That's right! I didn't! . . . [But] maybe someone else [in that situation], would [consider suicide]." Nene'na Limbong, when asked about suicidal feelings, says: "We must be patient [if there is something one desires but hasn't attained]. . . . we say [to ourselves], 'I myself will endeavor to make it happen!'" He then goes on to describe how he is in the middle of a personally trying situation regarding a debt that Paku Asu residents owe a wealthy and powerful townsperson, and how he has worked hard to come up with the money.

Nene'na Tandi(f) says that she has not had suicidal thoughts because "I'm happy, you know? People who kill themselves are those whose husbands like to go 'play' with women . . . or like to get angry . . . or like to command the household matters. . . . Those things would make us distressed [so that one would] want to commit suicide." However, Nene'na Tandi(f) has threatened to commit suicide so that her parents would allow her to marry Nene'na Tandi(m) (see Hollan and Wellenkamp n.d.).[7] To commit suicide, or even to threaten to commit suicide can be shameful for the victim's family because family members may be held liable for a suicide if their indifference to, or mistreatment of, the victim is thought to have contributed to the victim's despair. Because of notions of shared responsibility for family members' emotional states and well-being (see chapters 4 and 7), to threaten to commit suicide can be an especially effective means of mobilizing familial support and concern.

Although suicide is thought to be wrong, many people are familiar with accounts of suicide, and appear genuinely concerned lest family members or friends be placed in situations which might precipitate self-destructive behavior. Thus while suicide is negatively evaluated, it also is considered comprehensible, familiar, and even predictable.

Rates and Forms of Suicide

Official records on suicide rates and forms in Tana Toraja do not offer much information and may be unreliable. Our impression, based on our knowledge of five cases of suicide,[8] reviews of hospital records, and interviews with teachers and health and police officials, is that patterns of suicide in Tana Toraja closely resemble those reported elsewhere in the Pacific. One prevalent form found both in the Pacific and in Tana Toraja involves individuals who commit suicide after they have broken important social or moral rules of conduct. Such individuals kill themselves to avoid further public humiliation and to make amends to their families and communities. Durkheim (1951:241–76) termed this "altruistic" suicide. A second prevalent form, termed "indignant" by Hollan (1990), involves individuals who commit suicide because they feel they have been slighted, offended, or wrongfully deprived in some way, usually by a close family member.

While rates of suicide in Toraja appear to be much lower than the high rates reported for Micronesia and some other areas of Oceania (see, for example, Rubinstein 1983), the relative frequency of the two forms of suicide are similar: "indignant" suicides appear to be much more common than "altruistic" ones.

Among "altruistic" suicides in Toraja are those committed by individuals who are unable to repay their debts. Although the number of suicidal deaths linked to unpaid debts appears to be small, many people view such a situation as potentially very shameful and humiliating and possibly leading to suicide,[9] since one's ability to repay one's debts is considered a hallmark of mature, responsible adulthood. Also, the inability to repay one's debts has consequences for the debtor's family members, since their reputations are closely tied to the debtor's, and since the debtor's children eventually will become responsible for any unpaid debts.

Other situations that lead to intense feelings of shame also may precipitate "altruistic" suicides. For example, one man reportedly committed suicide because of the shame he felt for having physically abused his children, and a young, unmarried woman in a nearby village killed herself when she became pregnant.

"Indignant" suicides, which as noted above appear to be more common, involve situations in which an individual believes that he or she has been wronged by someone—often a close family member—and feeling intensely disappointed, ashamed, and angry, commits suicide.[10] The sense of having been wronged often involves the perception that one has been denied or deprived of things (or persons, such as marriage partners) that one either clearly deserves or strongly desires. The initial response to such a situation often involves passive withdrawal from, or active avoidance of, those held responsible for one's disappointment or mistreatment.

It is common, for instance, for children to run away from home when they feel that they have been mistreated by their parents (see Hollan and Wellenkamp n.d.), and adults may refuse to talk to household members or other individuals who they feel have mistreated them. Withdrawal and avoidance behaviors generally are interpreted as a sign of distress and possibly anger, and they often mobilize restitutive actions. Efforts are made to discover the source of the withdrawn person's discontent, and if necessary, to make recompense for actual or perceived slights. However, if the restitutive measures are viewed as insufficient or too slow in coming, withdrawal behavior may intensify and may lead to threats of suicide, or actual suicide attempts.

Many "indignant" suicides in Toraja involve young people whose requests (e.g., for business capital or money for schooling, etc.) have gone unheeded by family members and who consequently feel deprived.[11] From the suicide victim's perspective, that family members would ignore one's desires is especially upsetting given cultural beliefs about the dangers that unsatisfied or frustrated desires present to one's physical and mental health.[12] Having one's requests go unheeded also is upsetting to people given the value placed on reciprocal exchange in interpersonal relationships (see chapters 1 and 2). While the webs of reciprocal exchange may sometimes cause people to feel entrapped (see Hollan 1989), they also promote a strong sense of entitlement with regard to the satisfaction of one's needs.[13]

Both Indo'na Sapan and Nene'na Tandi(m) say that they have been careful in their interactions with their children so as not to precipitate suicidal responses. Indo'na Sapan says that she has heard of one case of suicide involving a young man whose parents would not give him money for schooling and "that's why I just go along with Sapan [her son, who is going to school]. . . . I have told him, 'I can't afford it.' But he . . . says, 'I want to go to school.' I say [to myself], 'Let it be [then].' " Similarly, Nene'na Tandi(m), in explaining why he doted on his only stepchild, says: "I never punished her! I gave her complete freedom! Because if I had gotten angry with her, she might have killed herself, and then I wouldn't have had any children. So she was completely free. If she asked for money, I gave it to her. [I would ask her], 'How much money do you want?' Then I would give it to her."

MENTAL DISTURBANCES

Local Views

We have noted that rumination and prolonged emotional distress are believed by the Toraja to possibly lead to physical or mental disorders. Insanity also is thought to be caused by hereditary factors, magical attacks, the repeated violation of prohibitions, the rapid acquisition of knowledge, and the possession of superior intelligence.

Locally recognized indications of mental disturbance include aggressiveness, a disheveled appearance—including the wearing of several layers of clothing—quietness, talking or laughing to oneself, and lewd joking or gestures (outside of special ritual contexts). Aggressive behavior, in particular, appears to be a salient identifying characteristic of mental disturbance for villagers (see Hollan 1984). For instance, a health officer at a local clinic said that one indication of mental disturbance was if people talked to themselves, but then he concluded by saying that truly crazy people yell, get angry, and hit others. The potential for violence on the part of disturbed individuals is something that is worrisome for villagers, as Indo'na Tiku's comments suggest: "(What do you think or feel when you see a crazy person?) We feel afraid. Afraid because later, we might be hit by them. So we must be cautious around them. We can't get too close."

Local terms reflect the belief that there are different degrees and forms of mental disturbance. For example, *to baga* refers to simpletons, *maro-maro* means "half-crazy," and *maro* and *bomboan* (from *bombo*, souls of the dead or those near death) refer to truly "crazy" individuals.[14]

Though disturbed individuals occasionally draw crowds of adults or children who may taunt or ridicule them, for the most part, such people are treated with much tolerance and cautiousness; villagers try to avoid them when possible, and otherwise try not to provoke or upset them. One informant said, You must give them whatever they want, because otherwise, they will just get angry and take whatever they want anyway. Particularly aggressive individuals, however, are restrained or placed in locked enclosures.

During our stay, we encountered a number of individuals who appeared both to us and to our Toraja companions to be mentally disturbed. These included:

A woman who appeared to be in her early thirties who was present at a ritual we attended in a nearby village. She demanded money from people, threw a stick on the ground, talked about hanging herself, and yelled at someone to go get her a machete. Supposedly she had tried to strangle her grandparent earlier that morning.

A woman who appeared to be in her middle twenties who we also encountered while attending a ritual in another village. She was dressed oddly, and apparently wanders from one celebration to the next, demanding food. More than once, some boys teased her and she chased after them with a stick.

A middle-aged man who lives near Paku Asu and is able to support himself by tending a garden. He is fairly solitary, although at a meat division, he once acted as our supporter and publicly demanded that we receive more meat. When we spoke to him on a couple of occasions, he was both more skeptical than most people, and more grandiose. For example, he said that it was not possible that in former times those who were possessed during the *ma'maro* were able to cut off their heads, as many people claim. It's not possible, he said, because he can't accomplish such a feat, and he is special, he is God.

A middle-aged man who works for, and lives with, a few different villagers, including Nene'na Limbong. One day, after drinking some palm wine, he took off his clothes in some ricefields and danced in a way characteristic of girls and young women.

In addition, there were other individuals who were identified by villagers as being disturbed in some way. These included:

A middle-aged man who became very angry at a meat division over the amount of meat he was given.

An elderly *to minaa* who is said to easily become angry and who once accused us of withholding secret knowledge.

An unknown, middle-aged man who walked through the village with an unsheathed machete.

Also, one of our respondents, Ambe'na Tangke, was viewed by at least some villagers as "crazy" or as having been "crazy." During the interviews, he described a period in his life when he claims he was attacked by a spirit during both waking and dreaming states:

When I was about to enter junior high school, I was always sick. [Once] when I was on the playing field . . . the sky looked red. Everywhere I looked, things looked red. It was a long time before I became conscious again, before I could walk. . . . (Were you frightened?) Yes, I was very frightened. I thought I had been attacked by a spirit. . . . I could feel its presence, but I couldn't see it! Sometimes it would come through the wall or from the sky. Sometimes I'd be sleeping [when the spirit attacked] and I couldn't move. I couldn't speak. [pause] (Could you see the spirit in your dream?) I couldn't see it, but I could feel it. . . . One time I grabbed its hand. I held on hard! I wanted to fight with it. I held on very hard! But it disappeared within my grasp! I never even opened my hand! [It] disappeared like the wind. . . . ([This was] when you were sleeping?) When I was sleeping. Even when there were other people [present] . . . I was the only one who was bothered [by the spirit]! Everyone else would sleep fine! (How often [did this happen]?) Oh, many times. Every month or so for several years.

Later in the interview, Ambe'na Tangke resumes his discussion of his period of illness: "(You said you saw red and yellow when the spirit came. What else did you see? What did you feel?) . . . I could see red on the walls. Everywhere I looked I saw red, yellow, different things. . . . (Were you dizzy or . . . ?) Yes! [I was] dizzy. (Did you faint?) No, I never fainted."

At this point in the interview, Ambe'na Tangke pauses for several seconds and then recalls how his father used to get angry at him and hit him on the head or push him into a wall. Although it is not entirely clear to us why Ambe'na Tangke reports this memory when he does, it seems that he draws some parallel between his experiences of being attacked by the spirit and being beaten by his father.[15]

Later, when Ambe'na Tangke is asked how he knew that it was a spirit that was attacking him, he replies:

> Oh, I was certain because when it came, I could feel it! I could feel it [even though] I couldn't see it. . . . And when the spirit came [in a dream], I couldn't speak. I couldn't move. (But you tried [to move or speak]?) Yes! I tried to move, but I couldn't. Probably the spirit left before I could move [again]. (Did you try to get up or . . . ?) Sometimes I would get up and sometimes I'd keep sleeping. Sometimes I'd struggle in my sleep. . . . When it left, I was conscious again. But when I tried to go back to sleep, it would come again! So I couldn't sleep. Finally, I became sick.

While many villagers experience spirit attack nightmares, Ambe'na Tangke's *tauan* were unusually frequent, and he is the only person who reported having such experiences during a waking state. Ambe'na Tangke says he sought treatment for his "illness" from a number of traditional healers, but claims that he was cured only after being "filled" with the Holy Spirit and joining the Pentecostal Church.

Mental disturbances are thought to be very difficult to cure, although treatments are attempted (see chapter 7).

Etic Perspectives

According to one Toraja psychiatrist, neurotic anxiety and symptoms of stress are commonly found in Tana Toraja, but psychosis is relatively infrequent. The psychiatrist was not aware of any cases of *amuk* or *latah*, but she said there were several instances of "hysteria"—which involved sudden collapses, blindness, paralysis, or instances of someone refusing to eat—among young female students (between 15 and 24 years of age) living in Rantepao. In one case, for example, a young woman fainted after watching a house burn down. After regaining consciousness, she was taken to the hospital where she refused to eat or talk. According to the psychiatrist, while her condition initially appeared serious, she recovered rapidly after being threatened with intravenous feeding and commitment at a mental hospital.

The data we collected on Toraja patients at the Rumah Sakit Jiwa (Mental Hospital) in Ujung Pandang indicated a preponderance of

patients diagnosed with "paranoid schizophrenia" and "paranoia."
There were very few patients diagnosed with depression.

A Case of Depression

Researchers interested in variations in the rate and manifestation of
depression cross-culturally (e.g., Marsella et al. 1985) have pointed out
the apparently low frequency of depression in Indonesia. In 1904,
Kraepelin reported that depression in Indonesia "when it did occur,
was usually mild and fleeting" (quoted in Marsella et al. 1985:302).
Other psychiatrically oriented researchers since have reported similar
findings (Maretzki 1981).

One of our respondents, however, has experienced a period of distress that from a Western perspective would be labeled "depressive
illness." Depressive illness in the West is identified by mood changes,
loss of appetite, sleep disturbances, diminished ability to think or con-
centrate, and by such feelings as hopelessness, guilt, and self-denigration (APA 1980:210–17; Kleinman and Good 1985).

While our respondent, Indo'na Sapan, does not report feelings of
hopelessness, guilt, and self-denigration, in other ways her experiences
appear similar to symptoms of "depressive illness." The Toraja language does not, however, have a specific term for "depression" per se,
and while Indo'na Sapan describes her experience as an "illness," she
attributes it to magic that was used against her by a man whose
romantic advances she rejected. The details of the case are as follows:

> Several years prior to our fieldwork, after Indo'na Sapan and her
> husband had divorced but when her sons were still young, In-
> do'na Sapan became very sick. She lost her appetite, she felt dizzy
> and could not think straight, and she often cried. Her mother
> prepared various foods for her in an attempt to find something
> she could eat, but she would not eat anything. "If I saw food, I
> started to cry, because I felt like vomiting if I saw food."
>
> Although she spent most of her time lying down, she slept only
> fitfully. Her whole body hurt and she felt weak and could not
> move. "How did I feel?! I wasn't comfortable. I didn't feel—I
> don't know how to describe that sickness. . . . [pause]. . . . If I
> wanted to go to church, and started to dress, I wouldn't be able
> to see. My eyes would well up with tears. Before I got that
> sickness, I was fat, very fat [healthy]. When I was still happy/
> content. But as soon as [I] started to get that illness, [I] became
> thin."

Indo'na Sapan reports that her "illness" lasted for nearly two years. Her distress was so great that she feared she was going to die. She eventually recovered, she says, when a relative took her to see a *to minaa* who diagnosed her as a victim of magic (see chapter 5), and treated her over a series of visits. The first time she went to see him, she could barely make it to his house. "I would walk a little ways, and then I would have to sit down [and then] lie down. Because I couldn't walk." After spending several nights at the healer's house, her condition greatly improved.[16] Later she returned for three shorter visits. She says that she now knows she was not meant to die then, that God had not yet let her go.[17]

While this is but a single case, it suggests the possibility that "depression" has been underreported in Indonesia. The source of evidence for the claim that depression only infrequently occurs in Indonesia has been psychiatric hospital data. However, it may be that cases of depression are not routinely brought to the attention of psychiatrists since behavior that is not aggressive or violent in nature is less likely to be viewed by others as problematic or disturbing (see above; cf. Connor 1982:253). In any case, studies of the epidemiology of depression in Indonesia have been narrowly focused and should be broadened to include unhospitalized cases outside the major urban areas.

7

COPING WITH DISORDER AND DYSPHORIA

Although villagers appear to experience a fair amount of personal distress and hardship in their lives, there are many culturally constituted means of coping with disorder and dysphoria. We have already discussed, for example, how dreams with ominous meanings can be reintepreted as having neutral or positive portents. We have also noted that there are many preventative techniques and means of increasing one's invulnerability to illness and other dangers (e.g., the use of preventative magic to guard against theft or poisoning and the use of amulets).[1] The extensive ritual life of the Toraja also offers means of coping with, or preventing, various forms of misfortune and disorder.

In this chapter, we focus on culturally prevalent means of coping used on a fairly frequent basis that have not yet been discussed.

EMOTION WORK

One common coping technique involves consciously attempting to alter one's feelings and perceptions regarding untoward and upsetting events. Villagers have several ways in which they consciously attempt to shape and manipulate their own and others' feelings and sensibilities, a process that can be thought of as a form of "emotion work" (Hochschild 1979, 1983). Hochschild (1979:561) defines emotion work as "the [deliberate and conscious] act of trying to change in degree or quality an emotion or feeling." That is, it is the active effort to evoke, shape, or suppress certain feelings—for example, trying not to feel disappointed or angry, or trying to feel happy or happier than one already is. "Emotion work" refers to the effort—the act of trying—and not to the outcome, which may or may not be successful (Hochschild 1979:561).

We begin by describing how villagers attempt to manage their own emotional states, and then turn to ways in which they seek to influence the emotional states of others.

Self-Directed Emotion Work

One prevalent technique of self-directed emotion work used by Paku Asu villagers is to remind oneself of the dangers of strong, negative emotions: that by expressing such feelings one may upset others and suffer public censure or provoke magical retaliation; that one may experience bad fortune in life as a consequence of getting angry and quarreling with others; and that by even experiencing negative emotions, one leaves oneself vulnerable to serious physical or mental illness.

Indo'na Tiku, for example, relates how she deals with her feelings of irritation and anger that arise during the course of her work as a teacher of elementary school children. According to Indo'na Tiku, since teachers are often getting angry at children,

> they often get . . . TBC [tuberculosis]. . . . So indeed . . . we must be careful about [our] anger. . . . if we can, we must limit it. [We] shouldn't always be angry. . . . (Does that mean [anger] is stored in one's heart, or is that not the case?) Actually lots of people store their anger in their hearts. . . . But I think it is better to let it out . . . (Then how is it limited?) For example . . . even if the children do something [upsetting] we just reprimand [them] but [we] don't let our hearts get hot. We must make ourselves aware/conscious. (How does one make oneself aware/conscious?) . . . for example, we want to get angry. But then we must remember, "Wah, if I get angry now, what's the use? My body will be disturbed/affected." The best thing—no matter what the children [do]—it's sufficient if [they] are well reprimanded. In order to prevent illness [in ourselves]. [Later she adds]: For example . . . if there is something that someone says to me [that she disagrees

with] and my heart starts to get *hot* [and] I want to get angry . . .
I then think within [myself], "Do I want to get angry or not?"
Wah, usually I am myself the one who makes myself aware/
conscious and then I say, "Disregard him/her!"

A second common strategy is to consciously suppress or avoid troubling thoughts or feelings. Nene'na Tandi(m), for example, says that
he tries not to think about his dead parents and grandparents, or to
visualize their faces for if he did,"I might get tuberculosis. Or go crazy.
That is how illnesses of the mind arise. Don't think [of them], don't
visualize [them]." Elsewhere, he comments:

> If people realize that someone's thinking is damaged/troubled,
> they know that that person will soon die. Everyone like that dies
> because they think/worry [too much]. . . . I always tell Nene'na
> Tandi [his wife], "Let's not think long, we must instead think of
> the time just ahead—tomorrow and the next day. . . . If we think
> at length, we'll be ruined. We, ourselves, will be ruined . . . every-
> thing will be ruined." . . . Thus, we must be quiet. . . . If you look
> at people who are thin, that arises from thinking. Anyone who is
> thin, thinks [too much].

Similarly, Indo'na Rante, when asked if she has ever felt angry at
herself, replies: "Yes, indeed. . . . But . . . I pull it back! . . . it's not
good, it will cause illness if we are angry at ourselves! It must be pulled
back."

The extent to which people attempt to avoid or suppress upsetting
thoughts and feelings was clearly demonstrated to us in the wake of
the forest fire that was started by two village boys (see chapter 4).
Although many villagers sustained losses from the fire, people in general declined to discuss the matter, saying that the deed was done and
there was no point in dwelling on it.[2]

A third common way of dealing with distressing events and feelings
is to remind oneself that the gods and ancestors, or God, assure that
people eventually get what they deserve. For example, the belief that
spiritual beings will eventually "replace" or "repay" unexpected or
unjustified losses is strongly held by some individuals. To Minaa Sattu
comments: "Imagine I had some rice and it's already harvested and
piled in the fields. I go to carry it home and discover it has been stolen.
But I don't feel loss/deprivation because the gods will exchange it, so
that things will be good/well for me." Nene'na Limbong says much the
same thing when asked if he felt anger toward a man who had cheated

him out of money: "I was not angry because later the gods will buy me an exchange. . . . That's the way it is if we are good hearted. That good heart must be returned by the gods and ancestors."

For Nene'na Tandi(m), his belief that God will replace one's losses is based on personal experience:

> Once my rice was eaten by a water buffalo. If I'm not incorrect, approximately 100 sheaves [were eaten]. Nene'na Tandi [his wife] was angry, [but] I said, "Don't be angry. It wasn't the buffalo's fault. A person [the buffalo tender] was in error, but don't [be angry]." . . . you may not believe this [but] at first I had put away [harvested and stored] 4,000 sheaves of rice. After [the rice] was eaten by the buffalo, why was it that I was able to put away 8,000 sheaves? Because I wasn't angry, I didn't order [the buffalo owner] to replace it [and so God helped me out]. . . . That's my opinion. Indeed it was [due to] God's help. He increased my [supply of] rice.

Indo'na Sapan reports that while other people have suggested that she take revenge against her ex-husband (who became involved with another woman and who, since their separation, has not provided Indo'na Sapan or her children with any income), she is content to leave the matter in God's hands. When people express surprise that she does not get angry at Ambe'na Sapan, she tells them, "I'm [just] a human, I can't respond [treat him in the way that he treated her]. Later, God will respond."

A fourth strategy involves avoiding potentially upsetting situations, and trying not to expect too much from life or strive too hard. Efforts to actively limit one's desires and so achieve a certain detachment from the world resemble Javanese efforts to be *iklas,* "not caring," and *trima,* "accepting" (Geertz 1960:241). Nene'na Tandi(m) says, for instance:

> Indeed, it is true when . . . elders say that when we are born, we already are holding our wealth [one's fate is determined at birth]. That's why I said earlier, we can't buy it [good fortune] and we can't take it by force, it can't be acquired through strength, and it can't be acquired through cleverness. It is all a gift from God. Health . . . long life, food—all of it is from God. There is not a human alive who can . . . [say], "Today I will be wealthy. Tomorrow I will be wealthy. The day after tomorrow I will be wealthy." No, that is not true. . . . Good fortune is only from God. . . . If,

for example, we deliberately try to take it . . . after awhile we'll get TBC [tuberculosis] . . . or we'll go crazy.

In handling feelings of loss and grief following a death, villagers commonly seek to remind themselves that death is inevitable. Indo'na Rante, for instance, says in reference to the deaths of one's parents, "We think, 'Wah, everyone must die. I also am going to die.' If their fate has arrived, who is going to refuse/prevent it?" Similarly, Nene'na Limbong, when discussing some of the difficulties he has experienced in life, including the deaths of his children, parents, grandparents, and first wife, says: "But I think about [how] every person [must] experience the death [of someone close to them]. Thus, yes, indeed it's their time to die."

Nene'na Tandi(m), speaking of his mother, who was a midwife skilled in massage, says:

If . . . she were still alive, she would attend to me and maybe my illness [his shortness of breath] would go away. . . . Her hands felt very sweet . . . That's why I said that if I remember my mother and father, I'll get tuberculosis. So in my opinion, it's better to [remind oneself that] indeed they've gone first, but later we must follow." [Elsewhere he says]: [while] my parents and grandparents indeed are dead . . . all humans must follow them. Even me. . . . All humans in the world, rich and poor, all will die. There aren't any who won't. Indeed they went first, but we must follow behind them. That's my opinion. If there is a dead person, everyone cries, but I don't! Because my opinion is that we all must die! . . . [If I] cry, [they'll] die, [if I] don't cry, [they'll] die [so it is better not to get upset].

At another time, Nene'na Tandi(m) discusses how he feels some regret because he was never able to provide for his parents as they had provided for him when he was a child, but that he knows there is nothing he can do about the fact that they are no longer alive: "Everything . . . like flowers . . . once it is old, it withers . . . That's how it is with humans, [too]. So it [the deaths of his parents] doesn't surprise me. And as I've told you before . . . it's not necessary for us to remember them, or to feel sad. Because . . . we all will follow . . . We just don't know when."

People also may remind themselves that others also experience death and misfortune. Ambe'na Toding, who has had several children die, reports:

Often it happens that I feel upset/hurt [about his children's deaths].
I usually say, "I'm not alone. Lots of other people are like that
[have had children die]." That's medicine [for me]. If . . . I were
to think about it [the deaths], probably I would be dead [by now].
[I would be] thin if I were to think of that, but— but lots of
people, lots of people throughout the world [have suffered losses].
. . . Indeed [I have] many hurt . . . feelings, but what can one do?
We are not the ones who have power [over such things].

Is it fair to describe the techniques and strategies discussed above as
forms of emotion "work," implying an expenditure of effort or energy
on the part of the actor? Our interview material strongly suggests that
respondents *do* expend much effort in managing their mental states.
The remarkable degree of emotional equanimity that villagers display
in their daily behavior involves much effort and vigilance and is not,
we believe, easily achieved (cf. Wikan 1991).

Other-Directed Emotion Work

Villagers may also seek to influence the emotional states of others, not
only indirectly (for example, by being respectful and polite and avoiding conflict), but also directly (for example, by taking measures to
facilitate others' efforts to remain calm and "conscious"). The particular strategies that are used depend to a certain extent on the situation
and the nature of the person's feelings.

In a society in which the open expression of negative or unpleasant
emotions is uncommon outside of certain special contexts, in order to
influence another's emotional state, one must first be sensitive to indirect cues that may indicate that someone is upset. It is our impression
that in the case of anger at least, villagers tend to overlabel signs of
distress in others. The strategy seems to be, Better to overdetect anger
in others than to underdetect it, and possibly risk exacerbating the
situation.

Once someone has been identified as being "angry," a common
response is to leave him or her alone. Ambe'na Toding states the basic
strategy:

For example, if there is an angry person, don't stay there [with
him or her]. We must go and hide ourselves first. They must be
cool before we return. They must already be calm/quiet. Because
no human is calm/quiet once they have become angry. So we
must hide ourselves first. Don't stay there, even if they order us

to stay! Because they are still angry. Don't stay with someone
who has already become hot or angry.

An avoidance strategy is used in many contexts, both public and
private. Nene'na Tandi(m) says of a meat division, for example:

That's why elders say that if someone gets up and starts speaking
coarsely, we can't respond! We must be silent. He/She [the angry
person] will . . . make him/herself aware/conscious. But if we
respond, then even coarser words will be spoken. . . . That's why
people say, "Wait first [before responding to the angry person]
. . . " Ah, then he/she thinks, "Oh yes . . . I was wrong." But if
he/she is right away [challenged], indeed, he/she becomes hot
again. That's why it's smarter to wait first [before responding].

The same principles apply in private contexts. Nene'na Tandi(m)
says of his wife:

So if I see that she has already become angry, it is better if I go
out [leave the house] first. If we want to improve things, we leave
for an hour or half an hour before returning. But if we want her
to get more angry, we just sit. That is like fanning a fire. But if
she is angry [and we leave], that is like putting water on a fire;
the fire must die. So when Nene'na Tandi is angry, usually I
immediately leave. When I return, she laughs [and asks], "Why
did you run away earlier?" I reply, "Wah, I knew that you were
like fire." That's how it must be before a household is quiet/
peaceful.

Most people seem to be grateful when others leave them alone when
they are angry. Indo'na Tiku, for instance, says of her former husband:

He often came to the house to visit the children. But . . . if there
were words [he said] that offended me, oh, my heart would get
hot again. But if he felt that my heart was getting hot again, right
away he would become silent. He would not respond [pause].
Indeed, that's the way it was when we were still together [still
married]. If he saw that I was starting to get angry, he would go
somewhere else, in order to hide [pause]. When he felt that [I]
was probably quiet/calm again, he'd return to the house. That
was his way. How was I going to get angry if he left?! Indeed . . .
he was a good man. A patient/sober man.

Indo'na Rante is unusual in that she reports feeling frustrated when
her husband fails to respond to her anger:

When I am angry at [my children's] father, and I'm not yet satisfied, I want to speak my mind, [but] he runs before [I can] . . . then I'm not happy, Belo! I'd be happy if for example we sat [down] and I said, "Don't you act that way!" . . . But how can I tell him if he immediately runs away?! Because . . . he doesn't want to hear an angry person. That's the way it is if I'm momentarily angry or if I reprimand the children, he leaves. . . . I'm not happy with that. . . . If I [begin to] argue . . . he thinks, "Be angry by yourself." I'm not happy with that [she laughs]. Sometimes I don't talk [to him] for an entire day.

If physical avoidance is not possible when someone is angry, then eye contact usually is avoided. Although this is not an explicitly stated strategy, on the few occasions when we were present when someone was visibly angry, other people tended to avoid eye contact with the angry person, and the angry person him- or herself also tended to look away from, or past others.

Also, once angry persons have regained composure, onlookers feel that it is incumbent upon them to insist upon a reconciliation between the angered parties. As Nene'na Tandi(m) says: "If we know that A has been angry with B, right away we will visit them and publicly repair [reconcile] them, so that there is peace. Because we feel that if there is a rift in the village, everything is ruined!"

With sad or grieving individuals, the techniques are somewhat different. Of primary importance is that others in the community demonstrate their solidarity with a misfortunate or bereaved individual, that they help to distract the individual, and that they provide him or her with verbal advice. Indo'na Rante explains:

If there is someone who has died . . . it's important for Toraja [that] we gather there [at the deceased's house] . . . We converse so that the person who has experienced the death is consoled. So that he/she doesn't continuously think troubling thoughts. . . . [People] talk about inconsequential things so that his/her thinking is divided [between] listening to the people who are relating [something], and thinking of the person who died.

Nene'na Tandi(m), in particular, stresses the importance of providing advice to those who are troubled or upset. When he asks about American death practices and is told that Americans in comparison to Toraja do not have as much contact with the remains of the deceased, he says:

Oh, indeed, people who don't want to see the deceased again . . . are "dizzy.". . . Why? Because they feel their loss. In America, doesn't anyone give advice [to the bereaved] . . . ? (Yes, it's good when that happens.) Yes. So that you can know a little about my opinions—[I think that] . . . when you return to America and someone dies, [the relatives] should be "medicated/treated." . . . Even if it's someone you don't know, their heart must be medicated/treated. They can't be treated with money! They can't be treated with gold, only with the mouth [with words]. That's the most powerful medicine [there is]! . . . If . . . someone has died, and we bring pigs . . . water buffalo [to the funeral], those are debts. . . . But if we give deep understanding [or] good advice [to the deceased's relatives], that's what they can consume, more so than buffalo, more so than gold.

In a later interview, Nene'na Tandi(m) returns to this topic:

For thinking/ruminating, there is no medicine. . . . Even according to the [westernized] doctor . . . there's no medicine, except for injecting them so they'll sleep. . . . Or, as I've told you before, we give them [people who are troubled] advice as a treatment. . . . We coax/flatter them . . . so that their heart is quiet, their thinking is healthy, ah that is effective. But when people . . . realize that, 'Oh, this person's thinking is damaged,' and they just watch [and don't offer any advice], [the person] will quickly die.

That sad or troubled people appreciate such efforts on the part of others is indicated by Nene'na Tandi(f)'s comments:

(If someone experiences a death, are they happier if lots of people come to the house, or would they prefer to be alone?) Eee, it's not good to be alone. If lots of people come, it consoles [one's] heart, what a pity. Yes, [one] doesn't feel good if no one comes. That's why people here, Belo . . . [think], "We must befriend everyone." Because of that—if something upsetting happens [a death] and no one comes [to the house], [it is because] we like to get angry at others! . . . [But if we befriend others], people will remember us, they will say, "What a pity, that person has a good heart, let's go sit with him/her.". . . So it's better if we are nice toward everyone. . . . [Otherwise], when something upsetting happens, no will look at us, not even with one eye.

MAKING AMENDS

While techniques of "emotion work" are used on a daily basis in an ongoing effort to maintain one's mental and physical health in the face of upsetting events and to maintain smooth interpersonal relationships with others, when misfortune of a greater magnitude arises—for example, illness, the death of livestock, the death of one's children—additional coping and restitutive measures are taken.

From a traditional or Alukta perspective, an individual's illness or misfortune may be associated with problematic social and spiritual relationships, which may be addressed through ritual means. While many Alukta rituals have the cure or prevention of illness as one of their aims (e.g., the *ma'bua'*, the *ma'bugi'*), one ceremony in particular, *massuru'*, is focused on absolution. The word *suru'* means "comb." In the context of atonement, "combing" figuratively describes the process whereby the disorder resulting from moral transgression is disentangled, straightened out, and ordered; the term also suggests that the process is a purification or cleansing, as one's hair and scalp are cleaned in the process of grooming. As the disentangling metaphor suggests, it is thought that some forms of illness or misfortune only can be cured or addressed by "straightening out" any disordered social and moral relations (cf. Watson-Gegeo and White 1990).[3]

The essential elements in the management of misfortune from an Alukta perspective are confession and sacrifice. When Alukta villagers engage in wrongdoing, they may immediately seek to correct the mistake, or they may wait until some misfortune occurs. In either case, a ritual specialist often is called so that the person may confess and perform a sacrifice if need be. By so doing, villagers hope to either prevent misfortune in the future, or avoid further calamity. Ambe'na Toding explains:

(What happens if someone makes a mistake but doesn't acknowledge it?) Oh, he/she must acknowledge it, because he/she is frightened. He/She . . . is frightened of the ancestors, or of religion, or of the *aluk*. So we are frightened. . . . (Why are you frightened?) We are frightened because if we have a promise [from spiritual beings that they will respond to misdeeds], we must feel/experience [misfortune] in our life. So indeed, we are frightened. . . . We are frightened that later [their] promise to us [to punish wrongdoers] will strike us. . . . So [we] must always acknowledge [mistakes] or ask forgiveness, so that whatever the promise is, [it doesn't strike] our family or household. If we don't acknowledge [our mistakes], and then there is a promise [calamity], we really feel it, "Oh, here it is [the punishment]." So in order to avoid that possibility, we acknowledge [our mistakes].

In some cases, however, villagers who have experienced misfortune are not certain what mistakes, if any, they have committed. In such instances, a *to minaa* or other specialist may be asked to help identify their transgressions through a process called *dipesaluan* (roughly translated as "the enumeration of mistakes"). As Nene'na Tandi(m) comments, the ritual specialist delves into the private corners of the afflicted person's life:

> If there are mistakes, the village people [Alukta adherents] must look for them until they are found, beginning at the "roots" all the way to the "leaves." . . . [They] start looking on the "outside" [of the afflicted] and then move to the "inside." Everything must be opened [to inspection]! . . . [They search] his/her legs, hands, eyes, mouth, [and] heart. Everything must be inspected! . . . [They] say, "Have you ever hit anyone?" And he/she will reply, "Yes, I have." "Have you ever abused people?" "I have." "Have you ever slandered someone?" "Yes.". . . So that's why I say [they] begin with his/her legs and arms and go to his/her eyes [looking for mistakes]. . . . Village people may even start [looking from the time the afflicted person was young] . . . until the sickness arose. . . . For example, maybe he/she threw [something at] someone when he/she was young and he/she must be sick before he/she will acknowledge it. . . . Indeed, everything is opened up [for inspection].

Part of the examination consists of the specialist asking the afflicted person whether he or she has ever committed particular mistakes. According to Ambe'na Toding, "[the person is told], 'Don't talk nonsense [tell the truth]. If you talk nonsense, you'll be burned in a fire.' That's *disumpa'* [to be interrogated]." But the specialist also interviews neighbors and family members in an attempt to gather a complete list of the person's misdeeds. In this way, the process allows individuals the opportunity to confess and right any wrongs that they may feel they have committed, and it potentially helps to improve community relationships.

Sometimes someone other than the afflicted person is identified as the wrongdoer. As noted previously, one's own misfortune is thought to be possibly caused by other people's—such as family members' or predecessors'—misdeeds. Ambe'na Toding provides an example:

> If people are crazy, very often it [insanity] is from their ancestors. Indeed, there were mistakes committed previously, for example, incest . . . and it may be many years—hundreds of years, thousands of years—before grandchildren or children are struck [become afflicted with insanity]. [Then people say], "Oh, indeed, our ancestors committed this or that mistake."[4]

Of the three *dipesaluan* that were conducted during our stay in Paku Asu, in one, a man's agricultural difficulties were attributed to the fact that one of his ancestors had sold his wife into slavery. In the second instance, a woman's insanity was found to be partly due to her having shaken her breast at her child (*dirodan susu*), a prohibited gesture interpreted as a curse. And in the third, a woman (Indo'na Rante's older sister) was said to be suffering from an eye disorder due in part to a visiting relative who had unwittingly violated a food taboo.

If the transgression, once identified, is not particularly serious, confession alone may be sufficient. Ambe'na Toding comments:

> All [mistakes] . . . are not the same. There are big ones and small ones. Likewise [sometimes] pigs [are required as a sacrifice] and [sometimes] chickens. [Sometimes] just the mouth alone! [So we] just acknowledge them. . . ."I have made a mistake." . . . [And we] are already cleansed. The point is, [we] have already acknowledged [the mistake].

To Minaa Sattu also says that confession alone may be adequate: "if there is a sick person and we [*to minaa*] are called to their house, we must go. We go their house and ask them questions. They reply, 'I made this mistake, I made that mistake.' They acknowledge their mistakes . . . [and] then they are well."

When the mistakes are of a more serious nature, however, a sacrifice is required. A major violation is seen as a debt that must be paid. The magnitude of the mistake determines the nature of the sacrifice. Also, larger sacrifices are required of high status, wealthy individuals and religious functionaries, since misbehavior on their part may have widespread consequences. To Minaa Sattu explains:

> For example, if we *to minaa* did things like that [adultery], all the crops would die. Pigs would die. Buffalo would die. So people would say [if there were a major catastrophe], "Oh, a *to minaa*

must have caused this [by his misbehavior]." The rice would be eaten by rats. . . . Bananas would be eaten by rats. Corn would also be destroyed. And the buffalo would all die. And the pigs and chickens. . . . So we are strict with the *to minaa* and rich people in the village. It's like poison [if high status people misbehave]. If *to minaa* were to do those things [misbehave], all prosperity would decline!

Once a mistake has been acknowledged and, if necessary, a sacrifice made, the wrongdoer is considered to be "as clean as a plate" (*masero pindan*). While the cleansing, sanctifying aspect of absolution is important, it is also important to note its pragmatic, somewhat mechanical tone. Ambe'na Toding, says, for example, "If we have already acknowledged [our mistakes] . . . asked forgiveness for our mistakes, we are already free of them. If we have acknowledged them, we are free. In other words, we've already paid our debt! . . . If we have already paid . . . it [the matter] is finished." At another time he remarks: "In the traditional religion, when there are people who make mistakes, questions are asked . . . in order to look for the mistakes. . . . So indeed, we have a medicine. What's the medicine? Those pigs and chickens that are burned/roasted [sacrificed] . . . so that the illness is cured."

The pragmatic tone of absolution is in keeping with the nature of the relationships among humans, gods, and ancestors that it seeks to repair. These relationships are based on reciprocal obligations which often concern, or are expressed in terms of, exchange.

Christian Responses

We noted in chapter 1 that some Christians, such as Nene'na Tandi(m), mistrust those who say that Christians need not abide by any of the traditional taboos. Similarly, Nene'na Tandi(m) doubts that Christian absolution is as thorough or efficacious as *Alukta* practices. When Christian villagers become sick, they may call together the minister and fellow church members to pray for them, something that Nene'na Tandi(m) has done four times in his adult life. According to Nene'na Tandi(m), the minister asks the ill person where he or she feels sick, how long he or she has felt sick, and so on, but in contrast to Alukta practices, he does *not* ask any personal questions about the sins or mistakes the person may have committed. Instead, he merely calls upon church members to pray for the sick person's recovery.

Nene'na Tandi(m) says that such a perfunctory examination allows

Christians "to hide their mistakes in their pockets" and he implies that this lack of rigor leaves open the possibility of continued illness and misfortune. From his perspective, it is only the public acknowledgement of wrongdoing and the disentangling and reordering of troubled social and spiritual relations which this acknowledgement promotes, that insures a return to individual and community well-being. Nene'na Tandi(m) explains:

> Village people [Alukta adherents] must look for [a mistake] until they find it, beginning from the roots all the way to the leaves [from foot to head]. But Christians don't, [they] only ask, "What kind of sickness do you have?" He/She may say, "I have a fever, I have a headache, I have a cough." After that, we just pray. . . . But it could be said that [this procedure] is not right. Why do I say not right? Because this questioning only looks on the outside [of the afflicted person], not the inside. The village [Alukta] people, it is true, start on the outside, too, but they also look on the inside. They open everything for inspection. We Christians just look with [our] eyes [perform a superficial examination]. . . . But village people [not only] look with their eyes, but search within the heart. . . . But we Christians don't! That's why I say that Christians store their sins in their pockets.

Like Nene'na Tandi(m), Ambe'na Toding also sees Christian means of absolution as less efficacious than Alukta ones. Ambe'na Toding, a Pentecostal who was an Alukta adherent for several years, says that when he is sick, he thinks about what mistakes he has committed so that he can acknowledge them to God.

> But if I admit one [mistake] there are ten more [that I have committed and haven't acknowledged]. So then what [he laughs]? The thing is . . . with the traditional religion, no matter how many mistakes there are, if we sacrifice a chicken or a pig, everything is well again. . . . Even if there are thousands of mistakes, we finish all of them. . . . No matter how many mistakes, we sacrifice a pig and acknowledge our mistakes . . . "I have this mistake, I have that mistake," and everything is well.

The shift among Christians to private confession and absolution is not a trivial change. Its immediate effect is that those experiencing illness and misfortune may not feel "absolved" of their mistakes and may lack a sense of reassurance that one's fortune will improve. The long-term effect probably will be an increase in a sense of personal as opposed to collective responsibility for people's health and well-being, and a shift away from the belief that others—human or spiritual—are either affected by one's misdeeds, or can be of assistance in times of stress.

OTHER APPROACHES TO HEALING

Several of our respondents have sought the services of a traditional healer (*to ma'dampi*) at some point in their lives. Indo'na Tiku, for example, went to a healer following her divorce when—contrary to cultural expectations—she continued to feel upset by it. A healer also once treated her when shortly after giving birth to her last child she felt nauseated and disoriented: "I just wanted to remain quiet in a dark room. I couldn't look at the daylight. If I did, I wanted to vomit. Wah, three weeks I [felt] that way. . . . I didn't want to eat; I didn't want to get up." Three times a small fire was built under the frame of her bed so that smoke enveloped her body. Only then, she says, did she begin to feel better. Also, Indo'na Sapan, Indo'na Rante, and Nene'na Tandi(m) each have been treated by healers for illnesses thought to be caused by magic.

In addition to a small number of midwives and bone setters, there are three persons in Paku Asu who have gained reputations as traditional healers. Two of these healers, in addition to treating ordinary illnesses (*saki biasa*), also specialize in the treatment of magically induced illnesses (*saki to lino*). One, Ne' Pare, says that he acquired his healing powers from an ancestor who came to him in a dream he had as a young man. The ancestor told him that he must mix soil with water and then say a spell over the mixture. This medicine, he was told, could treat most illnesses, except those caused by the *deata*. Ne' Pare says that there are many symptoms that might indicate magical causes: peculiar-smelling sweat and body excretions, yellow feces, teary eyes, and vomiting. He says that he cannot know with certainty if someone is suffering from magic until he has examined their body excretions after they have been treated with his magical water.

Ne' Atu says that he also acquired his healing powers in a dream, but from the *deata* rather than an ancestor. Among his talents is the ability to "know" immediately whether or not someone has been victimized by magic. He cannot, however, explain how this knowledge works. Like Ne' Pare, he uses one treatment for all illnesses, regardless of their cause—although he, too, is unable to treat *saki deata*. His treatment consists of massaging various parts of the body, paying particular attention to the head and stomach, while chewing *pangngan* and blowing on his patients.

The third healer, To Beluak, says that she acquired her healing and prophecy powers directly from *Puang Matua* (the creator deity in Alukta belief), who presented her with a gift of matted locks when she was around twenty years of age.[5] Unlike the other two healers, To Beluak claims that during sleep her soul is often in contact with the *deata* and the upperworld, which is why she must avoid all activities associated with death or funerals.[6] To Beluak claims to foretell the future by reading the markings of split areca nuts. She uses the same method to determine whether an illness is "ordinary" or caused by the *deata*. To cure *saki deata,* she orders chickens to be sacrificed. To cure *saki biasa,* she massages sick persons with an amulet (a monkey's hand) and/or splashes them with water that has been in contact with her matted locks.[7]

A variety of herbs and leaves are also commonly used for healing purposes.[8]

Generally, villagers are pragmatic when seeking the aid of healers. They may begin by asking an Alukta specialist or Christian minister to help them atone for any mistakes they may have committed, but if this fails to identify the cause of their distress or fails to ameliorate their symptoms, villagers may then seek the advice of other types of healers. However, the reverse also may occur: treatment by a healer or local health officer may precede that of a *to minaa* or minister.

In contrast to the more public proceedings of a *dipesaluan,* other healing encounters in the Paku Asu area (apart from rituals such as *ma'bua'* and *ma'bugi'*) are relatively informal, private affairs. A healer is approached and asked for a treatment for which he or she is generally well known. If the afflicted person improves, the healer is usually credited with the cure. But if the person does not improve, the healer's reputation is rarely tarnished, since it is usually assumed that the illness and the treatment simply were not well suited to one another. Healers are not expected to cure all afflictions, only certain types.

8

CULTURE AND EXPERIENCE IN TORAJA

The traditional approach of cultural anthropology, having as one of its primary goals a reliable account of differential modes of life found among the peoples of the world, has not been directly concerned with the behavior of individuals. It has been culture-centered, rather than behavior-centered. . . . No matter how reliable such data are, or whatever their value for comparative and analytic studies of *culture*, of necessity the material is presented from the standpoint of the outside observer. Presented to us in this form, these cultural data do not easily permit us to apprehend, in an integral fashion, the most significant and meaningful aspects of the world of the individual as experienced by him and in terms of which he thinks, is motivated to act, and satisfies his needs.   (Hallowell 1955:88; emphasis in original)

In this book, we have focused not on the elaborate culture and ritual of the Toraja per se, but rather on how Toraja life is viewed and experienced from the individual's perspective. We have done this for both ethnographic and theoretical reasons. From an ethnographic point of view, person-centered ethnographies of non-Western peoples are few in number; and several of those that are available focus on the life of a single individual (e.g., Crapanzano 1980; Shostak 1981). The detailed transcript material we present here has enabled us to highlight shared aspects of personal experience, while at the same conveying a sense of the individuality of each of our respondents. It also demonstrates that the personal experiences of Toraja individuals, whether shared or idiosyncratic, may clash with cultural expectations as well as be consistent with them.

The theoretical importance of this approach is suggested by the quotation cited at the head of this chapter. As Hallowell (1955:88) points out, an anthropological analysis focused on traditional cultural concerns and categories does not necessarily provide insight into "the most significant and meaningful aspects of the world of the individual as *experienced* by him and in terms of which he thinks, is motivated to act, and satisfies his needs" (emphasis added). We believe that it is important to investigate the emotional and cognitive "saliency" (Spiro 1984) or "directive force" (D'Andrade 1984) of cultural beliefs and symbols for particular actors. That is, the extent to which cultural beliefs and practices shape individuals' experience and behavior needs to be actively examined, rather than merely assumed. It is also important to realize that some aspects of a culture may be more instrumental in shaping personal experience than others, and that individuals may differ in the extent to which they "internalize" particular aspects of a culture.

In our research we have explored such issues by asking individual respondents to reflect upon their life experiences, and by observing the ways in which they use cultural beliefs and symbols to represent and make sense of their experiences. The emphasis throughout the present work has been on viewing anthropological subjects as actors, actively and creatively engaged in the construction of meaning, rather than as passive recipients of a cultural tradition.

What, then—to summarize briefly—are some of the personally salient aspects of life as experienced by the people of Paku Asu, especially our eleven respondents? For ease of exposition, we list a number of themes and topics discussed in the foregoing chapters, though the ordering is not meant to imply relative importance or saliency.

1. The cultural emphasis on "order," constraint, and smooth interpersonal relationships is highly valued on an individual, experiential level.

2. Optimal social and emotional relations (including those with spiritual beings) take much personal and collective effort to maintain, and individuals consciously experience more anger, distress, etc., than they express.

3. People strongly value cooperation and unity in village life, but they also have concerns about whether others can be trusted and relied upon for support, and they often worry that their own reputations as good citizens may be unfairly impugned.

4. Occasional periods of "disorder" are culturally encouraged but only some individuals participate, and in some instances there is conscious ambivalence about participating.

5. There is a strong cognitive orientation to the world, as exemplified in the many cognitive strategies used to manage emotions and by the appreciation of intelligence, cleverness, and riddles.

6. From an etic perspective, gender differences are relatively muted among the Toraja; emically, however, some gender differences are identified (regarding, for instance, cleverness and emotional experience).

7. While many individuals seem to strongly believe the cultural notion that one's fate is predetermined, they also believe that their fortunes are contingent upon their own efforts and "sacrifices" (both literal and metaphoric) and many strive hard to achieve good fortune (e.g., many people delay immediate gratification in order to achieve long range material, ritual, and educational goals).

8. Many villagers are concerned about status and seek to improve or maintain their position in the local status system through mostly indirect, symbolic ways. Some, however, like Nene'na Tandi(m), are no longer personally invested in traditional ways of marking status (e.g., through meat divisions at rituals).

9. In contradistinction to the desire for status, people also strongly value sharing and equality, especially in informal, everyday contexts and with close family members, and many find themselves torn between their desire for renown and the need to share (cf. Marcus 1978).

10. Despite the fact that many individuals continue to feel a strong obligation to participate in the traditional ritual system, many also report that their ritual obligations weigh heavily upon them, especially in combination with their responsibilities to provide for, and educate, their children.

11. Most villagers perceive life as being hard, and many speak of happiness and contentment as the occasional and fleeting absence of suffering and hardship.

12. Perhaps because of their awareness of suffering and hardship, people enjoy laughter and humor, and highly value advice from those who can make them laugh, or help them place their suffering in philosophical and religious perspective.

13. A sense of vulnerability and of being "acted upon" by outside forces is common, as are the use of traditional techniques designed to increase one's invulnerability.

14. When untoward events occur, there are ways of coping with them that do not put undo stress or blame on the self; people do not, for the most part, judge themselves harshly or seek to change themselves in fundamental ways.

15. While villagers are by no means unaware of the anger and hostility they sometimes feel toward others and which they assume others sometimes feel toward them, there appear to be aggressive as-

pects of the self that become organized outside of conscious awareness and that gain expression only indirectly (e.g., in possession trance behavior, kickfights, cockfights and buffalo fights, and dreams).

16. There is a tendency toward modesty and self-deflation in public (to avoid arousing envy and resentment, and to solicit nurturance and assistance), and toward self-inflation in private contexts and in dreams and fantasy.

17. As in many sociocentric societies, there are many contexts in which villagers closely identify with others, yet there are also occasions and contexts in which people assert their autonomy and protest vigorously when it is challenged.

In the remainder of this chapter, we explore a few of these key themes in greater detail. These are: the emphasis on social harmony and nonagression that coexists with interpersonal cautiousness and mistrust; the importance of emotional constraint, and the role of "emotion work" in maintaining such contraint; and, finally, the emphasis on suffering.

We have indicated that while behaviorally in Toraja there is much reciprocity and mutual aid, and little overt violence and aggression, experientially many individuals are cautious and mistrustful of others. As we suggested in chapter 5, these are not unrelated. The cultural emphasis on sharing, on nonaggressivity, and on openness exacerbates people's concerns about the motives and intents of others, since the more villagers are encouraged to cooperate with and assist one another, the more they tend to guard their own (threatened) interests. This in turn heightens people's fear of gossip and the use of retaliatory magic and it makes necessary an even greater emphasis on the ethic of giving, sharing, and mutual assistance.

This combination of marked social interdependency coupled with interpersonal cautiousness and tension in at least some contexts is not unique to the Toraja. Foster, for example, argues that it is typical generally of peasant societies, in which people perceive themselves as competing over limited resources. When, according to Foster (1965:302), an individual or family perceives that it can improve its position only at the expense of others,

> each minimal social unit (often the nuclear family and, in many situations, a single individual) sees itself in perpetual, unrelenting struggle with its fellows for possession or control over what it considers to be its share of scarce values. This is a position that calls for extreme caution and reserve, a reluctance to reveal true strength or position. It encourages

suspicion and mutual distrust, since things will not necessarily be what they seem to be.

It is also a situation that leads those who improve their lot to fear the envy and resentment of others, and one that leads those who are less fortunate to fear that they will be accused of gossiping about or employing other covert means of retaliation, whether or not they have in fact committed such acts.

Another, perhaps complementary, explanation for the existence of such social and personal tensions in Toraja is suggested by Edgerton (1971), who links the avoidance of direct conflict and interpersonal caution and anxiety to ecological variables. According to Edgerton, agriculturalists in the four East African cultures he investigated place a premium on the avoidance of direct conflict and on the promotion of social unity because they must live together on finite land resources, and because agriculturalists, unlike pastoralists, cannot physically disengage from their neighbors when disputes arise, but rather must remain sedentary in order to protect and cultivate their land. However, the caution, secrecy, and emotional constraint that result from the avoidance of direct conflict, together with the use of indirect forms of aggression such as gossip and witchcraft, in themselves generate anxiety and hostility (Edgerton 1971:275–76).

Hooper (1975) links the avoidance of hostility and violence, interpersonal cautiousness, and tentativeness to a third important variable. He argues that when, as in Tahiti, people are embedded in highly "multiplex" relationships—that is, when they are *simultaneously* related to the same relatively restricted set of individuals through ties of propinquity, religion, land ownership, kinship, marriage, gender, and broad age divisions—then generally speaking, they "do not directly oppose the actions of others and avoid confrontations whose only outcome can mean that one 'wins' all while the other 'loses.' Indirection and subtlety are called for. A second characteristic is that aggressiveness is very strictly controlled and down-played, as is its counterpart, individualism" (Hooper 1975:374). This is because:

> The open expression of anger and hostility in such a system has widespread ramifications. If directed by one person against a single other, then it affects not only the one aspect (or strand) of their relationship which might have provoked the reaction, but also all other strands of the relationship, which may then be seen as feeding back on one another. And it is also practically impossible for only two people to be involved. By the very nature of the situation the reaction must spread through the whole panoply of cliques, factions and coalitions, thus involving impli-

cations which are almost impossible to predict—even for those with life-long training in the calculus of such matters. A crucial feature here is that neither the angered person nor the person against whom the anger is directed, has room to move out of the social field, in the way that, for example, an urban worker may move to another job after a quarrel with boss or workmates, without disturbing unduly his or her other meaning-ful relationships. The open expression of anger is thus acutely disfunctional.

(Hooper 1975:376)

All three of the above explanations could apply to the Toraja, most of whom are peasant farmers involved in multiplex social relationships. These explanations, however, focus specifically on the avoidance of overt violence and aggression and interpersonal cautiousness. They do not, then, help to explain the more general emotional reserve that is also characteristic of the Toraja.

The Toraja share their controlled, reserved demeanor with a number of Malaysian and Indonesian groups. Several social and cultural factors appear to contribute to the prevalence of reserved demeanor in this particular culture area. Hollan suggests a number of these:

the commitment to and internalization of religious and cultural values that stress social harmony, cooperation, patience, and acceptance (C. Geertz 1976; Bonokamsi 1972); the role of complex patterns of etiquette and respectful behavior . . . (C. Geertz 1976; H. Geertz 1961); childrear-ing and enculturative practices that lead to behavioral patterns of passive withdrawal or fearful avoidance, and fear of intense emotional arousal, rather than to patterns of active assertion and aggression (Bateson and Mead 1942; H. Geertz 1961; Denton 1978; Robarchek 1977); illness beliefs that link the experience and/or expression of disturbing emotions to serious physical and mental ailments (H. Geertz 1961); and the impor-tance of dissociative mechanisms in splitting anger off from conscious awareness and limiting outwardly aggressive acts to circumscribed, well-controlled ritual or illness contexts (Bateson and Mead 1942; Connor 1979; Suryani 1984; Lee 1981; Hollan 1984).   (Hollan 1988a:52–53)

While other authors have highlighted the above factors when dis-cussing emotional and behavioral constraint in Indonesia and Malay-sia, we have in addition highlighted here the importance of "emotion work" (cf. Wikan 1991). It is our belief that the placidity of day-to-day behavior often requires active, conscious efforts to maintain, and fol-lowing Hochschild (1979, 1983), we have referred to such efforts as "emotion work."

According to Hochschild, the concept of "emotion work" fills a conceptual gap which exists between the approach of Freud, on the one hand, and that of Erving Goffman, on the other. Freud concentrates on what one might also call "emotion work," but it is work that is performed unconsciously and involuntarily through defense mechanisms, such as repression. Goffman, on the other hand, in his work on impression management (1959), concentrates on the management of one's outward behavior. He implies that managing one's behavioral displays (including displays of emotion) is accomplished fairly automatically, without much conscious effort or thought. The "actors" in Goffman's accounts "actively manage outer impressions, but they do not actively manage inner feelings" (Hochschild 1979:557). Hochschild, however, argues that to be successful at displaying the socially appropriate emotions at the appropriate times often requires "deep acting." She notes:

> The actor Goffman proposes does not seem to feel much, is not attuned to, does not monitor closely or assess, does not actively evoke, inhibit, shape—in a word *work on* feelings in a way an actor would have to do to accomplish what Goffman says is, in fact, accomplished in one encounter after another. We are left knowing about . . . [the] result, but knowing nothing of the process or techniques by which it is achieved.
> (Hochschild 1979:557, emphasis in original)

Hochschild (1979:562) outlines three general techniques of emotion work:

> One is *cognitive:* the attempt to change images, ideas, or thoughts in the service of changing the feelings associated with them. A second is *bodily:* the attempt to change somatic or other physical symptoms of emotion (e.g., trying to breath slowly, trying not to shake). Third, there is *expressive* emotion work: trying to change expressive gestures in the service of changing inner feeling (e.g., trying to smile, or to cry). This differs from simple display in that it is directed toward change in feeling. It differs from bodily emotion work in that the individual tries to alter or shape one or another of the classic public channels for the expression of feeling.   (emphasis in original)

Toraja individuals use all three techniques of emotion work at various times, yet cognitive techniques are the most highly developed and utilized ones (e.g., trying not to think about troubling thoughts).

While Hochschild recognizes that emotion work may be directed either toward the self or others (1979:562), she does not develop this distinction, and most of her examples (which are from the United States) are of self-directed emotion work. This may be because in a predominantly egocentric society like the United States—where ideally, people are "self-sufficient" and "autonomous"—other-directed emotion work remains relatively undeveloped. In contrast, the Toraja—who encourage a close identification of self with significant others throughout the life course—devote considerable efforts to managing the emotions of others as well as their own.

It is our guess that individuals in all or most societies engage to some degree in "emotion work," and that both self-directed, or "autocentric," emotion work as well as other-directed, or "allocentric," emotion work are used to some extent, although this obviously is an area of inquiry that needs further attention by psychocultural anthropologists. We would expect, however, that the relative emphasis placed on emotion work, and on the various techniques and forms, would vary considerably depending on cultural values, aspects of the self, and other social and cultural variables.

Last, what are we to make of our respondents' and informants' frequent talk of suffering? This is a complex issue. As we noted in the introduction to part 2, some of people's talk of hardship may be characterized as a rhetoric of suffering, which is self-consciously used to enlist the aid and sympathy of others or to avoid arousing their envy and resentment. In some respects, then, talk of hardship and suffering in Toraja is similar to the "rhetoric of complaint" found in many Mediterranean societies. As Gaines and Farmer (1986:305) describe it:

> One seeks to minimize the perceived risk of falling prey to supernatural and natural forces, the latter including the envy and jealousy of others, by presenting oneself as unfortunate, battered by the winds of fate and scarcely able to continue the struggle for life. The micropolitics of social life . . . demand that individuals conceal good fortune and demonstrate their social worthiness by a rhetoric indicative of a lack of success or good fortune. One verbalizes a social life of problems or mundane developments which try one's patience. This presentation of self seeks not to tempt others or make the self fall victim to the envy of others. One does not talk of glowing possibilities, plans and goals, and how well things are going; one complains.

Unlike Mediterranean peoples (Gaines and Farmer 1986:303–4, 320), however, the Toraja are unambivalent in their negative evaluation of misfortune; they also appear to derive little hidden masochistic pleasure from suffering; and they do not consider disclosure of one's suffering to be particularly ennobling.

When Toraja villagers talk about life's troubles in part they are using a familiar rhetoric; but talk of suffering is not *merely* rhetorical. Life in a village like Paku Asu *is* hard: rice yields vary, and one's supply of rice may not last through the year; the child mortality rate is high;

few people are fortunate enough to grow cash crops; the one money-making activity open to all Paku Asu families—the weaving of reed mats—is difficult, repetitive work; ritual and family obligations, though satisfying in many respects, are extensive; and death may come quickly and unexpectedly.

Thus, talk of suffering on the part of Toraja villagers is also a straightforward commentary on the challenging aspects of life in a small, relatively isolated mountain village. As such it reflects not so much depression or demoralization—although among certain individuals such underlying feelings may be present—as a remarkable ability to acknowledge life's pains, hardships, and disappointments as well as its moments of happiness and contentment.

This ability has cultural aspects to it. Toraja villagers need not necessarily blame themselves when their hopes and aspirations go un-fulfilled; there are others—family members, fellow villagers, ancestor figures, spirits, and God—who share responsibility with them. This allows Toraja villagers to acknowledge some of the failings and disap-pointments in life which many middle-class Americans—who value autonomy, self-sufficiency, and achievement—might deny or in some other way disavow, since not to do so would be to admit that one personally has failed to accomplish all that is ideally expected of one.

There is, finally, a philosophical dimension to talk about suffering in Toraja. From a Toraja perspective, life, of necessity, involves hard-ship as well as pleasure; suffering is not something that can be avoided. Such a view is different from that taken by many Americans, who consider the pursuit of happiness to be a central goal and right, and who assume that one can maximize happiness and minimize distress. In the United States, distress and suffering—whether in the form of poverty, illness, death, lack of physical beauty, etc.—are viewed as evidence of failure, and largely as a personal failure of the individual. Although it is hard to accept suffering, it seems to us that there is wisdom in the view that good and bad, contentment and suffering are both integral components of life.

AFTERWORD

In the summer of 1992, one of us made a return visit to Paku Asu. Some things had changed, but others remain the same.

Near the end of our stay in 1983, a dirt road was bulldozed into the village, for the first time making it possible to deliver goods and supplies via truck or auto rather than by foot. Although a few people resisted paying a tax that community members had levied to pay for the road, everyone seemed to agree that the road would be of great benefit to the village. The road was open long enough to deliver supplies for a new grade school building, but shortly after the annual rainy season began, it became heavily eroded and was soon closed to traffic.

Currently, the village road remains eroded in many places and is still impassable during the rainy season. Major roads in the surrounding area have been greatly improved, however, so that time and cost of travel to and from major market towns has been considerably reduced. Formerly, villagers had to walk thirty minutes over a mountainous trail to the nearest vehicle stop, pay a passanger fare of close to $5.00, and then withstand a bone-jarring, roundabout descent into the central valley that could last anywhere from two to three hours, depending upon weather and road conditions. Currently, villagers must still walk thirty minutes to the nearest stop, but they now pay a fare of approxiately $1.50 and descend into the valley in less than an hour. A mode of transport that was considered a luxury only ten years ago is now thought commonplace and indispensible. Evidence of this is that one of the area's major foot trails leading into the valley is now almost completely overgrown in places.

Some new construction has occurred. The largest Protestant church in the village was formerly a very simple wood-frame structure walled with split bamboo boards. Now it is a much more "modern" looking brick and mortar building complete with glass windows. Also, additions have been made to the teachers' houses, and several more Christian burial vaults have been built on the edges of one of the ritual fields, suggesting that fewer people are buried now in the limestone cliffs above the village.

One thing that has not changed is the continued outflow of youth in pursuit of employment and educational opportunities elsewhere in Indonesia. Although there were relatively few people between the ages of 15 and 30 living in Paku Asu ten years ago, there appear to be even fewer living there today. The village seems to be populated by the very young (grade-school age or less) and the relatively old, with few people in between. Even more so than ten years ago, then, there is a sense that the village is quiet, almost dormant, at least on non-ritual occasions. Such an impression is only reinforced by the gradual weathering of the village's magnificently carved ancestral houses.

What of our eleven respondents? Nine of them are still alive; two have died. Ambe'na Toding died of an illness a few years ago, long before he realized the business success he so sorely desired. Nene'na Tandi(m) died in Ujung Pandang in the spring of 1992 after he and his wife had moved there to live with their daughter. Nene'na Tandi(f) says that he died very suddenly, after only two or three days of illness, and before he could be taken to a hospital. He was buried in a cemetery in Ujung Pandang.

Nene'na Tandi(f) continues to live with her daughter in Ujung Pandang, returning to the village only to supervise the planting and harvesting of her rice fields. She remains a strong and relatively youthful-looking woman, though she is much more quiet and reserved since the death of her husband. Six months after Nene'na Tandi(m)'s death, she says that she still grieves for him, especially at night, when she lies in bed alone thinking of him.

Indo'na Tiku no longer lives in the village. She was transferred to a school in a nearby village several years ago, and continues to live with several of her children and grandchildren. She seems to like her new location, which is closer to a major road.

Most of the respondents still live in the village. Nene'na Limbong, now approaching 80 years of age, still spends part of the day working in his rice fields. He remains the self-assured aristocrat, though at the request of his children, he recently converted to Christianity. Ambe'na Kondo had once told us that he, too, would convert to Christianity after completing ritual obligations to his own and his wife's parents, and so he did several years ago. To Minaa Sattu's social and economic position is still precarious. He complains of having lost weight in recent years, and he was forced to move out of his ancestral house when he could not afford to repair its leaking roof. He remains, however, a warm and congenial man.

In closing, let us note an indication of the changes that are on the horizon for Paku Asu and other rural villages in Indonesia. One of the religious specialists we originally worked with, To Minaa Tanduk, still lives in his traditional-style ancestral house, and still joins the other men in replacing the thatched roofing of a rice barn. Yet when given a chance to talk about himself, he speaks not of rice harvests or of aspects of the traditional religion, as he might have several years ago, but rather of his recent trip to Europe to visit one of his children. To Minaa Tanduk has become a world traveler since the last time we met, and it is important for him that others know and appreciate this.

APPENDIX: CHECKLIST OF OPEN INTERVIEW TOPICS

This checklist is taken largely from Levy (1973:509–11), who devised it in part from a question schedule used by the Institute for Human Development at the University of California, Berkeley.

1. Locating data: name; birth date; birthplace; description of childhood house; childhood eating customs; languages and literacy; movements; schooling; travel.
2. Childhood household: members at various ages; sibling pattern; sleeping arrangement; caretaking agents for subject; time spent in and out of household; alternate households.
3. Nature of household relations (adult-adult, adult-children, children-children): leadership; quarrels; conflict resolution.
4. Data on significant caretakers: family background; where born; movements; languages; special statuses; illnesses; involvement and special roles in religion; death.
5. Responses to significant caretakers: evaluation; interaction pattern.
6. Patterns of identification: self compared to significant adults;

special qualities of family; special qualities of ancestors; heroes; negative role models.

7. Early learning in family: nursing; weaning; excretion training; discipline and teaching patterns; familial values.

8. Childhood play: with whom; how chosen; activities; conflicts; special roles in play group; solitary play.

9. Evaluation of childhood.

10. Special circumstances of childhood, including illnesses.

11. Puberty and adolescence: age at beginning; signs of transition; nature of transition; associations; relations with household; major concerns; ideas about the future; sexual life; religious life; formal and informal learning; transition to adulthood; evaluation.

12. History of occupations and special roles.

13. Present associations: with whom; length; activities; nature of the relationship; quality of relations with neighbors, relatives, villagers; enemies.

14. Stress: illnesses; theory of illness; energy/fatigue; headaches; eating problems; sleep difficulties; irritability; depression; fear; anxiety; altered consciousness; suicidal ideas; experience with healers; major mental illness.

15. Aggression: causes, objects, frequency of anger; associated feelings; actions taken; evaluation and interpretation.

16. Moral controls: nature of forbidden desires; why not acted on; results of wrongdoing; moral principles.

17. Religion and the spiritual: present involvement; development of involvement; private uses of religion.

18. Death: interpretations of and reactions to own death and death of others.

19. Dreams: frequency; examples of significant, recurring, and recent dreams; interpretation; theory of dreaming.

20. Drinking: frequency; interpretations and evaluations.

21. Spouse relationship: history; why chosen; evaluation; nature of the relationship; personal meanings of the relationship; conflict resolution.

22. Attitudes about gender roles: evaluation of male/female roles; interpretation of male/female differences; jealousy; romantic love.

23. Physical sexuality: play intercourse; onset of sexual feelings; sexual preferences; masturbation; nocturnal dreams and noc-

turnal orgasms; partners; frequencies; idea of orgasm; evaluations and meanings.

24. Reactions, interpretations, and evaluations of menarche, menstruation, menopause, childbirth.

25. Own children: meanings and evaluations, socialization goals and techniques.

26. Self: self-evaluation; self-disapproval; things to change; shifting selves; qualities of identity.

27. Past: evaluation of past, of ancestors, of the Toraja past.

28. Future: plans and expectations for the future; proposed actions; attitudes and expectations about aging.

29. Community identity: evaluations and interpretations of Toraja, of other groups.

30. Participation in specific cultural activities: scarification; supercision; kickfights; spirit possession; rituals; etc.

NOTES

Introduction

1. According to LeVine (1982:293), "standard ethnography produces a cultural description analagous to a map or aerial photograph of a community; person-centered ethnography tells us what it is like to live there—what features are salient to its inhabitants."

2. Benedict's global characterizations of several tribal groups became well-known in anthropology: the Dobuans of Melanesia, who practiced magic and sorcery and whose competing loyalties to family and spouse were intensified by their matrilineal kinship system were "paranoid"; the Kwakiutl of the northwest coast of North America, who competed for prestige and status through the destruction of property in the potlatch ceremony, were "megalomaniacs"; the Zuni of the southwestern United States, who prized sobriety and inoffensiveness above all other virtues, were "Apollonian"; and the Plains Indians of the central and northern United States, who sought supernatural powers in dreams and visions, were "Dionysian."

3. For example, according to Kardiner (1939:237–50), the "primary" institutions of the Marquesans of the south Pacific include polyandry (which results, in part, from female infanticide and a shortage of women); "maternal neglect" (resulting from the fact that Marquesan women value their roles as wives and erotic objects over their role as mothers); and paternal nurturance

and indulgence (due in part to the shortage of women and maternal care). Their "secondary" institutions include myths and folktales that portray women as cannibalistic demons who threaten children and steal their food, and a religious system whose gods remain somewhat distant and aloof, neither consistently punishing nor rewarding. On the basis of this cultural information, Kardiner argued that the "basic personality structure," which mediates between these two sets of institutions, is characterized by frustrated dependency needs, a muted or nonexistent Oedipus complex, and a relatively "realistic" image of the parents that does not inflate their powers of reward and punishment.

4. Margaret Mead used such tests as early as the 1920s, but their widespread use in anthropology came later.

5. For a recent defense of the cross-cultural use of psychological tests, see DeVos and Boyer (1989).

6. As Marcus and Fischer (1986:48) note, an interest in "ethnopsychologies" is not new to anthropology but "current works explore indigenous epistemologies, rhetorics, aesthetic criteria, and sensibilities with a richness comparable to the way in which only Greek, Roman, and European cultures (or more rarely the 'high cultural' strata of the Orient, such as India, China, and Japan) were previously treated."

7. As LeVine (1982:294) states, "the strategy of studying cultural meanings in detail rather than striving directly for psychological depth is based on the realization that depth interpretations are not valid without contextual evidence to support them."

8. The following comments from Shweder (1990:16) describe the major limitation of formal approaches to ethnopsychology (but his comments do not, in our view, apply to all ethnopsychology research): "ethnopsychology is a subdiscipline of ethnosemantics or ethnoscience. It is primarily concerned with the investigation of mind, self, body, and emotion as topics (along with, for example, botany or kinship) in the ethnographic study of folk beliefs. Ethnopsychology is thus less concerned [than the field of cultural psychology] with actual psychological functioning and subjective life of persons in the cultures whose doctrines about mind, representations of emotion, formal texts about the self, and gender ceremonies are under examination. Ethnopsychology is cultural psychology without the functioning psyche."

9. In a similar vein, Marcus and Fischer (1986:46–47) write: "Anthropologists have always collected information on such matters [indigenous conceptions of thought and feeling], but in using such material to pursue the experimental interest in an ethnography of experience, what is required now are innovations in writing strategies. These experiments are asking, centrally, what is a life for their subjects, and how do they conceive it to be experienced in various social contexts. This requires different sorts of framing categories and different modes of text organization than conventional fuctionalist ethnographies, which relied primarily upon the observation and exegesis of the collectively produced symbols of their subjects, to intuit the quality of their everyday life experience."

10. We were specially trained in the use of this interview technique through

a series of courses provided by the departments of Anthropology and Psychiatry at the University of California, San Diego.

11. We focus on the interview materials largely because space limitations preclude presenting much of our observational data. However, we also highlight them because interview data of this nature have infrequently been reported in the anthropological literature.

12. Levy interviewed rural and urban Tahitians, Kracke interviewed Kagwahiv political leaders and their followers, and Obeyesekere interviewed religious specialists in Sri Lanka.

13. The narratives we elicited can be interpreted as both life as told and life as experienced. According to Bruner (1984:7), a "life as told," a life history, is "a narrative, influenced by the cultural conventions of telling, and by the social context." A "life as experienced" consists of "images, feelings, sentiments, desires, thoughts, and meanings known to the person whose life it is. One can never know directly what another individual is experiencing, although we all interpret clues and make inferences about the experiences of others" (1984:7).

14. See also Herdt and Stoller (1990), who advocate the use of "clinical ethnography."

15. The open interview likely cannot be used in all cultural settings. Scheper-Hughes (1979:7) reports, for example, that given Irish interpersonal norms and preferences, the TAT was a much more useful source of information than direct questioning which "often resulted in stalemate."

16. See, for example, van der Veen (1965, 1966), Crystal (1971, 1974), Nooy-Palm (1978, 1979, 1986), Volkman (1984, 1985), Bigalke (1981), Waterson (1981), Coville (1988), and Adams (1988).

17. The Sa'dan Toraja are one of several related highland groups in South Sulawesi, collectively termed the "South Toraja" by Adriani and Kruyt, Dutch missionaries and linguists who began proselytizing in Central Sulawesi in the late nineteenth century (Bigalke 1981:15). Adriani and Kruyt originally believed that the South Toraja were closely related to the highland groups of Central Sulawesi, whom they termed the East or Bare'e speaking Toraja and the West Toraja. They later revised their classification, however, stating that linguistic evidence suggested that the South Toraja are more closely related to their South Sulawesi lowland neighbors, the Bugis and Makassar, than to the highland groups of Central Sulawesi (Waterson 1981:2). A linguistic study by Mills (1975) reaches a similar conclusion. Present-day Sa'dan Toraja are not familiar with the term "Sa'dan" and simply call themselves "Toraja." More precisely, since there is no 'j' in the local language, Toraja use the terms "Toraya" and "Toraa" instead of "Toraja" when communicating among themselves.

18. According to government statistics, the area of the district is 3,630 square kilometers.

19. See chapter 1 for some examples. Like many traditional religions in the central and eastern regions of Indonesia, Alukta has "dualistic" characteristics (cf. van der Kroef 1954; Kipp and Rodgers 1987:8–11; Weinstock 1987; Traube 1986).

20. According to Nooy-Palm (1975:77), rites of passage, with the exception

of funerals, are also considered smoke-ascending rituals. These include relatively unelaborate birth and marriage rites (see Nooy-Palm 1986 and Hollan and Wellenkamp n.d.).

21. There is some disagreement about whether the *ma'nene'* should be classified smoke-descending, smoke-ascending, or is intermediary between the two (see Wellenkamp 1984:48–49).

22. There are several levels of funeral ritual. Children and poor, low status adults are given the most simple funerals, while older, wealthy nobles are accorded the most elaborate, "highest" ones.

23. The *ma'nene'* is held annually in some areas of Toraja, while in others (including the region in which we worked) it occurs at seven to ten year intervals.

24. The main sacrificial animals are water buffalo, which are slaughtered primarily for smoke-descending events; chickens, which are slaughtered primarily for smoke-ascending events; and pigs, which are slaughtered at both types of events.

25. The traditional ritual system is intricate. For more information, see Nooy-Palm (1979, 1986), Volkman (1979, 1985), and Wellenkamp (1984, 1988a, 1991). Since this is a "person-centered" ethnography, we limit our discussion of ritual and religion to those elements that have a great deal of personal significance for our respondents.

26. These are the terms used in the area in which we worked. As mentioned above, terminology varies from region to region in Tana Toraja.

27. Four ritual specialists reside in Paku Asu: one *to burake*, a specialist who oversees "smoke-ascending" rituals, and three *to minaa*, who perform certain roles in both "smoke-ascending" and "smoke-descending" rituals (see Wellenkamp 1984:37–39). A number of traditional healers and midwives also live in Paku Asu.

28. When one of us was conducting an interview at our house, the other went to visit someone, took a walk, or if it was raining heavily, retreated to the kitchen or the work area at the back of our house.

1. Religious, Moral, and Philosophical Orientations

1. This invocation is part of the *merok* ritual as it is performed in the Kesu' area of Tana Toraja.

2. The names of these more horrific beings may vary somewhat from region to region. See, for example, Adams n.d.

3. See Nooy-Palm (1979) for a more detailed description of Toraja gods and cosmology.

4. Both Bigalke (1981:218–19) and Nooy-Palm (1979:118) suggest that the prominence of this god in relation to other traditional gods has increased since the introduction of Christianity. However, as Nooy-Palm observes, "the Sa'dan religious litanies which never tire of ascribing leading roles to Puang Matua, confirms the antiquity of his position so that we may assume that his stature has been immense for generations" (1979:118–19).

5. It is said that the souls of all those who die—with the possible exception

of those who die under unusual circumstances and whose souls do not enter Puya, the afterworld—become *nene'*. *To dolo* (forebears) and *to matua* (elders) are other terms used to refer to the souls of deceased ancestors.

6. It is said that those who happen to see a *bombo* should not forewarn the person of his or her impending death or else they themselves will be the first to die.

7. There are reportedly ritual procedures that can be used to either allow one to see *bombo* or prevent one from seeing them.

8. The belief in such spirits apparently is of relatively recent origin (Bas Plaisier, personal communication).

9. At the same time, however, since the introduction of Christianity, there seems to have been, and continues to be, a gradual relaxation of some of the traditional rules and regulations (e.g., the restriction of funerals to the period after harvest and before planting). See Hollan (1988b) for a more detailed analysis of religious change in the Toraja highlands.

10. However, Christian participation continues to various degrees in a number of places.

11. In place of smoke-ascending rituals, Christians now hold a thanksgiving feast for which many pigs are slaughtered. Christians also hold smaller celebrations for Christmas and New Year's and increasingly larger celebrations for marriages and baptisms.

12. It is believed that misfortune may be due to one's own misdeeds, or those of family members or forebears (see chapters 4 and 7).

13. In contrast, the traditional trickster figure, Dana', manages to prosper while avoiding labor (see chapter 5).

14. For example, there are rules regulating the location and orientation of houses and ricebarns and of certain plants and trees in the village, as well as the time of year during which specific foods can be consumed, rituals can be performed, and certain children's games can be played.

15. Prominent in smoke-ascending rituals, commonly referred to as "good" (*melo*) rituals, are rice and poultry; the colors white, pink, green, turquoise, and especially yellow; and the directions north, east, right, and up. Prominent in smoke-descending rituals, commonly referred to as "bad" (*kadake*) rituals, are water buffalo meat, corn, and sweet potato; the color black; and the directions south, west, left, and down.

16. There are also formal correspondences between certain smoke-ascending and smoke-descending rituals, and similar themes (see Wellenkamp 1984:30–31; Nooy-Palm and Schefold 1986:46–48; Nooy-Palm 1986:6–8; cf. Traube 1980:311–14).

17. There are several terms (e.g., forms of *osso'*, *tingga'*, and *salu*) meaning "to relate in a systematic sequence," as when relating a genealogy, a story, historical events, or a person's misdeeds.

18. For further discussion of the relationship between order and disorder, see Wellenkamp (1988a). Heider (1991a:34–38, 1991b:115–116) suggests that this theme is of central importance in many Indonesian cultures.

19. The food must be cooked and eaten in the garden or field and not taken home.

20. They are also valued *because* they symbolize relationships.

21. The following section focuses on moral behavior, but of course by implication, it also touches on what is considered to be immoral behavior. For a more detailed discussion of the latter topic, see chapter 4.

22. Here is another example: After Ambe'na Payung had become convinced that one of his in-laws, Ambe'na Tasik, had cheated him of money, he publicly accused Ambe'na Tasik of being a thief and demanded recompense. Though most people agreed that Ambe'na Tasik should not have cheated Ambe'na Payung, they were even more critical of Ambe'na Payung for humiliating Ambe'na Tasik in public. Interestingly, Ambe'na Payung's refusal to talk to Ambe'na Tasik in the days following the dispute was attributed to Ambe'na Payung's shame over having lost control of himself, not to the anger he felt toward Ambe'na Tasik.

23. *Masiri'* is more clearly connected to wrongdoing.

24. For example, "Don't stab the eye of the fish," meaning, it is impolite to speak too directly, or, "A person is not a cob of corn," meaning, a person should not be handled with bare hands, like a piece of corn.

25. For example: "To talk like a hawk," meaning, to talk with no purpose or aim; "to talk like an owl," meaning, someone whose words go back and forth; "to call like a cock," meaning, to talk, even though one has no reason to talk.

26. Villagers do occasionally boast about their special skills or talents, but in this chapter, we focus on ideal behavior.

2. Aspects of Interpersonal Relationships

1. *Sikande,* "to eat one another," has the general meaning of "connected" or "related." Similarly, the Bugis speak of two items in close association as "swallowing" or "gulping" one another (Errington 1983:564). Eating also is a colloquial way of referring to sexual intercourse in Toraja.

2. With biologically related individuals, reciprocal exchanges reflect the existence of a prior relationship based on shared ancestry, while reciprocal exchanges between non-kin make possible a social relationship.

3. The traditional greeting is *"Manasumo raka?"* ("Is [it] cooked yet?"), to which the polite reply is, *"Manasumo"* ("[It] is cooked").

4. The overriding importance of these exchanges is exemplified by the fact that Bugis and Toraja adherents of accommodationist Islam living in rural areas of Tana Toraja during the early twentieth century contributed livestock, including pigs, to reciprocal exchanges with non-Islamic families (Bigalke 1981:206).

5. Toraja terms for love and affection are similar in meaning to the Ifaluk (Micronesia) term, *fago,* "compassion/love/sadness" (see Lutz 1988). See also Heider (1991b:70–72) for a discussion of concepts of love in other Indonesian cultures.

6. Although it is customary to be called after one's first-born child or grandchild, this is not always the case. Also, sometimes those who are grand-

parents continue to be called "Mother of . . . " or "Father of . . . " especially if the grandchild does not live in the vicinity.

7. It is not uncommon for young couples to live for awhile with either the husband's or the wife's parents before establishing their own households (see Hollan and Wellenkamp n.d.).

8. Both Nene'na Limbong and Ambe'na Kondo seemed slightly offended when asked if they had ever fostered children. They each replied that they had no need to foster children since they had plenty of their own.

9. In contrast, in Tahiti a request to raise a child is usually made during the mother's pregnancy.

10. Geertz makes a similar distinction between "adoption" and "borrowing" in Java. According to Geertz, formal adoption is rare in Java (1961:38–39).

11. Waterson (1981:316) reports that some villagers are now utilizing the court system to make official adoptions.

12. A child may be adopted by one parent or by both.

13. Waterson (1981:314) makes a further distinction between two types of adoption, *mangiu'* and *urrampanan doke biang,* based on the extent and types of obligations and rights assumed by the adopted child.

14. Waterson (1981:330) also reports that formal adoption is infrequent in the area in which she worked (western Tana Toraja). Moreover, the distinction between foster and adopted children does not seem to be a very clear or rigid one. Waterson (1981:309), for example, reports the following: One couple had eight foster children and one "fully adopted" child who had been given *tekken;* when the foster father died, however, all of the children participated in his funeral and shared in the inheritance.

15. The stem of *passarak, sarak,* means generally "to part or to separate;" the same stem is also part of the verb "to wean," *sarakki.* The *passarak* is both weaned from his or her mother and separated from her.

16. Paku Asu villagers have heard rumors that in Java children may be sold to others. Such an idea is considered scandalous, although one villager with few resources once mentioned to us that he had been offered a car in exchange for one of his children.

17. These are *pa'indoran,* "just like a mother," and *pa'ambean,* "just like a father."

18. Based on our own observations, we believe that such claims are often accurate.

19. In fact, Indo'na Tiku's children had already suggested to Sampe that he was a foster child, a suggestion that made him cry and vigorously deny their claims. Interestingly, Indo'na Tiku seemed surprised by Sampe's response.

20. For information on raising children, see Hollan and Wellenkamp (n.d.).

21. Negative images of stepmothers also appear in stories and folktales. In one popular story, Indo' Oro-Oro, the stepmother gives her stepchildren excrement to eat instead of food.

22. Paku Asu villagers reported one recent instance of brother-sister incest. For a discussion of sexuality, see Hollan and Wellenkamp (n.d.).

23. Mediators also may assist in marital and other disputes.

24. Parties to a divorce may or may not have to pay a divorce fine, depending upon whether the separation is mutually agreed upon or initiated by one party against the wishes of the other. The most common reason to divorce is said to be adultery. Divorce may also occur because a couple has not had children.

25. According to our census of one of the hamlets of Paku Asu, 13 of 35 women and 11 of 29 men have divorced at least once. Of the 24 adults who have divorced, 13 already had children at the time of the divorce.

26. Once a couple have divorced, they are free to remarry. However, traditionally, when a marriage ends as a result of the death of a spouse, a special ceremony must be performed before the surviving spouse is free to marry whomever he or she pleases (see Hollan and Wellenkamp n.d.).

27. It could be that Nene'na Limbong and Nene'na Tandi(m) are unconsciously drawing from traditional narrative styles to compose their personal accounts (see Peacock 1988). Alternatively, the similarities between their accounts of their own experiences and traditional folktales could be due to the fact that both derive from, and reflect, important interpersonal concerns and patterns of behavior.

28. In contrast, the Fulani believe that fathers, at least, should be able to overcome the compassionate feelings aroused in them by their children, and should appear to have an unpredictable attitude towards their children's appeals (Riesman 1977:199–204).

29. According to Bigalke (1981:340), Makassar perceive Toraja as being slow to respond to provocation.

3. Aspects of Identity and Self

1. Most tourists, however, do not venture far beyond the central valley area where the towns of Rantepao and Makale are located.

2. See Volkman (1985) for further discussion of aspects of contemporary social identity.

3. See Volkman (1955:77) for a discussion of the village *saroan*, a meat- and labor-sharing group.

4. These are the distinctions and terms used in the Paku Asu area.

5. Paku Asu villagers used Toraja names to address us. The names we were given were Belo and Tandi.

6. The Toraja term for slaughter or sacrifice is *tunu*, "to burn/roast." For Alukta villagers, the sacrificial aspects of the slaughtering of livestock at rituals are very important; for Christians, slaughtering does not officially involve sacrifice. For both groups, slaughtering remains an emotionally charged activity.

7. Buffalo are individually killed in front of the assembled guests by a blow to the jugular vein with a machete.

8. Interestingly, however, most of the people we asked denied having conscious feelings of sorrow or compassion for slaughtered animals. In con-

trast, Levy's (1990:334) Bhaktapur respondents do report conscious feelings of empathy for slaughtered animals.

9. For a discussion of gender in other insular Southeast Asian cultures, see Atkinson and Errington (1990).

10. The absence of a "hypermasculine" sensibility among Toraja males perhaps is best illustrated by the fact that those few individual men who possess an especially bold and assertive manner are considered extraordinary and are viewed with awe.

11. For example, male respondents were much more hesitant in general to respond to the Rorschach than female respondents.

12. This makes sense given that, by his own account, Ambe'na Toding is more easily aroused to anger than many of his fellow villagers.

13. For example, like Balinese children, Toraja children may play with live insects that are attached to strings; Toraja children also play with buffalo hooves that are attached to thin pieces of cord. Language learning also is similar (see Bateson and Mead (1942:13).

14. According to Nene'na Limbong, "the meaning [of the dream] is that when there is a legal case. . . sometimes I am called [to surrounding regions] to [help] decide [the case]."

4. Mental States and Processes

1. See also Nooy-Palm (1979:128–129).

2. Respondents vary in their estimates of how frequently they dream. Nene'na Tandi(f) is unusual in that she says that she dreams every night. Most respondents say that they dream occasionally. Indo'na Rante, for instance, says that she dreams about once every month.

3. Indo'na Tiku spontaneously reported the following dream upon awakening from an afternoon nap: A female teacher at Laka, a nearby village, had killed a pig to pay for the labor needed to level some land (Indo'na Tiku at the time was herself building a house in Laka). The pig that was killed happened to be someone else's pig—some children had taken it. It was Nene'na Tandi's pig. Moreover, it had several baby pigs in its stomach/womb.

4. According to some informants, dreams of flying or of traveling to many places are indications that the dreamer is a po'pok (see chapter 1).

5. There is one healer in the village with matted locks (see chapter 7), and she is thought to communicate with the deata while dreaming. We were once invited to spend the night with her at Ambe'na Kondo's house so that we could hear her speak to the deata in her sleep (we were told that the deata would not visit her at the house of Christians). Her utterances were unintelligible to us and to Ambe'na Kondo's family, a fact that for some villagers lends credence to the belief that she engages in divine communication. The healer sometimes uses her dreams to help her identify the "mistakes" of her patients (see the discussion of healing in chapter 7).

6. Indo'na Sapan says that she has heard that Christians do not believe that dreams are portentous, "but as for me, I believe it! Because there's evidence, you know. So how could one not believe? Dreams are from God!"

7. Respondents vary in the way in which they use cultural beliefs and symbols to interpret specific dream experiences; see Hollan (1989) for a discussion of contrasts between Nene'na Limbong's and To Minaa Sattu's styles of dream interpretation.

8. Indo'na Rante reports that she had this dream shortly after a relative in the household in which she was living died. It is not uncommon for people to change residences after a misfortunate event has occurred.

9. Toraja avoid coercion in favor of more subtle means of pressuring and influencing others (see Hollan and Wellenkamp n.d. and chapter 5). Also Toraja believe that the use of coercion with children, particularly young children, can possibly damage a child's psyche.

10. One popular and highly respected former military commander is believed by Paku Asu villagers to possess an amulet (*balo'*) that contributed to his military successes in defending against Islamic troops. When we asked him about this, however, he said that it was not an amulet that had protected him and his men, but advice that he had received through dreams from his deceased father.

11. Other ill omens can also be *dibori,* for instance, when someone falls or rice or meat is spilled or dropped during a smoke-ascending ritual, or when the entrails of a sacrificial pig contain inauspicious signs.

12. When one commits a "mistake" of some sort, it is said to "be seen" (*ditiro*) by spiritual beings.

13. One informant said: The *penaa,* or spirit, travels throughout one's body. It's thinking, you know. Breath. Blood. The blood sends news to the nerves. If the blood stops, so does life.

14. *Penaa* and *inaa* also are used to refer to "nonemotional" states or processes (e.g., *langngo' penaa,* literally "slippery breath" but figuratively "willingness;" *kamoraian penaa,* "desire/passion").

15. *Ba'tang* is a related term used in ritual language.

16. For a discussion of cultural similarities and differences in folk models of the mind, see D'Andrade (1987).

17. Mental and physical states and processes also are not sharply distinguished conceptually or linguistically. For example, *masaki ulungku,*literally "my head hurts/is ill" may refer to either physical or mental distress.

18. One informant, when asked which was stronger, thinking or feeling, replied that they are the same, they must go together. If either one is stronger, he added, then mental disturbance of some sort will result.

19. Nene'na Limbong once found fault with an outside adjudicator who had been asked to help resolve a divorce case in the village; according to Nene'na Limbong, the man's thinking jumped around.

20. An example of *karume* is the following: Question: A coconut with seven eyes is . . . ? Answer: One's head (which has seven openings).

21. For a discussion of empathetic sadness and compassion among Toraja villagers, see Wellenkamp (1992).

22. Levy (1973:273) reports that during the interviews he conducted with his Tahitian respondents, people would simulate various emotions to add color to a story, but "the nonsimulated demonstration of a strong emotion during

the interviews was very rare and stood out in contrast to the usual expression of feeling." Our Toraja respondents also often used "willful dramatization" in their accounts and discussions, but rarely demonstrated strong, spontaneous emotions.

23. Sometimes when groups of men undertake strenuous work activities, some men will "hoot" exuberantly.

24. We use English glosses such as "anger" and "sadness" in a general way to refer to "anger-like," "sad-like," etc., emotions. Toraja terms overlap with, but are also different from, English emotion terms (see, for example, Wellen-kamp 1992). There are several Toraja terms relating to anger and sadness including, for anger, *malassu penaa, sengke, magi'gi'*, and *re'de ara'*, and for sadness, *mapa'di' penaa, ma'inaa-naa, masaki inaa,* and *masussa.*

25. Lighting fires apparently has been a common pasttime of boys for some time, at least in the Paku Asu area. Most fires do not spread far, but in this particular incident, 35 people incurred losses of property according to the official count.

26. We also observed villagers occasionally kicking dogs, throwing cats, and in one incident, forcing a water buffalo to struggle back to a slaughtering ground after its hind legs had been deeply slashed to prevent it from running away. Such actions toward domestic animals are not cause for comment usually, although Nene'na Tandi(m) once related a traditional story about how buffalo should not be beaten or they will not thrive.

27. According to Nene'na Limbong, murderous assaults were more common during the 1960s, when there was considerable political unrest.

28. However, outsiders, such as Western tourists, may be targets of hostile or aggressive actions, such as aggressive begging on the part of children.

29. As we note earlier in this chapter, dreams with violent themes also appear to be common.

30. As noted in chapter 3, most of those who publicly receive meat are men; adult women receive meat only if they are unmarried.

31. It is not clear why Ambe'na Kondo told To Minaa Sattu to leave, although it is likely that he thought To Minaa Sattu was attempting to receive greater attention and respect than he deserved.

32. Although Busa"s behavior sounds similar to *amuk* (see Spores 1988), none of our informants used this term in reference to Busa'. According to one Toraja psychiatrist, *amuk* behaviors are not common in Toraja (see chapter 6).

33. Indo'na Rante reports that a few years ago she earned a large sum of money by selling coffee and snacks at a funeral. She lent some of her earnings to a man who still has not repaid her. Although she says that the incident is best forgotten, she concedes that "often I think of it. He took a lot of money." Occasionally she sees the man who borrowed the money at the nearby market and then, she says, "I feel like I want to beat him." She is afraid, however, to ask for the return of the money for fear that the man might attempt to poison her (see chapter 5).

34. For more information on this topic, see Wellenkamp (1992).

35. Geertz (1976:97) reports that in Java, physical illness is believed (especially by "abangans") to result from the fact that when one is "upset, startled,

or severely depressed," one becomes "confused and disoriented, and one's soul is then empty and easily entered by spirits." The Bugis of Luwu hold similar beliefs. According to Errington (1983), the Bugis believe that emotional upset can lead to illness and that the mechanism by which this happens is loss of *sumange'*, spiritual potency. If one loses one's composure, or even if one is in the presence of others who lose theirs, one may experience "shock" (*aseddin-geng*). Shock entails a decrease in one's *sumange'* which, in turn, makes one more vulnerable to illness and other misfortune.

36. Like the Toraja, Tahitians (Levy 1973:285) and Chinese (Klineberg 1938:519) also speak of people dying from intense emotional experiences, and yet the Tahitians and Chinese speak of people dying from anger, while the Toraja usually talk about people dying from sadness and disappointment.

37. The Toraja terms are *malassu*, "hot," and *masakke, madingngin*, literally, "cool/cold," but metaphorically, "safe/healthy/prosperous."

38. For example, as discussed later, while crying and wailing occur in connection with death, crying is usually subdued and wailing, though often loud and dramatic, only should occur in the vicinity of the deceased or some representation of the deceased (such as an effigy [*tatau*] or the substitute body that is constructed when the bodily remains are not recovered [see Wellenkamp 1991]), and only at funerals of a certain level.

39. As older boys and men begin to join in, younger boys drop out, so that engagements usually involve men or boys of roughly the same age and size.

40. Formal kickfights (as opposed to small, impromptu ones during play) are structured along geopolitical lines. That is, groups of hamlets or villages compete against other allied groups. In the Paku Asu area, for example, Paku Asu joins the villages to the south of a nearby river in opposing those to the north. Within Paku Asu, those hamlets to the northwest end oppose those to the southeast.

41. Ambe'na Toding reports that he was often unintentionally kicked in the genital area when he played *sisemba'*.

42. Although, according to one informant, in former times only those villages that were *not* engaged in warfare with one another could compete in kickfights.

43. Cockfights (held recreationally as well as for high level funerals) and buffalo fights (also held for high level funerals)—events that are popular in Toraja—also are occasions when aggressive actions are prominent.

44. In addition, expressions of grief serve as demonstrations of attachment to the deceased, and crying and wailing are used to beseech the dead to bless the living (see Wellenkamp 1992).

45. Several forms of ritual combat similar to Toraja kickfights are found in other parts of Indonesia. In at least two cases, the Toba Batak of Sumatra and the Manggarai of western Flores, ritual combats take place in connection with planting and/or harvesting (Downs 1977:134–44).

46. See Wellenkamp (1988b) for a discussion of Toraja notions of "cathar-sis," which are linked to more general ideas concerning the periodic use of heat, disorder, and lack of constraint to attain "vitality" (Wellenkamp 1988a). For some, a certain degree of embarrassment and discomfort seems to

accompany such "cathartic" displays. For example, some spectators say they are afraid to watch those who are possessed during rituals and it is somewhat shameful afterwards for those who become possessed. In the presence of people wailing, men often look uncomfortable and some laugh nervously. In addition, it seems that some attempt is made to identify individuals who appear especially upset and efforts may be made to calm them. For instance, at one funeral, there was a young man who was close to tears as he angrily defended his father's distribution of the meat. One woman came over to him and gently placed her arm on his shoulder. Similar gestures are sometimes made toward people who are wailing.

47. One *ma'maro* was held in a village not far from Paku Asu, and the other some distance away. A *ma'bugi'* ritual was held in Paku Asu a few months before our arrival.

48. The place of *ma'maro* ceremonies in terms of the annual cycle of rituals in the Paku Asu area is after the annual rice harvest and death rituals, and after kickfights and house-building rituals (*ma'papa*).

49. In the Kesu' area, the construction of the *bate* varies somewhat (Nooy-Palm 1986:126).

50. Cf. Zerner (1981:103–4), who maintains that the recitation of ritual poems (described later) "acts like a switch in an electrical communication system, opening circuits between the realms of the spirits and the community. These poems activate or energize the ritual apparatus."

51. *To minaa* begin the recitation of *gelong* in advance of the main celebration.

52. In the *ma'maro* rituals that we witnessed, the pace of the singing and dancing increased as soon as one of the members of the dance circle—often an older woman—appeared to be possessed.

53. Broch (1985:276) notes that sexually provocative behavior occurs in Bonerate (South Sulawesi) possession ritual as well, though there it is only women who become possessed.

54. Possession trance in Toraja conforms in many ways to Bourguignon's (1979) observations regarding the cross-cultural distribution, means of inducing, and other features of possession trance. For example, according to Bourguignon (1979:233–69), possession trance is most likely to occur in stratified agricultural societies that place a high value on obedience, reliability, and nurturance (a description that characterizes the Toraja). In some ways, however, possession trance in Toraja differs from the "typical" pattern; for instance, while Bourguignon (1979:258) maintains that possession trance "appears to be a typically female phenomenon," among the Toraja, both men and women become possessed (see Hollan 1992b for a more in-depth discussion of such similarities and differences).

55. At least one informant claims that more people became possessed at *ma'maro* rituals when he was young than now do. Bourguignon (1979:261) suggests that possession trance typically is experienced by a minority of people in a community.

56. Nene'na Tandi(m) says that he once asked a *ma'maro* participant to stab his forehead (an accepted treatment for headaches), and yet he still suffers

from headaches. Ambe'na Kondo's wife says that she has considered receiving such a treatment, but that she is afraid that someone might use magic against her (see chapter 5) and that instead of just pricking her forehead, the knife would go into her head.

57. At the *ma'maro* rituals we observed, older women and younger men predominated among those who became possessed (see Hollan 1992b).

58. Some people say that participants may request permission from the *deata* to perform certain behaviors.

59. Possession trance behavior among the Toraja involves much individual choice and functions as a "personal symbol" (Obeyesekere 1981), having both personal and cultural meanings. For further elaboration of this point, see Hollan (1992b).

60. In former times, many people delight in saying, even more spectacular feats were performed by the possessed, including cutting off one's head and placing it on a ricebarn while one danced. Nowadays, however, people say, *to kandeatan* are no longer bold enough to attempt such feats because they fear that spectators will either intentionally or unintentionally jeopardize their safety by voicing skepticism or failing to observe a prohibition. Interestingly, the only person we met who said that it was impossible for people to cut off their heads even during a *ma'maro* is a man who is widely regarded as "crazy."

61. As we discuss in a later chapter, angry or violent behavior is considered a prominent identifying characteristic of insanity.

62. Participants' sense of shame probably also is related to the highly visible role they play, since merely being the object of other people's attention can be uncomfortable for some people.

63. To Minaa Sattu began to be possessed while he was a youth and for over twenty years he regularly attended *ma'maro* rituals.

64. Villagers also prefer to drink in the privacy of their own homes to avoid having to share what little *tuak* they can afford with neighbors and passersby.

65. People also are said to become dizzy when they inappropriately come into contact with persons or objects that are more sacred or powerful.

66. The techniques used to revive people when they faint include pinching people's stomachs, rubbing their nostrils, and blowing (*pamurru'*) on them.

67. According to a psychiatrist in Rantepao, many schoolgirls in town evince "hysterical" symptoms that include sudden collapses (see chapter 6).

68. Insanity also is conceptualized by the Toraja as a loss of "consciousness." We discuss insanity in chapter 5.

69. Trickery is viewed ambivalently, however, as we discuss in chapter 5.

70. Since according to Alukta beliefs, misfortune may be due to either one's own misconduct, or that of others (such as family members, forebears, or others in the community), villagers have an interest in insuring that other people behave properly and atone for any transgressions they commit (see chapter 6).

71. Another Christian said that the inhabitants of a particular village in Toraja experienced repeated incidents of misfortune for several generations until it was recalled that a Christian missionary had once been murdered by

village residents. Only after the crime was publicly acknowledged and God's forgiveness was sought, according to our informant, did the fortune of the residents improve.

72. For a discussion of Alukta and Christian conceptions of the afterlife, see Hollan and Wellenkamp (n.d.).

73. In Toraja, one's sense of conscience and moral awareness are directly linked to the evaluations and opinions of others (cf. Levy 1973; Shore 1982).

5. Prevalent Interpersonal Concerns and Anxieties

1. As we discuss, some of the concerns people have seem well-justified, while others less so.

2. In 1982, according to police records there were only 45 cases of theft for the entire administrative region of Tana Toraja; both police officials and officials in the Justice Department claimed that many of these thefts were committed by non-Toraja in the towns of Makale and Rantepao. In that same year, there was only one theft reported from the rural district in which Paku Asu is located.

Not all thefts are reported to police, however. Villagers who engage in petty theft may receive a warning from village elders before they are reported to the police. Also, more recently, several of the wooden effigies of the dead (*tatau*) have been stolen from cliffside balconies in the central valley area.

3. Most people own at least one or more dogs. Though the Toraja also raise dogs for food, a dog that is vigilant and barks loudly is less likely to be slaughtered.

4. Our neighbors probably also were concerned about possibly being suspected of stealing from us if something were to turn up missing. Similarly, villagers on the whole probably were concerned that if something were stolen from us by a resident from another village, Paku Asu residents would be suspected and the village's reputation would suffer.

5. According to one informant, there is magic that one can use to protect one's gardens from theft.

6. In contrast, other historical sources (see Bigalke 1981) indicate that Pong Tiku and his forces were under siege and at a distinct military disadvantage at the time of their capture.

7. Nene'na Limbong's first three accounts, which have to do with outwitting powerful foreign occupiers, are reminiscent of popular folktales in which the wily Toraja consistently outsmart and defeat their more powerful and oppressive neighbors, the Bugis (see chapter 3).

8. Villagers' views about whether, in fact, the parents were responsible for the boys' actions, and about what should be done to the boys varied considerably.

9. For example, one villager complained that he was "tricked" by his own relatives into beginning construction on a new ancestral house (*tongkonan*). His kin persuaded him to pay for and build the foundation and frame of the house with the promise that other relatives would pay for the roofing. Once

the house was half completed however, his relatives claimed they could not afford to pay for their share of the costs. Our informant was then left to watch his new foundation and frame rot or pay for the roofing himself.

In another instance, a neighbor said she was "tricked" by a couple in the next hamlet who have refused to repay a buffalo debt. This couple, according our neighbor, regularly receive money from their financially successful children and so could repay the debt if they wished to, but whenever she asks them to do so, they claim they cannot afford it at the moment. Our neighbor claimed that cultural norms of etiquette do not allow her to confront the couple with their deceit; she cannot "force" them to honor their debt and thus she may never be repaid.

See Hollan (1984) for other examples.

10. For further discussion of cultural conventions relating to the exchange of resources and services, see Wellenkamp (1984).

11. Terms for gossip and slander include *kada langko*, "empty words," *ma'kada boko'*, "to speak behind someone," and *boko kada*, "to steal someone's words/name."

12. Someone who disrupts the community by spreading false rumors is called a *peruso kalando*.

13. In another example of how someone might try to destroy a marriage, Nene'na Tandi (m) imagines a case where a wife is falsely told that her husband is accumulating large debts. Such a rumor is bound to make the wife angry, since the use of household resources should be decided on jointly, and if she believes the rumor, she might then seek a divorce.

14. Demands for concrete evidence are particularly salient in the course of formal disputes. Thus when a man in the village produced an unsigned love letter addressed to his wife as proof that she had committed adultery, many people would not accept it as evidence, saying that the husband (or one of his cohorts) could have forged the letter in order to incriminate his wife. If the husband wished to prove that adultery had occurred, some people said, he should name the man who had allegedly slept with his wife and have him publicly confess.

15. One expression for "to commit adultery" is *ma'pangngan buni*, "to chew *pangngan* in secrecy."

16. As noted in the Introduction, this made it difficult for us to conduct private interviews with members of the opposite gender.

17. Ideally couples should not engage in sex for up to six months following the birth of a child (see Hollan and Wellenkamp n.d.).

18. One Protestant minister in a nearby village bemoaned the fact that the traditional "big men" among the Toraja are often best known for what he considered to be their vices: illicit sex, gambling at cockfights, and competitive slaughtering of livestock at rituals.

19. Elsewhere Ambe'na Toding reports that he has occasionally had short affairs with other women.

20. She suspected that her children's deaths were the result of her husband's transgressions.

21. Selby (1974) has suggested that extramarital sexual affairs often are

evaluated differently depending on who commits them, under what circumstances, and whether or not they are eventually recognized and labeled by the community. In Toraja, it appears that extramarital affairs may be tolerated in certain circumstances. See Waterson (1981) and Hollan (1984).

22. However, Waterson (1981) notes that in the western area of Tana Toraja, it is not uncommon for a married man to have sexual liaisons, and even children, with several women, and that wives may be cognizant of these relationships but tolerate them.

23. In one traditional story, a beautiful newlywed woman, who is at home alone while her husband is gone collecting wood for a new house, seduces a young man by the name of Dakku Rarana by taking his golden top and then luring him into her home. With the help of the couple's bird, the husband eventually discovers that Dakku Rarana has had sexual relations with his wife. The husband then burns Dakku Rarana to death in retribution for his deed, and yet Dakku Rarana is brought back to life by his father. The wife then leaves her husband for Dakku Rarana, and the two live happily together, while the husband is burned to death after Dakku Rarana sets fire to his house.

24. It is not clear if Nene'na Tandi(m) means that the resulting illness is caused by human powers of magic or by the power of the spirits.

25. The belief that magically induced illness has increased in recent years probably is related to several factors including: 1) the increased contact that now occurs between "distant" people (those most likely to arouse fear and suspicion) due to pacification and the development of roads; 2) the introduction of Christianity and modern medicine, which undermine the belief in spiritually caused illnesses; 3) the expansion of a cash economy, which has increased interpersonal tensions over status competition; and 4) the disappearance or decline of more traditional ways of expressing and managing fear and hostility, such as head hunting, warfare, possession trance, and kickfights.

26. The theme of seduction by a female is prominent in the traditional story, Dakku Rarana.

6. Dysphoria and Disorder

1. We personally did not encounter any intense odors when visiting houses in which bodies were stored.

2. We collected data from the health clinics located closest to Paku Asu.

3. It may be that Toraja dream interpretations provide Nene'na Limbong and other villagers with a kind of "built-in cultural secondary elaboration" (Kracke 1979:163) that allows one to dream in a relatively open fashion about threatening aspects of interpersonal relationships (see Hollan 1989).

4. It makes sense that To Minaa Sattu was not given any of the meat since close relatives of the deceased are not allowed to have meat from the funeral buffalo that represents the deceased.

5. When Nene'na Tandi(m) is asked if he has ever had a nightmare, he replies, "Not yet! Not yet, because I've never been angry with anyone!" In a later interview, he suggests that daytime encounters with *deata* (spirits) or with a sacred spot also can cause one to have nightmares.

6. "Bygone" is the English trade name for one of the most commonly used pesticides in Tana Toraja. Sometimes people joke that when someone ingests pesticide in order to commit suicide, they are "bye, bye, and gone!"

7. Also Nene'na Tandi(f)'s husband says that she has threatened to commit suicide if he were to leave her for another woman.

8. In two cases, women committed suicide after being mistreated or abandoned by men; in two cases, young men killed themselves because their families refused to provide them with money for business ventures or schooling; and in the fifth case, a teenage boy suffering from a severe and debilitating disease hung himself.

9. However, Indo'na Sapan says that unpaid debts do not usually lead to suicide: "As for debts, people say, 'If you will be patient, we will pay you back a little at a time.'"

10. That suicide is viewed as an impulsive act is suggested by the verb *mentuyo*, which means both to commit suicide and to fling oneself about in unhappiness, as when a child is upset.

11. MacPherson and MacPherson (1985, 1987) describe a similar situation in Western Samoa. They refer to such suicides as "anomic." However, in the Toraja instance, such suicides are not related to a lessening of commitment to traditional norms and values, which is the hallmark of "anomic" suicide as described by Durkheim. Rather, young people's sense of deprivation is based on traditional assumptions regarding interpersonal relationships; thus "indignant" suicide seems a more appropriate term (see Hollan 1990).

12. Infants, in particular, are seen as needing to have their desires met, and yet persons of all ages are thought to be vulnerable to excessive frustration, and it is thought wise to minimize frustration whenever possible.

13. Among close family members, a sense of entitlement is reinforced by the inherent ambiguity of the rules of generalized exchange (cf. Popkin 1979). Since the specific rights and obligations of the individual parties are rather vaguely defined, family members are free to suppose that most, if not all, of their self-defined needs should be satisfied by other family members.

14. The souls of those near death are thought to be greedy, capricious, and potentially violent.

15. As we discuss elsewhere (Hollan and Wellenkamp n.d.), by Toraja standards, Ambe'na Tangke's father seems to have been uncharacteristically harsh in his treatment of his son.

16. Her treatment consisted of drinking water containing herbs over which the healer had spoken a spell, a common treatment procedure used in response to a variety of complaints in Toraja (see chapter 7).

17. See Wellenkamp (1989) for further analysis of this case.

7. Coping with Disorder and Dysphoria

1. Traditionally, omens also offered assistance in making decisions about potentially dangerous actions, such as traveling outside of the village.

2. Some people say that the ability to suppress or avoid troubling thoughts

or feelings is facilitated by the use of *pangngan* and tobacco, which reportedly help to relax the body and clear the mind.

3. During our stay, we did not observe any *masurru'* performances. However, another process, called *dipesaluan*, occurred on more than one occasion in Paku Asu.

4. While Nene'na Tandi(m) emphasizes the thorough and potentially very shameful aspects of examining the afflicted person's mistakes, in practice, the process often shields people from too much exposure by displacing responsibility for wrongdoing onto forebears, or by identifying the wrongdoer's misdeeds as relatively innocuous—for example, the violation of food taboos.

5. There are some parallels between To Beluak's life experiences and those of the women with matted locks interviewed by Obeyesekere (1981).

6. According to To Minaa Sattu and Nene'na Tandi(m), To Beluak is not technically a *to ma'dampi* but a *tutungan bia'*, which refers to "lighting a torch," a metaphor for "to lead into lightness/safety."

7. To Beluak's young nephew also has matted locks and has treated a few individuals.

8. A lotion containing herbs and leaves may be used to help heal a supercision wound, for example (see Hollan and Wellenkamp n.d.).

Glossary

All terms are Toraja words except those marked with an (I), which are Indonesian.

adi younger sibling

aluk rite, ritual

Aluk Nene' way of the ancestors, traditional religion

aluk pare rice ritual

Alukta our way, traditional religion

Aluk To Dolo way of the people of before, traditional religion

ambe' father

ambe' poro' stepfather

amuk (I) a behavioral reaction characterized by impulsive, indiscriminate violence

anak child

anak poro' stepchild

ara' chest, breast

Bahasa Indonesia (I) Indonesian language

baine woman, wife

balo' amulet

barani brave, courageous

Basa Toraa Toraja language

bate trident-shaped banner

biung pu'pu' orphan

bombo soul (especially, of recently deceased or of someone about to die

bomboan crazy

dalle' good fortune

dapo' hearth, household

datu Ruler

deata gods, spirits; also a person's vital force

deatan soul

desa (I) administrative region comprising, in Toraja, several villages or *kampung*

dibori "limited" or reinterpreted (e.g., a bad dream or omen)

dikasiri' honored or respected

dilebang "limited" or reinterpreted (e.g., a bad dream or omen)

dipandan invested

dipesaluan process to identify transgressions

disapan blocked up (e.g., the good portents of a dream)

disumpa' interrogated

ditantang divorced, let go

doti magic spell

gelong paired verses

inaa mind, heart, insight

indo' mother

indo' poro' stepmother

induk sugar palm tree

kabupaten (I) regency, administrative area

kadake bad, ugly

kaka older sibling

kampung (I) village, administrative area

kapa' divorce payment

kapua penaa lit. big breath, happy, proud

karume riddle

kaunan dependent, slave

kendu have sex

lampa bamboo carrying vessel

latah (I) startle reaction characterized by verbal and behavioral mimicry

lobang boko' spirit of a woman who has died in childbirth

ma'badong to perform a type of funeral song

ma'bua' to perform a type of "smoke-ascending" ritual oriented toward fertility and prosperity

ma'bugi' to perform a ritual oriented toward the prevention or cure of illness; involves possession trance

ma'deata to be possessed

madingngin cool, cold

ma'dondi' to perform a type of funeral song

ma'inaa-naa to think of, yearn for

ma'ipu to faint

ma'kada boko' to gossip

ma'kada melo to speak well, pleasingly

malango intoxicated

malassu warm, hot

malassu penaa lit. hot breath, upset, angry

malippang to faint

malongko' embarrassed, shamed

mamali' lako to love

ma'maro to perform a "smoke-ascending" ritual involving possesion trance

mamase feel compassion

mamintu baine daughter-in-law

mamintu muane son-in-law

manarang knowledgeable, skilled

ma'nene' to perform a form of secondary burial

ma'pakaboro' to love

ma'pangngan bunt lit. to chew *pangngan* in secrecy, to commit adultery

ma'papa to perform a house-building ritual

marapuan bilaterally related kin who trace descent from a common ancestor

maro crazy

maro-maro half crazy

masaki inaa sad, hurt, distressed

masakke cool, cold; safe, healthy

ma'sakkun are to sit with one's chin cupped in one's hand

masiri' embarrassed, shamed

massuru' to perform an absolution ceremony

masussa distressed

mataku' afraid

ma'tangnga' to think, also to trick, deceive

matusa baine mother-in-law

matusa muane father-in-law

melo good, nice

mengkilala conscious

mentuyo commit suicide; fling about in unhappiness

merok to perform a type of "smoke-ascending" ritual oriented toward thanksgiving and celebration

misa penaa one breath, one mind

muane man, husband

nene' grandparent, soul of a deceased ancestor

pakena to trick, deceive

palaku request

pamurru' to blow

pangngan areca nut, betel, and lime

parannu joyful

pa'rapuan bilaterally related kin who trace descent from a common ancestor

passarak a foster child separated from his or her mother at the time of weaning

pemali prohibition

penaa breath, heart, mind

penaa masallo' generous, willing

penaa melo lit. good breath, good-hearted, fair

peruso kalando someone who destroys community harmony by spreading false rumors

po'pok a vampire-like being

porai like, desire

Puang Matua important and powerful creator god

rambu solo' smoke-descending (ritual sphere)

rambu tuka' smoke-ascending (ritual sphere)

rante funeral ground

rapa' penaa calm, patient

rara buku lit. blood bones, family

rasun poison

sa'bara' calm, patient

sadang specter that appears at night as a shining torch

sa'ding to experience, feel

saki sick, illness

saki biasa "ordinary" illness

saki deata illness due to having violated a religious prescription or prohibition

saki to lino illness caused by humans

salego highly prized spotted water buffalo

sanginaa one mind

sarong (I) cylindrical piece of clothing

sengke angry

setang spirit

sikande lit. to eat one another; connected, related

siporai to agree with one another, mutually compatible

sisemba' to kickfight with one another

sukaran aluk rites and rituals of the traditional religion

sumanga' life force

sunga' span of life

suru' comb

tabang a plant (Cordyline terminalis) considered sacred

taibaro semen

tambuk stomach, wound

tatau statue of the dead

tauan nightmare, spirit attack

tedong water buffalo

tekken land that is given to an heir for his or her use until the owner dies, at which point the heir becomes the legal owner

tindo dream (in particular, a vivid dream)

tiro to see, look at

to person, people

to arasan person prone to anger

to baga simpleton

to biasa commoner

to boko thief

to buda commoner

to burake specialist who oversees smoke-ascending rituals

to diala anak lit. person taken as a child; foster child

to didadian lit. person given birth to

to dipakasalle lit. "raised" person; foster child

to dolo forebear

to kandeatan possessed person

to kapua lit. big person; important person

to lino human

to ma'dampi healer

to makaka noble

to ma'pakianak midwife

to masipa polite, well-behaved person

to matua elder

to mentaa meat divider

to minaa religious specialist

tongkonan ancestral house

to sa'bara' patient, tolerant person

to sengkean person prone to anger

to sugi' wealthy person

tuak palm wine

tumange' to cry, wail

tunu to burn, roast; to slaughter, sacrifice

ulu head

umbating to wail, cry

REFERENCES

Adams, K. 1988. Carving a New Identity: Ethnic and Artistic Change in Tana Toraja, Indonesia. Ph.D. dissertation. University of Washington.
—— n.d. The Discourse of Souls in Tana Toraja (Indonesia): Indigenous Notions and Christian Conceptions.
Anderson, B. 1972. The Idea of Power in Javanese Culture. In C. Holt, B. Anderson, and J. Siegel, eds., *Culture and Politics in Indonesia*. Ithaca: Cornell University Press.
APA (American Psychiatric Association). 1980. *Diagnostic and Statistical Manual of Mental Disorders (DSM-III)*. 3d ed. Washington, D.C.: American Psychiatric Association.
Atkinson, J. 1983. Religions in Dialogue: The Construction of an Indonesian Minority Religion. *American Ethnologist* 10:684–96.
—— 1989. The Art and Politics of Wana Shamanship. Berkeley: University of California Press.
Atkinson, J. and S. Errington. 1990. *Power and Difference: Gender in Island Southeast Asia*. Stanford: Stanford University Press.
Bateson, G. 1976. Some Components of Socialization for Trance. In T. Schwartz, ed., *Socialization as Cultural Communication: Development of a Theme in the Work of Margaret Mead*. Berkeley: University of California Press.
Bateson, G. and M. Mead 1942. *Balinese Character*. New York: New York Academy of Sciences.

Belo, J. 1970. The Balinese Temper. In *Traditional Balinese Culture*. New York: Columbia University Press.

Benedict, R. 1934. *Patterns of Culture*. New York: Houghton Mifflin.

Bigalke, T. 1981. A Social History of "Tana Toraja," 1870–1965. Ph.D. dissertation, University of Wisconsin, Madison.

Bock, P. K. 1988. *Rethinking Psychological Anthropology: Continuity and Change in the Study of Human Action*. New York: Freeman.

Bonokamsi, D. 1972. Javanese Mystical Groups. In W. Lebra, ed., *Transcultural Research in Mental Health*. Honolulu: University of Hawaii Press.

Bourguignon, E. 1979. *Psychological Anthropology: An Introduction to Human Nature and Cultural Differences*. New York: Holt, Rinehart, and Winston.

Broch, H.B. 1985. "Crazy Women Are Performing in Sombali": A Possession-Trance Ritual on Bonerate, Indonesia. *Ethos* 13:262–82.

Bruner, E.M. 1984. The Opening Up of Anthropology. In Bruner, ed., *Text, Play, and Story*. Proceedings of the American Ethnological Society. Washington, D.C.: AES.

Cole, M. 1978. Ethnographic Psychology of Cognition—So Far. In G. D. Spindler, ed., *The Making of Psychological Anthropology*. Berkeley: University of California Press.

Connor, L. 1979. Corpse Abuse and Trance in Bali: The Cultural Mediation of Aggression. *Mankind* 12:104–18.

——— 1982. The Unbounded Self: Balinese Therapy in Theory and Practice. In A. Marsella and G. White, eds. *Cultural Conceptions of Mental Health and Therapy*. Dordrecht: D. Reidel.

Coville, E. 1988. A Single Word Brings to Life: The Maro Ritual in Tana Toraja. Ph.D. dissertation. University of Chicago.

Crapanzano, V. 1980. *Tuhami: Portrait of a Moroccan*. Chicago: University of Chicago Press.

Crystal, E. 1971. Toradja Town. Ph.D. dissertation, University of California, Berkeley.

——— 1974. Cooking Pot Politics: A Toraja Village Study. *Indonesia* 18:119–51. 1986.

——— 1986. Souls and Spirits: Reflections of Life in Toraja Rituals of Death. Manuscript.

Crystal, E. and S. Yamashita. 1987. Power of Gods: Ma'bugi' Ritual of the Sa'dan Toraja. In R. S. Kipp and S. Rodgers, eds., *Indonesian Religions in Transition*. Tucson: University of Arizona Press.

D'Andrade, R. G. 1984. Cultural Meaning Systems. In R. A. Shweder and R. A. LeVine, eds., *Culture Theory: Essays on Mind, Self, and Emotion*. Cambridge: Cambridge University Press.

——— 1987. A Folk Model of the Mind. In D. Holland and N. Quinn, eds., *Cultural Models in Language and Thought*. Cambridge: Cambridge University Press.

Denton, R. K. 1978. Notes on Childhood in a Nonviolent Context: The Semai Case (Malaysia). In A. Montagu, ed., *Learning Non-Aggression*. Oxford: Oxford University Press.

DeVos, G. A. and L. B. Boyer. 1989. Humans as Symbolic Animals: A Psycho-cultural Perspective. In DeVos and Boyer, eds., *Symbolic Analysis Cross-Culturally.* Berkeley: University of California Press.

Downs, R. E. 1977. Head-Hunting in Indonesia. In P. E. de Josselin de Jong, ed., *Structural Anthropology in the Netherlands.* The Hague: Excelsior.

DuBois, Cora. 1961 (1944). *The People of Alor: A Social-Psychological Study of an East Indian Island.* New York: Harper.

Durkheim, E. 1951. *Suicide.* New York: Free Press.

Edgerton, R. B. 1971. *The Individual in Cultural Adaptation: A Study of Four East African Societies.* Los Angeles: University of California Press.

———— 1992. *Sick Societies: Challenging the Myth of Primitive Harmony.* New York: Free Press.

Errington, F. K. 1984. *Manners and Meaning in West Sumatra: The Social Context of Consciousness.* New Haven: Yale University Press.

Errington, S. 1979. The Cosmic House of the Buginese. *Asia* 1:8–14.

———— 1983a. Embodied *Sumange'* in Luwu. *Journal of Asian Studies* 43:545–70.

———— 1983b. The Place of Regalia in Luwu. In L. Gesick, ed., *Centers, Symbols, and Hierarchies: Essays on the Classical States of Southeast Asia.* New Haven: Yale University Southeast Asia Monographs. No. 26.

———— 1989. *Meaning and Power in a Southeast Asian Realm.* Princeton: Princeton University Press.

Farmer, P. 1988. Bad Blood, Spoiled Milk: Bodily Fluids as Barometers in Rural Haiti. *American Ethnologist* 15:62–83.

Foster, G. 1965. Peasant Society and the Image of Limited Good. *American Anthropologist* 67:293–315.

Fox, J. J., ed. 1980. *The Flow of Life: Essays on Eastern Indonesia.* Cambridge: Cambridge University Press.

Gaines, A. D. and P. E. Farmer. 1986. Visible Saints: Social Cynosures and Dysphoria in the Mediterranean Tradition. *Culture, Medicine, and Psychiatry* 10:295–330.

Geertz, C. 1973. *The Interpretation of Cultures.* New York: Basic Books.

———— 1976. *The Religion of Java.* Chicago: University of Chicago Press.

———— 1983. *Local Knowledge: Further Essays in Interpretive Anthropology.* New York: Basic.

Geertz, H. 1961. *The Javanese Family.* New York: Free Press of Glencoe.

Geertz, H. and C. Geertz. 1975. *Kinship in Bali.* Chicago: University of Chicago Press.

Goffman, E. 1959. *The Presentation of Self in Everyday Life.* Garden City, N.Y.: Doubleday.

Hallowell, A. I. 1955. *Culture and Experience.* Philadelphia: University of Pennsylvania Press.

Harvey, B. S. 1974. Tradition, Islam, and Rebellion: South Sulawesi 1950–1965. Ph.D. dissertation, Cornell University.

———— 1977. *Permesta: Half a Rebellion.* Ithaca: Cornell Modern Indonesia Project.

Heelas, P. L. K. 1981. The Model Applied: Anthropology and Indigenous

Psychologies. In P. L. K. Heelas and A. J. Lock, eds., *Indigenous Psychologies: The Anthropology of Self.* New York: Academic Press.

Heider, K. G. 1991a. *Indonesian Cinema: National Culture on Screen.* Honolulu: University of Hawaii Press.

―――― 1991b. *Landscapes of Emotion: Mapping Three Cultures of Emotion in Indonesia.* Cambridge: Cambridge University Press.

Herdt, G. and R. J. Stoller. 1990. *Intimate Communications: Erotics and the Study of Culture.* New York: Columbia University Press.

Hertz, R. 1960. *Death and the Right Hand* (translation of the 1907 essay by R. and C. Needham). New York: Free Press and Aberdeen University Press.

Hochschild, A. 1979. Emotion Work, Feeling Rules, and Social Structure. *American Journal of Sociology* 85:551–75.

―――― 1983. *The Managed Heart: Commercialization of Human Feeling.* Berkeley: University of California Press.

Hollan, D. 1984. "Disruptive" Behavior in a Toraja Community. Ph.D. dissertation, University of California, San Diego.

―――― 1988a. Staying "Cool" in Toraja: Informal Strategies for the Management of Anger and Hostility in a Nonviolent Society. *Ethos* 16:52–72.

―――― 1988b. Pockets Full of Mistakes: The Personal Consequences of Religious Change in a Toraja Village. *Oceania* 58: 275–89.

―――― 1989. The Personal Use of Dream Beliefs in the Toraja Highlands. *Ethos* 17:166–86.

―――― 1990. Indignant Suicide in the Pacific: An Example From the Toraja Highlands of Indonesia. *Culture, Medicine, and Psychiatry* 14:365–79.

―――― 1992a. Emotion Work and the Value of Emotional Equanimity Among the Toraja. *Ethnology* 31:45–56.

―――― 1992b. Cultural and Experiential Aspects of Spirit Beliefs Among the Toraja. Paper presented in the symposium, "Spirits in the Pacific," Annual Meeting of the Association for Social Anthropology in Oceania, New Orleans, February 1992.

―――― 1992c. Cross-Cultural Differences in the Self. *Journal of Anthropological Research* 48:283–300.

―――― in press. Suffering and the Work of Culture: A Case of Magical Poisoning in Toraja. *American Ethnologist.*

Hollan, D. W. and J. C. Wellenkamp. n.d. *The Thread of Life: Toraja Reflections on the Life-Cycle.*

Hooper, A. 1975. Review article of *Tahitians: Mind and Experience in the Society Islands* by R.I. Levy. *Journal of the Polynesian Society* 84:369–78.

Howard, A. 1985. Ethnopsychology and the Prospects for a Cultural Psychology. In G. M. White and J. Kirkpatrick, eds., *Person, Self, and Experience: Exploring Pacific Ethnopsychologies.* Berkeley: University of California Press.

Howell, S. 1981. Rules Not Words. In P. L. K. Heelas and A. J. Lock, eds., *Indigenous Psychologies: The Anthropology of Self.* New York: Academic Press.

Huntington, R. and P. Metcalf. 1979. *Celebrations of Death: The Anthropology of Mortuary Ritual.* New York: Cambridge University Press.

Jones, E. 1951. *On the Nightmare*. New York: Liveright.

Kardiner, A. 1939. *The Individual and His Society*. New York: Columbia University Press.

—— 1945. *The Psychological Frontiers of Society*. New York: Columbia University Press.

Keeler, W. 1987. *Javanese Shadow Plays, Javanese Selves*. Princeton: Princeton University Press.

Kipp, R. S. and S. Rodgers, eds. 1987. *Indonesian Religions in Transition*. Tucson: University of Arizona Press.

Kleinman, A. and B. Good, eds. 1985. *Culture and Depression: Studies in the Anthropology and Cross-Cultural Psychiatry of Affect and Disorder*. Berkeley: University of California Press.

Kleinman, A. and J. Kleinman. 1991. Suffering and Its Professional Transformation: Toward an Ethnography of Interpersonal Experience. *Culture, Medicine, and Psychiatry* 15:275–301.

Klineberg, O. 1938. Emotional Expression in Chinese Literature. *Journal of Abnormal and Social Psychology* 33:517–20.

Knauft, B. M. 1985. *Good Company and Violence: Sorcery and Social Action in a Lowland New Guinea Society*. Berkeley: University of California Press.

Kobong, Th., A. Rumpa, Sr., Y. R. Pasolon, B. Plaisier, Y. A. Sarira, and Y. Lebang. 1983. *Manusia Toraja*. Rantepao: Institut Theologia Gereja Toraja.

Koentjaraningrat. 1975. *Anthropology in Indonesia*. 's-Gravenhage: Verhandelingen van het Koninklijk Instituut voor Taal-, Landen Volkenkunde.

Kohut, H. 1971. *The Analysis of Self*. New York: International Universities Press.

Kracke, W. 1978. *Force and Persuasion: Leadership in an Amazonian Society*. Chicago: University of Chicago Press.

—— 1979. Dreaming in Kagwahiv: Dream Beliefs and Their Psychic Uses in an Amazonian Indian Culture. *Psychoanalytic Study of Society* 8:119–71.

Langness, L. L. 1987. *The Study of Culture*. Novato: Chandler and Sharp.

Lee, R. L. M. 1981. Structure and Anti-Structure in the Culture-Bound Syndromes: The Malay Case. *Culture, Medicine, and Psychiatry* 5:233–48.

LeVine, R. A. 1982. *Culture, Behavior, and Personality: An Introduction to the Comparative Study of Psychosocial Adaptation*. New York: Aldine.

Levy, R. I. 1973. *Tahitians: Mind and Experience in the Society Islands*. Chicago: University of Chicago Press.

—— 1990. *Mesocosm: Hinduism and the Organization of a Traditional Newar City in Nepal*. Berkeley: University of California Press.

Levy, R. I. and J. C. Wellenkamp. 1989. Methodology in the Anthropological Study of Emotion. In R. Plutchik and H. Kellerman, eds., *Emotion: Theory, Research, and Experience*. Vol. 4: *The Measurement of Emotions*. New York: Academic Press.

Lincoln, J. S. 1935. *The Dream in Primitive Cultures*. London: Cressett Press.

Lindholm, C. 1982. *Generosity and Jealousy: The Swat Pukhtun of Northern Pakistan*. New York: Columbia University Press.

Lock, A. J. 1981. Universals in Human Conception. In P. L. K. Heelas and A. J. Lock, eds., *Indigenous Psychologies: The Anthropology of Self.* New York: Academic Press.

Lutz, C. A. 1988. *Unnatural Emotions: Everyday Sentiments on a Micronesian Atoll and Their Challenge to Western Theory.* Chicago: University of Chicago Press.

MacPherson, C. and L. MacPherson. 1985. Suicide in Western Samoa: A Sociological Perspective. In F. X. Hezel, D. H. Rubenstein, and G. M. White, eds., *Culture, Youth, and Suicide in the Pacific.* Honolulu: Institute of Culture and Communication, East-West Center.

―――― 1987. Towards an Explanation of Recent Trends in Suicide in Western Samoa. *Man* 22:305–30.

Marcus, G. E. 1978. Status Rivalry in a Polynesian Steady-State Society. *Ethos* 6:242–69.

Marcus, G. E. and M. M. J. Fischer. 1986. *Anthropology as Cultural Critique: An Experimental Moment in the Human Sciences.* Chicago: University of Chicago Press.

Maretzki, T. 1981. Culture and Psychopathology in Indonesia. *Transcultural Psychiatric Research Review* 18:237–56.

Marsella, A., N. Sartorius, A. Jablensky, and F. Fenton. 1985. Cross-Cultural Studies of Depressive Disorders: An Overview. In A. Kleinman and B. Good, eds., *Culture and Depression: Studies in the Anthropology and Cross-Cultural Psychiatry of Affect and Disorder.* Berkeley: University of California Press.

Meeker, M. 1990. Natural Objects and Substitutive Acts: The Symbolic Process in the Anthropologies of Durkheim and Freud. In D. K. Jordan and M. J. Swartz, eds., *Personality and the Cultural Construction of Society.* Tuscaloosa: University of Alabama Press.

Mills, R. 1975. The Reconstruction of Proto South Sulawesi. *Archipel* 10:205–25.

Milner, G. B., ed. 1978. *Natural Symbols in South East Asia.* School of Oriental and African Studies, University of London.

Miner, H. M. and G. A. DeVos. 1960. *Oasis and Casbah: Algerian Culture and Personality in Change.* Ann Arbor: University of Michigan Press.

―――― 1989. Some Individual Sketches. In G. A. DeVos and L. B. Boyer, eds., *Symbolic Analysis Cross-Culturally.* Berkeley: University of California Press.

Nooy-Palm, H. 1969. Dress and Adornment of the Sa'dan Toradja (Celebes, Indonesia). *Tropical Man* 2:162–94.

―――― 1975. Introduction to the Sa'dan Toraja People and Their Country. *Archipel* 10:53–92.

―――― 1978. Survey of Studies on the Anthropology of Tana Toraja, Sulawesi. *Archipel* 10:52–92.

―――― 1979. *The Sa'dan-Toraja: A Study of Their Social Life and Religion.* Vol. 1: *Organization, Symbols, and Beliefs.* The Hague: Martinus Nijhoff.

―――― 1986. *The Sa'dan-Toraja: A Study of Their Social Life and Religion.* Vol. 2: *Rituals of the East and West.* Dordrecht: Foris.

Nooy-Palm, H. and R. Schefold. 1986. Colour and Anti-Colour in the Death Ritual of the Toraja. *Archipel* 32:39–49.

Obeyesekere, G. 1981. *Medusa's Hair: An Essay on Personal Symbols and Religious Experience.* Chicago: University of Chicago Press.

Peacock, J. 1988. Religion and Life History: An Exploration in Cultural Psychology. In E. M. Bruner, ed., *Text, Play, and Story: The Construction and Reconstruction of Self and Society.* Prospect Heights: Waveland Press.

Popkin, S. L. 1979. *The Rational Peasant: The Political Economy of Rural Society in Vietnam.* Berkeley: University of California Press.

Price-Williams, D. 1978. Cognition: Anthropological and Psychological Nexus. In G. D. Spindler, ed., *The Making of Psychological Anthropology.* Berkeley: University of California Press.

Quinn, N. and D. Holland. 1987. Culture and Cognition. In D. Holland and N. Quinn, eds., *Cultural Models in Language and Thought.* Cambridge: Cambridge University Press.

Ramsden, P. G. 1991. Alice in the Afterlife: A Glimpse in the Mirror. In D. R. Counts and D. A. Counts, eds., *Coping With the Final Tragedy: Cultural Variation in Dying and Grieving.* Amityville, N.Y.: Baywood.

Reid, A. 1988. *Southeast Asia in the Age of Commerce, 1450–1680.* New Haven: Yale University Press.

Riesman, P. 1977. *Freedom in Fulani Social Life: An Introspective Ethnography.* Chicago: University of Chicago Press.

Robarchek, C. A. 1977. Frustration, Aggression, and the Nonviolent Semai. *American Ethnologist* 4:762–79.

Rosaldo, M. Z. 1980. *Knowledge and Passion: Ilongot Notions of Self and Social Life.* Cambridge: Cambridge University Press.

Rubinstein, D. H. 1983. Epidemic Suicide Among Micronesian Adolescents. *Social Science and Medicine* 17:657–65.

Scheper-Hughes, N. 1979. *Saints, Scholars, and Schizophrenics.* Berkeley: University of California Press.

Schieffelin, E. L. 1976. *The Sorrow of the Lonely and the Burning of the Dancers.* New York: St. Martin's Press.

—— 1985a. The Cultural Analysis of Depressive Affect: An Example from New Guinea. In A. Kleinman and B. Good, eds., *Culture and Depression: Studies in the Anthropology and Cross-Cultural Psychiatry of Affect and Disorder.* Berkeley: University of California Press.

—— 1985b. Anger, Grief, and Shame: Towards a Kaluli Ethnopsychology. In G. M. White and J. Kirkpatrick, eds., *Person, Self, and Experience: Exploring Pacific Ethnopsychologies.* Berkeley: University of California Press.

Schwartz, T. 1973. Cult and Context: The Paranoid Ethos in Melanesia. *Ethos* 1:153–74.

Selby, H. 1974. *Zapotec Deviance.* Austin: University of Texas Press.

Shostak, M. 1981. *Nisa: The Life and Words of a !Kung Woman.* Cambridge: Harvard University Press.

Shweder, R. A. 1990. Cultural Psychology—What Is It? In J. W. Stigler, R. A. Shweder, and G. Herdt, eds., *Cultural Psychology: Essays on Comparative Human Development.* Cambridge: Cambridge University Press.

Siegel, J. T. 1966. Prayer and Play in Atjeh: A Comment on Two Photographs. *Indonesia* 1:1–21.

—— 1986. *Solo in the New Order: Language and Hierarchy in an Indonesian City*. Princeton: Princeton University Press.

Spiro, M. E. 1978. *Burmese Supernaturalism*. Philadelphia: Institute for the Study of Human Issues.

—— 1984. Some Reflections on Cultural Determinism and Relativism with Special Reference to Emotion and Reason. In R. A. Shweder and R. A. LeVine, eds., *Culture Theory: Essays on Mind, Self, and Emotion*. Cambridge: Cambridge University Press.

Spores, J. C. 1988. *Running Amok: An Historical Inquiry*. Athens: Ohio University Center for International Studies.

Suryani, L. K. 1984. Culture and Mental Disorder: The Case of Bebainan in Bali. *Culture, Medicine, and Psychiatry* 8:95–114.

Swellengrebel, J. L. 1960. Patterns of Cosmic Order. Bali: Studies in Life, Thought, and Ritual. *Selected Studies on Indonesia* 5:36–53.

Traube, E. G. 1986. *Cosmology and Social Life: Ritual Exchange Among the Mambai of East Timor*. Chicago: University of Chicago Press.

Valeri, V. 1985. *Kingship and Sacrifice: Ritual and Society in Ancient Hawaii*. Chicago: University of Chicago Press.

van der Kroef, J. M. 1954. Dualism and Symbolic Antithesis in Indonesian Society. *American Anthropologist* 56:847–62.

van der Veen, H. 1965. *The Merok Feast of the Sa'dan Toradja*. 's-Gravenhage: Martinus Nijhoff.

—— 1966. *The Sa'dan Toradja Chant for the Deceased*. 's-Gravenhage: Martinus Nijhoff.

Volkman, T. 1979. The Arts of Dying in Sulawesi. *Asia* 2(2):24–31.

—— 1980. *The Pig Has Eaten the Vegetable: Ritual and Change in Tana Toraja*. Ph.D. dissertation. Cornell University.

—— 1984. Great Performances: Toraja Cultural Identity in the 1970s. *American Ethnologist* 11:152–69.

—— 1985. *Feasts of Honor: Ritual and Change in the Toraja Highlands*. Urbana: University of Illinois Press.

Wallace, A. F. C. 1952. The Modal Personality Structure of the Tuscarora Indians as Revealed by the Rorschach Test. Bureau of American Ethnology *Bulletin No. 150*. Washington, D.C.: Smithsonian Institution.

Waterson, R. 1981. *The Economic and Social Position of Women in Tana Toraja*. Ph.D. dissertation. University of Cambridge.

Watson-Gegeo, K. and G. White, eds. 1990. *Disentangling: Conflict Discourse in Pacific Societies*. Stanford: Stanford University Press.

Weinstock, J. A. 1987. Kararingan: Life and Death in Southern Borneo. In R. S. Kipp and S. Rodgers, eds., *Indonesian Religions in Transition*. Tucson: University of Arizona Press.

Wellenkamp, J. C. 1984. *A Psychocultural Study of Loss and Death Among the Toraja*. Ph.D. dissertation, University of California, San Diego.

—— 1988a. Order and Disorder in Toraja Thought and Ritual. *Ethnology* 27:311–26.

—— 1988b. Notions of Grief and Catharsis Among the Toraja. *American Ethnologist* 15:486–500.

—— 1989. Love Magic and Depression: A Case Study from Toraja. Paper presented in the symposium, "Culture and Emotion in Indonesia," 88th Annual Meeting of the American Anthropological Association, Washington, D.C.

—— 1991. Fallen Leaves: Death and Grieving in Toraja. In D. R. Counts and D. A. Counts, eds., *Coping with the Final Tragedy: Cultural Variation in Dying and Grieving*. Amityville, N.Y.: Baywood.

—— 1992. Variation in the Social and Cultural Organization of Emotions: The Meaning of Crying and the Importance of Compassion in Toraja, Indonesia. In D. F. Franks and V. Gecas, eds., *Social Perspectives on Emotion*. Greenwich, Conn.: JAI Press.

White, G. M. 1990. Emotion Talk and Social Inference: Disentangling in Santa Isabel, Solomon Islands. In K. A. Watson-Gegeo and G. M. White, eds., *Disentangling: Conflict Discourse in Pacific Societies*. Stanford: Stanford University Press.

White, G. M. and J. Kirkpatrick, eds. 1985. *Person, Self, and Experience: Exploring Pacific Ethnopsychologies*. Berkeley: University of California Press.

Whiting, B. and C. P. Edwards. 1974. A Cross-Cultural Analysis of Sex Differences in the Behavior of Children Aged Three Through Eleven. In R. A. LeVine, ed., *Culture and Personality: Contemporary Readings*. Chicago: Aldine.

Whiting, J. and B. Whiting. 1978. A Strategy for Psychocultural Research. In G. D. Spindler, ed., *The Making of Psychological Anthropology*. Berkeley: University of California Press.

Wikan, U. 1991. *Managing Turbulent Hearts: A Balinese Formula for Living*. Chicago: University of Chicago Press.

Worsley, P. 1982. Non-Western Medical Systems. *Annual Review of Anthropology* 11:315–48.

Zerner, C. 1981. Signs of the Spirits, Signature of the Smith: Iron Forging in Tana Toraja. *Indonesia* 31:89–112.

INDEX

Designer: Susan Clark
Text: Sabon
Compositor: Maple-Vail
Printer: Maple-Vail
Binder: Maple-Vail